Instructor's Manual and Test Bank to Accompany

Experiencing Intercultural Communication

An Introduction

Judith N. Martin and Thomas K. Nakayama

Francisca Trujillo-Dalbey
Portland State University

Anneliese Harper
Scottsdale Community College

With contributions from
Lisa Bradford
University of Wisconsin–Milwaukee

Mayfield Publishing Company
Mountain View, California
London • Toronto

International Standard Book Number: 0-7674-2335-6

Manufactured in the United States of America
10   9   8   7   6   5   4   3   2   1

Mayfield Publishing Company
1280 Villa Street
Mountain View, California 94041

CONTENTS

PREFACE

Teaching intercultural communication can be an exciting and challenging experience for instructors. This newest textbook by Judith N. Martin and Thomas K. Nakayama, *Experiencing Intercultural Communication*, provides an opportunity for instructors to meet the needs of their freshman and sophomore students while not talking down to them or minimizing the complexity of the topic. Instructors will find that this book is interesting and stimulating for students at all levels, as it addresses issues such as class, power dynamics, and written and unwritten histories that are not covered in other intercultural textbooks. Also of note are the final four chapters, in the "applications" section of the text, which focus on intercultural communication and tourism, business, education, and health care, respectively. These chapters in particular will help students understand how intercultural communication applies to their daily lives and future occupations and experiences.

One of the many strengths of this and others of Martin and Nakayama's works is that the authors share with readers personal information about themselves and locate themselves within the context of their writing. In this tradition, I would like to introduce myself and tell you what I bring to this subject and to the writing of this manual. My name is Francisca Trujillo-Dalbey, and I grew up in West Los Angeles with bilingual parents whose first language was Spanish. I am second-generation Mexican on my mother's side, and my father's family (which self-identifies as Spanish) has lived for many generations in New Mexico. I moved to Oregon twenty-five years ago, where I met my husband of twenty-three years, and have raised a bicultural family. We have two granddaughters, and my mother and our three dogs share our home. I have a very personal interest in intercultural communication as I have lived my entire life with its challenges and rewards, and it continues to be crucial to my identity as a Latina woman. My personal experiences with cultural differences inform my approach to teaching and learning by focusing my attention as a woman of color with a commitment to facilitating intercultural learning.

I am on the faculty of Portland State University's communication studies department in Portland, Oregon. Among other communication classes, I teach Introduction to Intercultural Communication to freshman and sophomore students. In addition, I am an associate faculty member of the Intercultural Communication Institute's and Antioch University's master of arts program in intercultural relations. Twice a year Dr. Milton Bennett, director of the Intercultural Communication Institute, and I teach students from around the world a course titled Concepts of Intercultural Relations. For the past two summers I have had the opportunity to cofacilitate a week-long workshop with one of the authors of this textbook, Dr. Judith N. Martin, on Teaching Intercultural Communication at the Summer Institute for Intercultural Communication. I have also taught Introduction to Intercultural Communication at community colleges.

I earned a bachelor's degree in communication with an emphasis on intercultural communication from Marylhurst College, and a master of science in communication with an emphasis on intercultural communication from Portland State University. I am in a doctoral program at Portland State University in the School of Urban Studies.

I am pleased to have been asked to apply my years of study and teaching intercultural communication to the writing of this instructor's manual. Last year I was asked to contribute to the second edition of the instructor's manual for Judith N. Martin and Thomas K. Nakayama's textbook *Intercultural Communication in Contexts* by adding to the classroom exercises and chapter assignments written by my colleagues Lisa Bradford and Jolanta A. Drzewiecka. While I wrote the majority of this manual, I drew heavily on Lisa and Jolanta's work, and I would like to thank them for developing the foundation on which this manual is built.

This instructor's manual is designed to assist instructors in preparing for and teaching a course in Intercultural Communication. I have included resources, ideas, and chapter outlines to help both new and seasoned instructors get the most out of the main text, *Experiencing Intercultural Communication.*

With that goal in mind, this manual is divided into three parts. Part One gives general information about teaching intercultural communication, reading and video resources, and sample syllabi. Part Two of the manual is a detailed outline for each of the chapters in the textbook, complete with chapter objectives, discussion questions, classroom exercises and assignments, and video resources. Part Three is the test bank, which contains a chapter-by-chapter list of multiple choice, true/false, and essay test questions, written by Anneliese Harper of Scottsdale Community College. The questions are a combination of factual and application items designed to complement the chapter's learning objectives. The test bank is available in computerized format in the Microtest III program. This testing program allows you to design tests using the questions provided and to include your own questions. Microtest is available in both Windows and Macintosh formats. For more information on this software program, contact your Mayfield sales representative or call our marketing and sales department at (800) 433-1279.

Part One
General Introduction

Teaching Intercultural Communication

Intercultural communication is one of the most exciting and rewarding courses to teach, and it can also be one of the most challenging. Intercultural communication courses ask students to examine their values, beliefs, attitudes, and behavior in ways other courses do not. Students' reactions to the course material may range from intense curiosity to sometimes overtly defensive behavior. Therefore, it is crucial that teachers of intercultural communication be prepared to handle this wide range of reactions. One way to do this is for instructors to examine their own values, beliefs, and attitudes prior to teaching this course.

There are also some pedagogical issues that should be examined in preparation for teaching intercultural communication. Many of these suggestions and issues come from my work with Judith N. Martin at the Summer Institute for Intercultural Communication. The purpose of raising these pedagogical issues is not to dichotomize or privilege one way of thinking over another, or to suggest that instructors subscribe to teaching from one perspective only. The goal is simply to offer a range of issues, approaches, and ideas to help instructors make choices about how they will prepare for and teach their classes.

GOALS FOR THE CLASS

The first question we need to ask ourselves is, What are our goals when teaching intercultural communication? That is, do we want to bring about cognitive, affective, or behavioral changes in our students? Often we want to do all three, yet our teaching will tend to focus more on one goal than the others. When seeking a cognitive goal, the focus is on imparting conceptual knowledge to students, ensuring that students learn theories and concepts relating to the subject. Some instructors who teach intercultural communication are less interested in teaching theoretical concepts; instead, they emphasize the attitudinal and emotional issues involved. These instructors might take a more affective approach in their assignments, activities, and lectures, focusing on issues of racism, classism, and so on. Other instructors believe that it is important to focus on changing students' behavior by encouraging and reinforcing skills development so that students will behave in a more culturally competent manner when communicating with those who are different from them. They may provide many opportunities to practice a variety of skills during class. This textbook has been written in such a way as to allow instructors to focus their course on all three of these goals—guiding students through each chapter by touching on the cognitive, affective, and behavioral aspects of each.

THEORETICAL FRAMEWORK

The theoretical framework that instructors bring to teaching intercultural communication will affect the approach they use. Instructors may have been trained in the social science, interpretative, ethnographic, critical, perceptual, or communication approach to intercultural communication. Each of these approaches has its roots in different disciplines such as psychology, anthropology, sociolinguistics, and communication, and each framework influences research goals, assumptions about reality, assumptions about human behavior, methods of study, and perceptions of the relationship between culture and communication (Martin & Nakayama, 2000, pp. 26–27). While it is not necessary for students at the introductory level to learn about these frameworks, instructors need to recognize which framework informs their teaching. It is important to our teaching and to students' learning that we do not privilege one framework over another and yet be aware that personally we may have a particular preference. All of the frameworks offer valuable insights into intercultural communication and contribute to our growing understanding of this field through theory building, research, and so on. Unlike other textbooks on intercultural communication, *Experiencing Intercultural Communication* offers research, examples, and references from all of these frameworks to enhance student learning.

THE FOCUS OF THE CLASS

The next issue concerns the focus of the class. That is, will the instructor focus on teaching intercultural communication from a culture-specific perspective or a culture-general one? Will the class be focused on international issues or domestic diversity issues? And will the focus be on intercultural, intracultural, or cross-cultural interaction?

A culture-specific approach means that the course content revolves around teaching how to communicate primarily with persons from one particular culture. The curriculum may focus on how to act in a certain culture and on what types of behaviors, values, and beliefs members of that culture hold. A culture-general focus involves covering issues in intercultural communication that affect interactions across cultures in general and describing ranges of behaviors. Many instructors tend to use a combination of approaches, teaching culture-general concepts and using culture-specific examples.

Another consideration is whether the course will be taught from an international or a domestic perspective. Often this depends on the particular interests and personal experiences of the instructor, and the makeup of the class. Some instructors have more experience with domestic diversity, and their examples tend to illustrate this focus, while others may have more experience with international differences. Striving for a balance between an international and a domestic focus demonstrates the complexities and breadth of the field of intercultural communication, and challenges instructors to stress the importance of understanding both contexts.

Whether a course focuses on intercultural, intracultural, or cross-cultural issues may depend on the interests of the instructor, the institutional requirements of the course, and the interests of the students. A course with an intercultural focus (as in this textbook) examines what occurs when people from two or more cultures interact within a communication context. An intracultural focus involves cultural differences within a particular culture, and a cross-cultural focus is one in which one culture is compared to another in some manner. Usually, a course titled "Intercultural Communication" will focus primarily on the communication interaction between persons from different cultures while not ignoring the intracultural and cross-cultural issues.

WHAT INSTRUCTORS BRING TO THE INTERCULTURAL COMMUNICATION CLASSROOM

Ideally, instructors selected to teach intercultural communication have some formal training in both communication studies and intercultural communication. However, at times instructors find themselves faced with the task of teaching intercultural communication for the first time with little or no academic background in communication studies generally or intercultural communication specifically. While this instructor's manual contains a reading list, suggested course outlines, and other resources for teaching intercultural communication, we cannot stress enough the importance of taking time to do some background reading in the field of intercultural communication. We also recommend that instructors attend workshops on teaching intercultural communication or in some other way become knowledgeable about the complexities of the field before entering the classroom. Some instructors may have an academic background in a related discipline, such as anthropology, sociology, or linguistics, and may need only to understand the communication perspective to do quite well in teaching intercultural communication.

Many persons are interested in the field and come to teach intercultural communication because of their international or domestic intercultural experiences. Often instructors possess some international experience but have little experience with domestic diversity, or vice versa. Again, the ideal is a solid combination of academic and experiential learning in both international and domestic contexts. However, most teachers of intercultural communication are stronger in either international or domestic issues and have some academic background in some aspect of intercultural communication or a related field.

It is important for instructors to examine their strengths in terms of both academic background and intercultural experience prior to entering the classroom. Students will want to hear about both international and domestic issues in intercultural communication; therefore, instructors need to be able to discuss both. In recent years, the number of books about domestic and international cultures from an intercultural communication perspective has risen steadily, and it is now quite easy to locate books, videos, Web Sites, and other sources of information about intercultural communication. While this will not substitute for personal experiences or formal training, it will help prepare new instructors to teach intercultural communication.

TEACHING AND LEARNING STYLES

As instructors, we all have our own preferred style of teaching and learning. A popular model that assesses learning styles is the Kolb Learning-Style Inventory (1993), which asks a series of questions to determine which of four learning styles one prefers. The four styles identified by Kolb are concrete experience ("feeling"), reflective observation ("watching"), abstract conceptualization ("thinking"), and active experimentation ("doing") (Kolb, 1993). Generally, the Kolb learning styles are based on the notion that we tend to learn and thus teach according to one preferred style, which may or may not be the preferred learning style of our students. Knowledge of the styles and our own preferences allows us to approach topics in more than one way, thus honoring the diversity of learning styles of our students and, in turn, enhancing their learning experiences.

It is important to note that Kolb does not give preference to one style over another, but rather argues that all styles are equally valid modes of learning. However, Kolb also contends that, the more one is able to learn in all four styles, the more sophisticated and flexible a learner one will be. The implications for teaching intercultural communication involve whether an instructor is more comfortable instructing students in a more experiential, passive, reflective, or affective mode. For instance, an instructor whose preferred learning style is abstract conceptualization may primarily lecture and be less comfortable conducting experiential learning activities.

Kolb maintains that to facilitate student learning, instructors need to guide students through all four styles. For example, the instructor may have students do some sort of topic-related activity. Next, students may conduct research on the topic, or the instructor may choose to lecture on the topic. Students may then discuss, either in large or small groups, how they react to or feel about the topic. And the lesson may culminate with students reflecting on their learning by synthesizing the topic in writing. There is no "right" order to these learning activities, and where instructors begin is often related to their own learning style preferences.

There are other learning style models available for assessing learning and teaching styles, and Kolb's Learning-Style Inventory is simply one of the most well known. The point here is not to single out Kolb's as the best one, but to stress the importance of knowing one's own style and understanding how that style impacts one's teaching.

ATTITUDES AND BIASES

It is important for instructors to gauge their own attitudes and biases toward the topic of intercultural communication prior to entering the classroom. A useful model for thinking about attitudes and biases is Milton J. Bennett's developmental model of intercultural sensitivity (1993). This model offers a progression of stages people may go through as they become more interculturally sensitive to the way they construe differences.

The model consists of six stages; the first three are ethnocentric, and the last three are ethnorelative. The ethnocentric stages are denial, defense, and minimization. Bennett defines "ethnocentric" as "assuming that the worldview of one's own culture is central to all reality" (1993, p. 10).

A total denial of cultural differences is somewhat rare in today's technologically connected world, yet some people maintain some semblance of this position through "either the isolation of physical circumstance or . . . the separation created by intentional physical and social barriers" (Bennett, 1993, p. 10).

People who are aware that there are differences and perceive the differences as threatening characterize the defense stage. As Bennett states, "The threat is to one's sense of reality and thus to one's identity" (1993, p. 15). It is likely that instructors will come across some students who exhibit attitudes and behaviors that place them within this stage. It is important to note that, when a person is taking a defensive posture toward cultural differences, care must be taken to avoid exacerbating the person's stance. Arguing with the person, trying to convince the person that she or he is wrong, and otherwise trying to talk him or her out of those beliefs may have the reverse effect, causing the person to defend her or his position ever more strongly.

The last stage in the ethnocentric group is minimization. This stage represents movement away from defense and focuses instead on the relative smallness of cultural differences, thus minimizing their importance. Minimization appears benign compared to defense, and Bennett describes it as "an alluring position, because adherents to it manifest an orientation that is associated with human sensitivity" (1993, p. 21). People in this stage may be ready to move into the ethnorelative stages through training and education, but they can just as easily retreat back to the defense stage if challenged too quickly or with too much force.

The ethnorelative stages are based on the assumption that "cultures can only be understood relative to one another and that particular behavior can only be understood within a cultural context" (Bennett, 1993, p. 26). The three stages in this ethnorelative frame are acceptance, adaptation, and integration.

Acceptance is characterized by an acknowledgment of and respect for cultural differences. As Bennett states, "Rather than being evaluated negatively or positively as part of a defensive strategy, the existence of difference is accepted as a necessary and preferable human condition" (1993, p. 28). Adaptation focuses on the person's ability to develop new skills appropriate for interacting with people who have a different worldview from his or her own. There is an emphasis on the ability to shift cultural frames of reference to enhance communication. And integration reflects a person's attempt "to integrate disparate aspects of one's identity into a new whole while remaining culturally marginal" (Bennett, 1993, p. 40).

Bennett suggests that when using this model "teachers of a beginning intercultural communication class whose goal for students is acceptance could operate effectively from adaptation" (1993, p. 46). One of the strengths of the Bennett model is that it can assist instructors in evaluating their own level of sensitivity toward cultural differences and in assessing the level of students' intercultural sensitivity. Instructors can use this information to guide their planning and teaching activities based on their students' development.

In addition to assessing their own intercultural sensitivity, instructors must also be aware that we all have our own personal "hot buttons," or statements, subjects, or issues that can trigger a negative reaction toward students. One of the challenges when teaching intercultural communication is setting up a classroom atmosphere in which students feel comfortable discussing and exploring their feelings, attitudes, and beliefs while simultaneously being respectful of others in the class, including the instructor.

One proactive technique is to set up ground rules for communication behavior that allows students (and instructors) to discuss sometimes difficult issues in a manner that does not hurt, insult, or otherwise offend others. These ground rules can be posted in the classroom or handed out to students. Some instructors include some basic ground rules in their syllabi and then ask students to add to them during a class discussion. Sample ground rules include refraining from name-calling, listening without interrupting, and avoiding put-downs.

However, even the best ground rules will not guard against instructors having their emotions or values triggered by what may be racist-sounding or ethnocentrically biased remarks. If the instructor reacts negatively or harshly to the student's remark, it can have a chilling effect on the future participation of students in the classroom. A strong negative response may also cause some students to revert to a previous stage in their learning such as defensiveness. Once instructors are aware that certain issues are hot-button issues for them, they can be prepared to deal with these situations in ways that enhance learning and participation rather than thwart it.

It is important to become aware of the physiological responses to hot-button topics. This is the first step toward controlling one's reaction to them in class. Common physiological responses such as a knot in the stomach, tight shoulders, or a pounding heart can act as warning signs of the need to control one's response. Lee Warren (1997) of the Derek Bok Center for Teaching and Learning at Harvard University offers these suggestions for controlling emotional hot buttons in class:

1. Listen without interrupting while taking several deep breaths to help control your physical reactions.
2. Take an inventory of your own feelings.
3. Acknowledge the student's feelings.
4. Make a conscious choice about your own response. That is, you can get angry, try to address the situation, have other students respond, or ignore it.
5. Ask open-ended, objective questions for clarification before responding.
6. Try to see the student's point of view. Agree when you can, and feed back what you are hearing.
7. Be patient. Some issues don't have immediate solutions.
8. Express your point of view. Present your evidence without backing the student into a corner.
9. Explain why. A reasonable explanation can often take the sting out of an emotional issue as well as shed some light for other students.
10. Involve others in the discussion. Don't get caught in a "class versus you" scenario.
11. Reframe the problematic comment or point. Try to elicit a positive point from the comment.
12. Take a break to give yourself time to calm down and gather your thoughts.
13. Enforce the ground rules. Once the class has agreed to them, remind the students that they made an agreement, and you will hold them to it.

It is not easy for us to control our emotions, and nonverbal behaviors have a tendency to "leak out" for many of us. Students are quite astute and may comment on an instructor's unintentional nonverbal response. At this point the instructor may want to acknowledge that the statement or behavior has provoked a response and calmly explain her or his reasons in a nonblaming, neutral manner. This will humanize the instructor and can even provide good role modeling for the students on appropriate ways to handle opinions and beliefs different from their own.

WHAT STUDENTS BRING TO THE INTERCULTURAL COMMUNICATION CLASSROOM

Students in intercultural communication classes tend to come from a wide variety of academic disciplines, and many have not yet declared a major. When students have some idea of their educational goals, their chosen disciplinary perspective may affect their goals in and motivations for taking an intercultural communication class. For example, business majors will be more motivated to learn about intercultural communication if they can see the benefits associated with an increasingly global economic environment. Or computer science majors may need assistance making connections between their career choices and the importance of learning how to be an effective intercultural communicator. Also, if a class is filled with students from a particular major (I once taught intercultural communication to a class of administration of justice majors), then the instructor can tailor the course content to the students' particular needs and motivate them to learn about intercultural communication.

Some students take an intercultural communication course purely out of personal interest. This may be the case for international students, students of color, and students who have had some type of previous intercultural experience. Others take the course for many of the same reasons they take other courses: It fits their schedule, it's a requirement for their major, it's one of the few courses that's available, and so on. With some students, the instructor may discover that the subject of intercultural communication is so compelling that motivating them to learn is quite easy. With other students, the instructor may need to demonstrate the importance of learning about intercultural communication and how it will help them become more successful in their careers and their daily interactions.

As mentioned, some students will have a significant amount of previous intercultural experience either as international students, immigrants, or members of a nondominant culture. These cultural experiences can add richness to the class, particularly if students are willing to share their cultural and ethnic perspectives. Indeed, it is tempting to call directly on students to act as "cultural informants" for their particular group. In fact, sometimes students wonder why instructors don't ask international and ethnic minority students for their opinions, observations, and experiences.

While having students share their cultural experiences can be very valuable in an intercultural communication class, there are some risks. Some students may feel uncomfortable being asked to speak for their entire culture. Other students may feel put on the spot when asked a question for which they may not have an answer. And still others may feel singled out to once again educate people about their culture. This is not to imply that students should not be asked for their cultural perspective; rather, it is to point out that as instructors we need to be sensitive to students' feelings and responses.

One possible strategy is to ask those students who have already been freely providing their thoughts and opinions. Another is to ask students privately before or after class if they are comfortable being asked to provide their personal cultural insights. And, to ensure that all the students provide input during class discussions, the instructor might ask the dominant culture students the same questions that he or she normally would have asked only an international student or a nondominant culture minority student. The result may be that students are less likely to object to being asked to share their personal experiences.

To complicate matters, some students are accustomed to being called upon by name before speaking, depending on their cultural rules for teacher–student interaction. So, when a student does not offer to speak in class, the instructor must be careful not to misinterpret this behavior as an unwillingness to share her or his cultural perspective. Again, it may be useful to ask certain students privately if they are comfortable being asked to speak about their cultural experiences.

Another strategy for encouraging students to share their cultural perspectives is to have them work in small groups, as some students are more comfortable talking with just a few people about their experiences. Small groups tend to provide each person with more chances to talk and may encourage a more equal exchange of information, as well as lessen the chance that one cultural perspective is privileged over another. Students in small groups may also feel less singled out to speak as cultural informants.

Students bring to the intercultural communication classroom varying levels of knowledge, expertise, and intercultural sensitivity. Introductory exercises and discussions can provide invaluable clues about students' attitudes, behaviors and receptivity toward intercultural communication. This information, in turn, allows instructors to tailor their teaching style, class activities, and assignments to the particular needs of the class. Also, by paying close attention to the students' attitudes toward and knowledge about intercultural communication issues, instructors can determine in general terms where the class falls along Bennett's continuum of intercultural sensitivity.

Questionnaires can be given to the class to determine intercultural competency levels and levels of sensitivity, and many intercultural communication instructors choose to administer such assessment instruments early on as instructional aids. Some of these instruments (such as Bennett's Intercultural Developmental Inventory based on the developmental model of intercultural sensitivity) require certification while others (such as Kelley and Meyer's Cross-Cultural Adaptability Inventory) do not require any form of certification.

Another consideration when teaching intercultural communication involves the homogeneity or heterogeneity of the students. Often the geographic location of the college or university affects the level of homogeneity of its students in terms of ethnic and cultural differences. For example, it is not unusual in the Pacific Northwest to have an entire classroom of White, dominant culture students. In other parts of the United States, the classroom may be more heterogeneous or even homogeneously Hispanic, Asian American, or African American. Similarly, the neighborhood or community in which the school is located, regardless of the state or region, can affect the ethnic and cultural makeup of the class.

Of course, the "ideal" intercultural communication class will contain a variety of persons from different cultural and ethnic backgrounds, genders, religions, and so on. Diverse classes of students allow for the richness of diverse viewpoints to emerge and flourish. One of the most challenging classes to teach is one in which a dramatic imbalance of minority and majority cultural group members exists. Instructors who find themselves teaching classes with such an imbalance have to be sensitive to the possible marginalization of the minority students by the majority and should carefully monitor the power dynamics among students during discussions and group activities. This is true whether the numerical minority in the class are dominant or nondominant culture students.

The ethnicity and culture of the instructor may play a role in the power dynamics of the classroom as well, and the teacher from a nondominant culture who is teaching in a dominant culture classroom may encounter resistance and defensiveness from some students. This can also occur in a more heterogeneous classroom, but sometimes students are more willing to monitor their comments when the class contains students from a variety of cultures and ethnicities. In any case, instructors should remember that the cultural and ethnic make-up of the class, as well as their own cultural background, affect interaction and other dynamics in the intercultural communication class.

The final issue to consider when teaching intercultural communication (as well as any course) is the learning styles of the students. As discussed previously, it is useful to understand the learning styles students prefer in the particular class and the teaching style preferred by the instructor. Some instructors administer some type of learning styles assessment instrument to their students at the beginning of the course to help them choose their teaching strategies. Other instructors are familiar enough with either Kolb's or others' work on learning styles to be able to assess their students' preferred learning styles through close observation. Still other instructors develop their curriculum and plan their teaching activities in such a manner that they consistently employ all four learning styles in their teaching. Since the students are unlikely to all prefer the same style, teaching in all four styles will ensure that each student gets to learn in his or her preferred way, allowing everyone an opportunity to succeed.

MANAGING LARGE CLASSES

Depending on the particular institutional requirements, instructors may be asked to teach a large number of students in one intercultural communication course. Of course, the ideal class size depends on the topic, the instructor, and the students but in any case instructors may find themselves teaching a class of 100 or more. While this subject matter lends itself better to small class sizes, which maximizes interaction among students, models such as the intercultural communication workshop provide a way to accommodate large numbers of students, depending on the number of graduate students available to serve as facilitators.

The intercultural communication workshop model can be configured in a number of ways, and one effective model was instituted and directed by Milton J. Bennett at Portland State University. Graduate students from various disciplines were recruited to cofacilitate small groups of interculturally diverse freshmen and sophomores. The graduate students earned advanced credits for their weekly facilitation of the groups and weekly class attendance with Dr. Bennett. This model allowed 200 students to participate in experientially based learning.

Another method of handling large classes is for the instructor to use a lecture style of teaching interspersed with periodic small group work. This works best when the course is taught in a classroom that has movable chairs or desks and enough room to form small groups. It is clearly more difficult to debrief a small-group activity with 10 to 15 groups; however, it can be done by employing a portable microphone or other means to allow students to hear one another. Large class discussions are also challenging and again are facilitated by a microphone.

Another technique that can be used with large groups is to have students work in dyads. This eliminates the need for large numbers of students to move their desks (which can be time-consuming and chaotic) by having students discuss questions or work on projects with the person next to them. Although students get less variety in their interactions when only meeting in dyads, at least they have an opportunity to talk with another person rather than simply listening to lectures.

If instructors have access to teaching assistants or other helpers, each assistant can occasionally facilitate a large group simultaneously with the other assistants, allowing students to interact a bit more than in a large-group discussion format. Additional classrooms may be needed if the classroom is not big enough for larger groups to meet all at once.

Yet another strategy for teaching large sections is to have students work together on small-group projects during class time, but outside of the classroom. Students must be held accountable for work done in this manner, and we suggest that students report back to their classroom before and after their small-group meetings to ensure that they have attended their group meeting and are actually working on the project. Students can share the results of their projects in a class "fair" for which they bring a visual representation of their project and circulate around the classroom to see one another's work. It is useful for students to have some sort of assignment that requires them to visit a number of the exhibits to ensure full student participation.

Teaching large sections can be challenging for instructors, but with some planning and creativity both instructors and students can find the course as rewarding and interesting as a smaller class. Variety is the key to successfully teaching a large section, and instructors who are able to intersperse activities tailored for the larger classroom with lectures will keep students involved and engaged.

RESOURCES FOR TEACHING INTERCULTURAL COMMUNICATION

Suggested Readings and Resources for Instructors

The following list is by no means inclusive of the vast number of readings available for persons wanting to know more about intercultural communication. Some of the references focus on teaching intercultural communication; others provide a theoretical foundation for much of what is included in the textbook; still others are useful resources for experiential activities that can be used as launching points for developing activities, small-group projects, and so on.

Bennett, M. J. (1993). Towards ethnorelativism: A developmental model of intercultural sensitivity. In R. M. Paige (Ed.), *Education for the intercultural experience* (pp. 1–51). Yarmouth, ME: Intercultural Press.

Bennett, M. J. (Ed.). (1998). *Basic concepts of intercultural communication: Selected readings.* Yarmouth, ME: Intercultural Press.

Brislin, R. W. (1993). *Understanding culture's influence on behavior.* Fort Worth, TX: Harcourt Brace Jovanovich.

Brislin, R. W., & Yoshida, T. (1994). *Intercultural communication training: An introduction.* Thousand Oaks, CA: Sage.

Byrd, M. L. (1992). *The intercultural communication book.* New York: McGraw-Hill.

Carbaugh, D. (Ed.). (1990). *Cultural communication and intercultural contact*. Hillsdale, NJ: Erlbaum.

Chen, G. M., & Starosta, W. J. (1998). *Foundations in intercultural communication*. Boston: Allyn & Bacon

Cushner, K., & Brislin, R. W. (Eds.). (1997). *Improving intercultural interactions: Modules for cross-cultural training programs* (Vol. 2). Thousand Oaks, CA: Sage.

Fowler, S. M., & Mumford, M. G. (Eds.). (1995-1999). *Intercultural sourcebook: Cross-cultural training methods* (Vols. 1–2). Yarmouth, ME: Intercultural Press.

Gochenour, T. (Ed.). (1993). *Beyond experience: The experiential approach to cross-cultural education*. Yarmouth, ME: Intercultural Press.

Gonzalez, A., Houston, M., & Chen, V. (Eds.). (2000). *Our voices: Essays in culture, ethnicity, and communication: An intercultural anthology* (3rd ed.). Los Angeles: Roxbury.

Groth, G. A. (1997). Managing conflict and hostilities during diversity discussions and training. In C. D. Brown, C. Snedeker, & B. Sykes (Eds.), *Conflict and diversity* (pp. 266–279). Cresskill, NJ: Hampton Press.

Gudykunst, W. B., & Nishida, T. (1989). Theoretical perspectives for studying intercultural communication. In M. K. Asante & W. B. Gudykunst (Eds.), *Handbook of international and intercultural communication* (pp. 17–46). Newbury Park, CA: Sage.

Hall, B. J. (1992). Theories of culture and communication. *Communication Theory, 1*, 50–70.

Hall, E. T. (1981). *Beyond culture*. New York: Doubleday.

Kohls, L. R. (1996). *Survival kit for overseas living* (3rd ed.). Yarmouth, ME: Intercultural Press.

Kohls, L. R., & Knight, J.M. (1994). *Developing intercultural awareness: A cross-cultural training handbook* (2nd ed.). Yarmouth, ME: Intercultural Press.

Kolb, D. A. (1993). *Learning-Style Inventory: Self-scoring inventory and interpretation booklet*. Boston: Hay/McBer Training Resources Group.

Martin, J. N., & Nakayama, T. K. (1999). Thinking dialectically about culture and communication. *Communication Monographs, 9*, 1–26.

Martin, J. N., & Nakayama, T. K. (2000). *Intercultural communication in contexts* (2nd ed.). Mountain View, CA: Mayfield.

Martin. J. N., Nakayama, T. K., & Flores, L. A. (1998). *Readings in intercultural contexts*. Mountain View, CA: Mayfield.

Paige, R. M. (Ed.). (1993). *Education for the intercultural experience*. Yarmouth, ME: Intercultural Press.

Paige, R. M. & Martin, J. N. (1983). Ethical issues and ethics in cross-cultural training. In D. Landis & R. Brislin (Eds.), *Handbook of intercultural training*. Elmsford, NY: Pergamon.

Ponterotto, J., & Pedersen, P. (1993). *Preventing prejudice: A guide for counselors and educators*. Newbury Park, CA: Sage.

Pusch, M. D. (Ed.). (1979). *Multicultural education: A cross-cultural training approach*. Yarmouth, ME: Intercultural Press.

Samovar, L., & Porter, R. (Eds.). *Intercultural communication: A reader* (9th ed.). Belmont, CA: Wadsworth.

Seelye, H. N., (Ed.) (1996). *Experiential activities for intercultural learning* (Vol. 1). Yarmouth, ME: Intercultural Press.

Singer, M. R. (1998). *Perception and identity in intercultural communication*. Yarmouth, ME: Intercultural Press.

Smith, D., & Kolb, D. A. (1985). *User guide for the Learning-Style Inventory*. Boston: McBer.

Steward, E. C., & Bennett, M. J. (1991). *American cultural patterns: A cross-cultural perspective*. Yarmouth, ME: Intercultural Press.

Summerfield, E. (1993). *Crossing cultures through film*. Yarmouth, ME: Intercultural Press.

Thiagarajan, S. (1990). *Barnga: Simulation*. Yarmouth, ME: Intercultural Press.

Ting-Toomey, S. (1999). *Communicating across cultures*. New York: Guilford.

Warren, L. (1997). *15 suggestions for controlling emotional "hot buttons" in class*. Derek Bok Center for Teaching and Learning, Harvard University. www.fas.harvard.edu/~bok_cen/docs.

Wildman, S.M. (1996). Privilege revealed: How invisible preference undermines America. New York: New York University Press.

Film and Video Distributors

This is a list of the distributors of the films and videos recommended in Part Two of the manual.

ABC Nightline: ABCNewstore.com: (800) CALL-ABC

Annenburg/CPB Project: (800) 532-7637; fax (802) 864-9846

Bbcamerica.com/videos: (800) 216-1BBC ext. 18

Beacon Films: (800) 323-9084; fax (847) 328-6706

California Newsreel: (800) 621-6196; fax (415) 621-6522

Cambridge Documentary Films: (617) 484-3993; fax (617) 484-0754

CCHCP Cross Cultural Health Care Program: (206) 621-4161

CNAM Film Library: (800) 343-5540; fax (201) 652-1973

CRM Films: (800) 421-0833, (619) 431-9800; fax (619) 931-5792

Encyclopaedia Britannica Educational Corporation: (800) 621-3900; fax (800) 480-0553

Facets Multimedia, Inc. (800) 331-6197; fax (773) 929-5437

Fanlight Productions: (800) 937-4113; fax (617) 524-8838

Film & Video Rental Center: (800) 345-6797

Filmakers Library: (212) 808-4980; fax (212) 808-4983

Filmic Archives: (800) 366-1920; fax (203) 268-1796

Films for the Humanities and Sciences: (800) 257-5126; fax (609) 275-3767

Frameline: (415) 703-8650; fax (415) 861-1404

Goodmeasure, Inc.: (617) 621-3838

Griggs Productions: (800) 210-4200; fax (415) 668-6004

Indiana University: (800) 552-8620; fax (812) 855-8404

Insight Media: (800) 233-9910; fax (212) 799-5309

Intercultural Communication Institute: (503) 297-4622; fax (503) 297-4695

IRIS Films: (800) 343-5540; fax (510) 841-3336

Kit Parker Films: (800) 538-5838; fax (408) 393-0304

LCA (c/o New World Video): (310) 444-8100; fax (310) 444-8101

McGraw-Hill Publishing Company: (800) 338-3987

MPI Home Video: (800) 323-0442

MTI/Film and Video: See Phoenix Coronet

NAFSA Association of International Educators: (800) 836-4994; fax (412) 741-0609

New Day Films: (201) 652-6590; fax (201) 652-1973

PBS Video: (800) 344-3337; fax (703) 739-5269

Phoenix Coronet: (800) 221-1274; fax (314) 569-2834

Prentice-Hall Publishing Company: (800) 922-0579; fax (201) 767-2993

Pyramid Film & Video: (800) 421-2304; fax (310) 453-9083

Rosenstein Productions: P.O. Box 2483, Champaign, IL 61825-2483

Sai Communications: (800) 343-5540; fax (201) 652-1973

Society for Visual Education, Inc.: (800) 829-1900; fax (800) 624-1678

SVE and Churchill Media: (800) 829-1900; fax (800) 624-1678

University of California Extension Media Center: (510) 642-0460; fax (510) 643-9271

Utah Valley State College, Behavioral Science Department: (801) 222-8083

Video Knowledge: (516) 367-4250; fax (576) 637-1006

West Glen Films: (800) 325-8677; fax (212) 944-9055

USING THIS INSTRUCTOR'S MANUAL

This manual can be used in any number of ways depending on the particular needs of the instructor. The chapter outlines are quite detailed, with the intention that instructors will be able to review the chapter in its entirety and then determine which sections of each chapter to include in the classroom lecture and which parts to have students read on their own. The class discussion questions can be used in small or large groups, as written assignments, or as jumping-off points to help instructors frame questions suited for their particular classroom. The class exercises and chapter assignments can be used as they are written or modified to fit instructors' needs. These exercises and assignments can also inspire instructors to develop their own activities. And the suggested videos are but a very few that are available to help students experience this subject in various ways. Many more videos can be located through on-line Web Sites on a variety of topics, as well as through campus and even municipal libraries. One of the best guides for using videos as teaching aides (Summerfield's *Crossing Cultures Through Films*) can be found in the suggested readings. Summerfield's book provides some useful tips and considerations when using videos in class, and she reviews a number of the most popular videos in use today.

Suggested Course Outlines

This textbook was specially designed for freshmen and sophomores in both community colleges and 4-year schools. The book contains nine main chapters and four shorter chapters that focus on applications of intercultural communication. For instructors teaching on a 15-week, 45-hour semester schedule, all 13 chapters can be included. For those teaching a 10-week, 40-hour quarter course, some choices will need to be made as to which material to include and which material to condense or exclude. Sample course schedules for both semester and quarter schedules are provided here as a guide to planning the course.

Sample Semester Course Schedule
15-week, 45-hour semester

Class Period	Topic	Weekly Reading
Week 1	Introduction to course Introduction activity Reasons for studying intercultural communication Classroom exercise/video	Chapter 1
Week 2	Four building blocks of intercultural communication Classroom exercise/video Attitude and behavioral barriers	Chapter 2
Week 3	History and intercultural communication History and identity Classroom exercise/video Intercultural communication and history	Chapter 3
Week 4	Understanding identity Social and cultural identities Identity development Classroom exercise/video	Chapter 4
Week 5	Multicultural identity Identity, language, and intercultural communication Classroom exercise/video Catch up and review	Chapter 4
Week 6	Exam 1 Verbal issues in intercultural communication The study of language Cultural variations in language Language and power Moving between languages	Chapter 5
Week 7	Nonverbal issues in intercultural communication Defining nonverbal communication Classroom exercise/video Cultural variations in nonverbal codes Defining cultural space	Chapter 6
Week 8	Popular culture and intercultural communication Defining popular culture Consuming and resisting popular culture Classroom exercise/video Representing cultural groups U.S. popular culture and power	Chapter 7

Week 9	Culture, communication, and conflict Characteristics of intercultural conflict Conflict types, strategies, and contexts Cultural influences on conflict management	Chapter 8
Week 10	Classroom exercise on conflict Managing intercultural conflict Understanding conflict and society	
Week 11	Intercultural communication in everyday life Benefits and challenges of intercultural relationships Foundations of intercultural relationships Intercultural dating and marriage Classroom exercise/video Exam 2	Chapter 9
Week 12	Intercultural communication and tourism Social norms, culture shock, and language issues Communication styles Classroom exercise	Chapter 10
Week 13	Intercultural communication and business Work-related values Cultural differences in management styles Language issues and communication styles Affirmative action Guest speaker	Chapter 11
Week 14	Intercultural communication and education Different kinds of educational experiences Communication, education, and cultural identity Social issues and education	Chapter 12
Week 15	Intercultural communication and health care Growing importance of health communication Intercultural barriers to effective health care Power in health communication Catch up and review Final exam	Chapter 13

Sample Quarter Course Schedule
10-week, 40-hour quarter

Class Period	Topic	Weekly Reading
Week 1	Introduction to course Introduction activity Reasons for studying intercultural communication Classroom exercise/video	Chapter 1
Week 2	Four building blocks of intercultural communication Classroom exercise/video Attitude and behavioral barriers	Chapter 2
Week 3	History and intercultural communication History and identity Classroom exercise/video Intercultural communication and history	Chapter 3
Week 4	Understanding identity Social and cultural identities Identity development Multicultural identity Identity, language, and intercultural communication	Chapter 4
Week 5	The study of language Cultural variations in language Language and power Moving between languages Midterm Exam	Chapter 5
Week 6	Defining nonverbal communication Classroom exercise/video Cultural variations in nonverbal codes Defining cultural space	Chapter 6
Week 7	Defining popular culture Consuming and resisting popular culture Classroom exercise/video U.S. popular culture and power	Chapter 7
Week 8	Characteristics of intercultural conflict Conflict types, strategies, and contexts Cultural influences on conflict management Managing intercultural conflict	Chapter 8
Week 9	Intercultural communication in everyday life Benefits and challenges of intercultural relationships Foundations of intercultural relationships Intercultural dating and marriage	Chapter 9

Week 10	Applying intercultural communication to:	Selected readings from:
	Tourism	Chapter 10
	Business	Chapter 11
	Education	Chapter 12
	Health care	Chapter 13

Alternative Week 10	Applying intercultural communication to:	Selected readings from:
	Either tourism or business	Chapters 10–11
	and	
	Either education or health care	Chapters 12–13
	Final exam	

Part Two
Chapter Resources

CHAPTER 1

Studying Intercultural Communication

LEARNING OBJECTIVES

After studying the material in this chapter, students should be able to:

Identify six imperatives that motivate interest in intercultural communication.

Describe how advances in technology and increased mobility have influenced intercultural communication.

List ways in which immigration patterns affect relationships between nations and cultures.

Explain how the history of immigration influences cultural relations within the United States.

Identify ways in which studying intercultural communication may contribute to promoting world peace.

Describe how the study of intercultural communication is important to the economy of the United States.

Explain how understanding other cultures improves our awareness of our own cultures.

Describe some of the ethical issues that arise in the study of intercultural communication.

Explain what it means to be an ethical intercultural communicator.

KEY TERMS

assimilatable	ethics	melting pot metaphor
class structure	global village	mobility
cross-cultural trainers	globalization	relativist position
demographics	heterogeneity	self-awareness
diversity	immigration	self-reflexivity
enclaves	*maquiladoras*	universalist position

DETAILED CHAPTER OUTLINE

Intercultural communication can be exciting and scary, frustrating and enlightening. There is no one "right" way to experience intercultural interaction. The authors of this book present their personal experiences in intercultural communication, as well as ones from other sources. Don't be overwhelmed by the apparent complexity of intercultural communication; instead, accept this as part of the intercultural communication experience. This chapter offers six reasons or imperatives for studying intercultural communication: economics, technology, demographics, peace, self-awareness, and ethics.

I. The Economic Imperative: Tremendous changes in the workplace are coming, and knowing about intercultural communication is strategically important for U.S. businesses in the emerging transnational economy.
   A. The Workplace
      1. Businesses must be more attentive to diversity issues.
      2. As the workforce becomes more diverse, many businesses are seeking to capitalize on these differences.
      3. Benefiting from cultural differences in the workplace involves:
         a. Working with diverse employees and employers.
         b. Seeing new business markets.
         c. Developing new products for differing cultural contexts.
         d. Marketing products in culturally appropriate and effective ways.
      4. Diversity is a potentially powerful economic tool for business organizations.
   B. The Global Economy
      1. U.S. businesses are expanding into world markets (globalization).
      2. As U.S. businesses expand, the ability of their employees to communicate effectively in intercultural contexts becomes crucial.
      3. This globalization process has not been as easy or profitable as one might think.
      4. To be competitive on a global scale, companies need to understand how business is conducted in other countries and negotiate deals that are advantageous to the U.S. economy.
      5. Increasingly, multinational corporations are moving their operations overseas to take advantage of lower labor costs—for example, *maquiladoras* (foreign-owned plants that use domestic labor) just across the U.S.–Mexican border.
      6. To bridge the cultural gap, many companies employ cross-cultural trainers who assist people going abroad by giving them information and strategies for dealing with cultural differences.
         a. Some countries, like Japan, have their personnel spend years in the United States studying English and learning about the country before building factories or investing money.
         b. By contrast, many U.S. companies provide little or no training before sending their workers overseas.
            i. They expect business deals to be completed very quickly with little regard for cultural idiosyncrasies.
            ii. This can cause ill will and mistrust, and enhance negative stereotypes, resulting in lost business opportunities.
      7. Economic development in Latin American, Japan, and other Asian countries will increase the demand for intercultural communication.
         a. Economic exchanges will drive intercultural interactions.
         b. This will create more jobs but also more consumers to purchase goods and to travel around the world.
II. The Technological Imperative: In the 1960s Marshall McLuhan coined the term "global village" to describe a world in which communication technology (TV, radio, news services) brings news and information to the most remote parts of the world. Today, people are connected via answering machines, faxes, e-mail, electronic bulletin boards, and the Internet to people they have never met face-to-face. Complex relationships can develop through technology.
   A. Technology and Human Communication
      1. Kenneth Gergen describes the changes that occur as technology alters patterns of communication.
         a. In past centuries, relationships were circumscribed by how far one could walk.
         b. With each technological advance (railroad, automobile, telephone, radio, TV, movies) the relationships expanded exponentially.

    c. With e-mail, faxes, phones, and so on, we can be involved simultaneously in many different relationships without face-to-face contact.

  2. Through high-tech communication, we come into contact with people who are very different from ourselves, often in ways we don't understand.

  3. Technology has increased the frequency with which many people encounter multilingual situations and so must decide which language will be used.

  4. Contrast this with the situation 100 years ago, when people rarely communicated with others outside their own villages, much less people speaking different languages.

  5. People seek out intercultural communication for many different reasons, including the use of other languages to express their thoughts and feelings.

B. Mobility and Its Effect on Communication

  1. We come into contact with more people physically and electronically these days.

  2. In the United States, families move on average five times although there are still communities in which people are born, live, and die.

  3. Mobility changes the nature of our society and the individuals involved.

  4. Many families move due to divorce.

    a. In 1988, only half of U.S. youths ages 15–17 lived with both birth parents.

    b. Of the other half, some lived with one parent, in stepfamilies, or in extended families (grandparents), or shuttled back and forth between parents, or commuted between different geographical regions of the United States.

    c. These new family configurations increase intercultural contact as generational, regional, and sometimes cultural differences influence the cultural notion of what constitutes "family."

    d. Increasing mobility increases the probability of encountering cultural differences related to food, languages, and regional ways of life.

  5. Families also relocate for economic reasons.

  6. Increasing technology and mobility means we can no longer afford to be culturally illiterate; rather, we all need to be more aware of cultural differences and learn to bridge those differences.

  7. Even people who never move may encounter others who are culturally different and so need to learn new strategies to communicate with them.

III. The Demographic Imperative: Changes come from two sources: changing demographics within the United States and changing immigration patterns.

A. Changing U.S. Demographics

  1. Demographics refer to the general characteristics of a given population.

  2. *Workforce 2000* and *Workforce 2020* document the changing demographics of the U.S. workforce as we enter the 21st century.

    a. The U.S. workforce will be older than it is now, with workers remaining in the workforce longer as Social Security and other benefits decline.

    b. More women will be working, and it is expected the United States will reach gender parity in the workforce, as opposed to the 1950s when only 30% of the workforce was female.

    c. The workforce will be more ethnically and racially diverse, but the diversity will not be evenly distributed across the nation. Changes will be felt most strongly in the West and South and less so in the Northeast and Midwest.

B. Changing Immigration Patterns

  1. There is a contradiction when discussing immigration in the United States.

    a. The United States is described as a nation of immigrants.

    b. It is also a nation that established itself by subjugating the original inhabitants of the land and prospering economically while forcibly importing millions of Africans to slave labor.

2. Patterns of immigration are having a significant effect on the social landscape of the United States.
   a. Prior to the 1960s, most immigrants came from Europe.
   b. Now, 90% of the million or so immigrants are from Latin America and Asia.
   c. In 2050, according to the Population Reference Bureau, the United States will be a global society in which nearly half of all inhabitants will be African Americans, Asian Americans, Pacific Islanders, Latinos/Latinas, and Native Americans.
   d. The United States is becoming more heterogeneous or diverse.
3. These demographic changes present many opportunities and challenges for students of intercultural communication and for society.
   a. The tension among different racial and ethnic groups and the fear on the part of politically dominant groups must be acknowledged.
      i.   For example, California has not made the transition to a more diverse society as smoothly as hoped.
      ii. During the 1990s, California passed laws eliminating affirmative action, restricting access to medical and social services, and eliminating bilingual education in schools.
   b. Many states with the highest percentages of non-White residents are the same states with very contentious racial histories—for example, Alabama, Mississippi, and South Carolina.
   c. Hawaii is a very diverse state in which no one group forms a majority, and it has largely avoided racial strife.
4. Intercultural conflict is not necessarily a consequence of diversity.
   a. Cultural diversity expands our linguistic, political, and social horizons as various lifestyles and ways of thinking merge.
   b. We often profit from being exposed to different ways of doing things and incorporate these customs into our own lifestyles.
C. Historical Overview: We have to look at the history of immigration in the United States to get a better sense of the sociocultural situation.
   1. An estimated 8–10 million Native Americans already lived here when Europeans began arriving.
      a. The outcome of the encounters between the colonizing Europeans and the native peoples is well known. By 1940, the Native American population of the United States had been reduced to an estimated 250,000.
      b. Today there are about 1.9 million Native Americans from 542 recognized tribes living in the United States.
   2. African Americans are a special case in U.S. immigration history because they were brought to this country involuntarily.
      a. Some Europeans and Asians also arrived in the country as indentured or contract labor. By the middle of the 17th century, this system had been dissolved because it was not economically viable for farmers and did not solve chronic labor shortages.
      b. Landowners needed captive workers who could neither escape servitude nor become competitors, and the answer was slavery.
      c. The slave trade lasted about 350 years during which time 9–10 million Africans reached the Americas (the vast majority died in the brutal overseas passage).
      d. James Baldwin has suggested that slavery is what makes U.S. history and current interracial relations different from those in Europe.
      e. Although slavery presented a moral dilemma for many Whites, a common response today is to ignore history.
         i.   Many Whites say that, because not all Whites owned slaves, we should simply forget it and move on.

       ii. For most African Americans, this is unacceptable, and Cornel West suggests that we should begin by acknowledging the historical flaws in U.S. society and recognize the historical consequences of slavery.

      iii. The recent controversy over the flying of the Confederate flag above the South Carolina state capitol building reflects a desire to remember that past in a different way.

      iv. There are several Holocaust museums in the United States, but no organized, official recognition of the horrors of slavery.

3. Relationships between residents and immigrants, between old-timers and newcomers, often have been contentious.
   a. For example, in the 19th century, Native Americans were sometimes caught in the middle of U.S.–European rivalries.
   b. As waves of immigrants continued to come from Europe, the more firmly established European (mainly English) immigrants tried to protect their way of life, language, and culture.

4. As immigrants from northern and western Europe came to dominate U.S. culture, immigrants from southern, central, and eastern Europe were expected to assimilate into mainstream culture—to jump into the "melting pot" and come out "American."

5. In the late 19th and early 20th centuries, an anti-immigrant, nativistic movement promoted violence against newer immigrants.

6. The U.S. government supported this anti-immigrant, nativistic sentiment.
   a. In 1882, Congress passed the Chinese Exclusion Act, officially prohibiting Chinese from immigrating to this country.
   b. In 1924, the Johnson-Read Act and the Oriental Exclusion Act established strict quotas on immigration and barred the immigration of Asians.
   c. The underlying rationale for these laws was that economic and political opportunities should be reserved for Whites whether or not they were native-born Americans.
   d. The dominance of Whites in the United States is not simply the result of more Europeans wanting to come here; the U.S. government designed our society this way.

7. By the 1930s, immigrants from southern and eastern Europe were considered assimilatable (able to become members of White society), and the concept of race assumed new meaning.
   a. All the so-called White races were now considered one, so racial hostilities were directed toward members of non-White ethnic groups.
   b. This bias was particularly devastating for African Americans because, in the first half of the 20th century, only White workers were assured a place.
   c. White immigrants did earn low wages, but they also were given "psychological" wages in the form of better schools, increased access to public facilities, and more public deference.

8. Economic conditions affect attitudes toward foreign workers and immigration policies.
   a. During the Great Depression of the 1930s, Mexicans and Mexican Americans were forced to return to Mexico to free up jobs for White Americans.
   b. When prosperity returned in the 1940s, Mexicans were welcomed back as a source of cheap labor.
   c. This pattern occurs around the world.

D. The Current Situation
   1. The tradition of tension and conflict between cultures continues.
   2. The conflicts in Southern California in the 1990s have their roots in the demographic changes in the United States.

      a. The California dream of Hollywood, as portrayed in TV shows and movies reflects unrealistic images that prevent us from recognizing intercultural tensions.

      b. One manifestation of these tensions was the 1991 Los Angeles riots that followed the Rodney King verdict. These and other kinds of tensions are fueled by recent allegations of widespread police corruption in the LAPD.

      c. Some of the conflict in Los Angeles among Latinos, African Americans, Korean Americans, and European Americans can be examined on a variety of levels.

         i. Some of the conflict is due to different languages, values, and lifestyles.

         ii. Some African Americans resent the success of recent Korean immigrants.

         iii. Conflict may also be due to the pattern of settlement that results in cultural enclaves: Blacks in South Central Los Angeles, Latinos in Inglewood and east Los Angeles, Koreans in the "Miracle Mile," and Whites on the west side of the city.

         iv. In other parts of the country, 86% of White suburban U.S. Americans live in neighborhoods that are less than 1% Black.

3. Economic disparity among these groups may also cause conflict.

      a. Most Americans are reluctant to admit that a class structure exists, let alone admit how difficult it is to move up in this structure.

      b. Most people live their lives in the same economic class into which they were born.

      c. The U.S. cultural myth that anyone can move up in the class structure through hard work is known as the Horatio Alger myth.

      d. The myth reinforces middle- and upper-class beliefs in members' superiority and perpetuates a false hope among working-class members that they can get ahead.

      e. Stories of easy upward mobility, such as the cases of Ross Perot, Roseanne, and Madonna, perpetuate the myth.

4. Have economic conditions changed for the various classes, and what might the future hold?

      a. *Workforce 2020* notes that the number of people at the high and low ends of the pay scale is increasing, while the number in the middle is decreasing.

      b. Concurrently, the stable industrial jobs in the cities have been disappearing as companies move overseas.

         i. Between 1979 and 1984, 11.5 million U.S. workers lost their jobs due to plant shutdowns or relocations.

         ii. Only 60% of these workers were able to find new jobs, and about half of these new jobs were for lower pay.

      c. The recent economic boom in the United States has made the rich even richer but has only increased income disparities between the rich and the poor.

      d. The increasing diversity presents a challenge for us as a society and as individuals to look beyond the Hollywood stereotypes and try to apply what we know about intercultural communication.

         i. A first step is to realize that the melting pot metaphor, in which all immigrants enter and blend into U.S. society, was probably never viable. Not all immigrants could be assimilated into the United States in the same way.

         ii. Many U.S. Americans believe they live in the most diverse society on earth; however, the United States is hardly a model of diversity, and many countries are much more ethnically diverse.

         iii. Nigeria has about 200 ethnic groups, as does Indonesia.

      e. Fortunately, most people negotiate day-to-day activities in schools, businesses, and other settings in spite of cultural differences.

      f. Demographic diversity in the United States has provided linguistic richness and culinary variety, generated resources to meet new social challenges, and created domestic and international business opportunities.

IV. The Peace Imperative: The key issue is, can individuals of different sexes, ages, ethnicities, races, languages, and cultural backgrounds coexist on the planet?
  A. Contact among different cultural groups often leads to disharmony.
      1. Consider the ethnic struggles in Bosnia and in the former Soviet Union, the conflicts between the Indonesians and East Timorese, and the racial and ethnic tensions in various U.S. cities.
      2. Some of these conflicts represent a legacy of colonialism around the world in which European powers forced diverse groups differing in language, culture, religion, or identity to form one state.
  B. Conflict is also tied to economic disparities and economic colonialism.
      1. The influence of U.S. technology and media is seen as a benefit by some and as a cause for resistance by others.
      2. Fernando Delgado states that cultural dominance "can spark intercultural conflicts because it inhibits the development of other nations' indigenous popular culture products, stunts their economic development and foists U.S. values and perspectives on other cultures."
      3. In Delgado's trip to Europe, he noticed anti-American sentiments in graffiti, newspapers, and TV programs, and resentment, frustration, and disdain among the locals.
  C. It would be naïve to assume that simply understanding something about intercultural communication will end war and intercultural conflict, but these problems underscore the need for us to learn more about groups of which we are not members.
  D. We need to remember that individuals often are born into and caught up in conflicts that they neither started nor chose and that are impacted by the larger forces.
V. The Self-Awareness Imperative
  A. One of the most important (but less obvious) reasons for studying intercultural communication is to gain an awareness of one's own cultural identity and background.
  B. Peter Adler observes that the study of intercultural communication begins as a journey into another culture and reality, and ends as a journey into one's own culture.
VI. The Ethical Imperative
  A. Ethical Judgments and Cultural Values: Living in an intercultural world presents challenging ethical issues that can be addressed by the study of intercultural communication.
      1. Ethics are principles of conduct that help govern the behavior of individuals and groups. They often arise from communities' views on what is good and bad behavior.
      2. Cultural values tell us what is "good" and what "ought" to be, and ethical judgments focus more on the degrees of rightness and wrongness in human behavior than do cultural values.
          a. Some judgments are stated very explicitly, like the Ten Commandments or the Golden Rule.
          b. Laws often reflect the cultural values of dominant groups. For example, many states had laws prohibiting interracial marriage (miscegenation laws), and today in many states there are debates about legalizing same-sex marriage.
          c. Less explicit principles arise from our cultural experiences, such as that people should be treated equally and that they should work hard.
      3. Several issues arise in any discussion of ethics in intercultural communication.
          a. One issue focuses on what happens when two ethical systems collide.
              i. The desire to do the right thing is an important motivation, but it is not easy to know what is "right" in specific situations in intercultural communication.
              ii. Ethical principles are often culture-bound, and intercultural conflicts arise from varying notions of what constitutes ethical behavior.

    b. Another ethical dilemma involves standards of conducting business in multinational corporations.

       i. The U.S. Congress and the Securities and Exchange Commission consider it unethical for corporations to make payments to government officials in other countries, as such payments smack of bribery.

       ii. In many countries, government officials are paid in this informal way instead of being supported by taxes.

       iii. This dilemma raises the issue of what is ethical behavior for personnel in multinational subsidiaries.

4. This book stresses the relativity of cultural behavior—that no cultural pattern is inherently right or wrong. This raises such questions as, Is there any universality in ethics? Are any cultural behaviors always right or always wrong?

5. The answers to these questions depend on one's perspective.

    a. According to the universalist position, we need to identify those rules that apply across cultures.

       i. A universalist might try to identify acts and conditions that most societies think of as wrong (murder, treason, theft).

       ii. An extreme universalist would insist that cultural differences are only superficial and that fundamental notions of right and wrong are universal.

       iii. Some religions take universal positions such as the Ten Commandments, although Christian groups often disagree about the universality of the Bible.

    b. By contrast, the relativist position holds that any cultural behavior can be judged only within the cultural context in which it occurs.

       i. This means that only a community can truly judge the ethics of its members.

       ii. William S. Howell explains the relativist position as "all moral choices flow from the perceptions of the decision maker, and those perceptions are produced by unique experiences in one person's life, in the context in which the choices are made."

6. Philosophers and anthropologists have struggled to develop ethical guidelines that are universally applicable but that also reflect the tremendous cultural variability in the world.

    a. David W. Kale has proposed a universal code of ethics for intercultural communicators based on a universal belief in the sanctity of the human spirit and the desirability of peace.

    b. While we may wish to believe that universal ethical principles exist, we must be careful not to assume that others share our ethical principles.

    c. When we encounter other ethical principles, it is often difficult to know if we are imposing our ethical principles on others and whether we should.

7. The study of intercultural communication should provide insights into cultural patterns and help us address these ethical issues.

    a. We should be able to judge what is ethical and unethical behavior given variations in cultural priorities.

    b. We should be able to identify guidelines for ethical behavior in intercultural contexts in which ethics clash.

8. Another ethical issue concerns the application of intercultural communication scholarship.

    a. Everett Kleinjans stresses that intercultural education differs from other kinds of education in that intercultural contact is particularly transformative as it deals with fundamental aspects of human behavior.

    b. Learning about intercultural communication sometimes calls into question the very core of our assumptive framework and challenges existing beliefs, values, and patterns of behavior.

B. Becoming an Ethical Student of Culture
1. Practicing self-reflexivity, the process by which we "look in the mirror" to see ourselves
    a. It is vital when studying intercultural communication to understand ourselves and our position in society.
    b. Intercultural experiences teach us about how we react and interact in different cultural contexts, and help us evaluate situations and deal with uncertainty.
    c. When considering ethical issues in intercultural communication, we need to recognize the strengths and limitations of our own intercultural experiences, and when we gain more intercultural experiences, our views on ethics may change.
    d. Many cultural attitudes and ideas are instilled in us and are difficult to unravel and identify. Discovering who we are is not easy but is an ongoing process.
    3. By understanding which social categories we belong to and their implications, we should better understand how to communicate.
2. Learning about others
    a. The study of cultures is actually the study of other people, and we must never lose sight of the humanity of the topic of study.
    b. We must remember we are studying real people who have real lives, and your conclusions about them may have very real consequences for them and for you.
    c. We should refrain from viewing people who are different from us as if their cultural practices are for the display and entertainment of others.
    d. Students of cultures should speak "with" and "to" others instead of "for" and "about" others.
3. Listening to the voices of others
    a. Hearing about the experiences of people who are different can lead to different ways of viewing the world.
    b. Listening carefully as people relate their experiences and their knowledge helps us learn about other cultures.
4. Changing through intercultural contact
    a. Sometimes communities lose their uniqueness because of intercultural contact.
    b. Some cultures resist the influence of contact whereas others do not.
5. Unethical applications for intercultural information
    a. One is the pursuit of intercultural information to proselytize others without their consent.
    b. Another involves trainers who misrepresent or exaggerate their ability to change prejudices or racism in brief, one-shot training sessions.

DISCUSSION QUESTIONS

1. How do electronic means of communication (e-mail, the Internet, fax, and so on) differ from face-to-face interactions?

2. How does increased mobility of our society affect us as individuals? How does it affect the way we form relationships?

3. What are some of the challenges that organizations face as they become more diverse?

4. How might organizations benefit from increased diversity in the workplace? How might individuals benefit?

5. How do economic situations affect intergroup relations?

6. What roles do ethics play in intercultural communication?

7. Why are some immigrant groups subject to prejudice while others are not?

8. How can diverse groups of people work together successfully in business?

9. How can we apply what we learn about intercultural communication in an ethical way?

10. How has technology changed your relationships with friends, family, and others?

11. How do you feel about the changes described in *Workforce 2020*? Do the changes impact you in a positive or negative way?

12. How can learning about intercultural communication reinforce the peace imperative?

CLASSROOM EXERCISES AND CHAPTER ACTIVITIES

1. *Introduction Exercise:* At the beginning of the course, it is useful to provide opportunities for the students to become familiar with one another so that they will feel more comfortable contributing to class discussions. This may be facilitated by dividing students into pairs. Each student has 5 minutes to play the role of interviewer and 5 minutes to be interviewed. At the end of 10 minutes, the student pairs take turns introducing each other to class members. The following questions are useful in becoming acquainted with students and the repertoire of cultural experiences they bring to class:

    a. Where did you grow up?

    b. What other languages besides English do you speak?

    c. What areas outside the United States have you visited?

    d. Have you lived outside of the United States? Where?

    e. What was one intercultural experience you have had?

    f. What was one ritual your family practiced as you were growing up?

    g. Why are you taking this class?

    h. Would you like to live in another country? Why?

    The length of time needed for this exercise depends on the class size and the number of questions you suggest to the students. Typically, 10–15 minutes are provided for the interviews; you can alert students when it is time to switch from being the interviewer to the interviewee. The oral introductions average about 2–3 minutes per pair. If you need to cut down on the time allotted for the oral introductions, limit the students to telling four or five things they learned about their partners.

2. *Intercultural Issues Exercise:* Use this activity to increase student awareness of the impact and prevalence of the imperatives (for example, technological, demographic) described in this chapter. You need an edition (if the class size is large, multiple editions may be used) of a fairly large local newspaper. Divide the class into groups of two to four individuals and give each group a section of the paper with news articles of some type (for example, local, state, national, international, sports, business). Then assign the groups of students to skim through their sections of the paper for articles that report on issues related to the imperatives. One member of the group should record on a piece of paper the number of articles found for each imperative and write a brief description of the subject of each article. You may want to show them one or two example from another paper/edition. Students will need 10–20 minutes to work as groups, unless their assigned sections are small. When they have finished, record on the board the number of articles found by each group for each imperative. After tallying the total in each column, ask students to discuss why there were more articles concerning some initiatives than others (were there any precipitating events that generated more articles?) and to share examples of some of the articles.

3. *Local Immigration Assignment:* The focus of this assignment is on familiarizing students with the way immigration patterns may have affected their own communities. Assign students to research the community in which they grew up or currently live to discover some of the motives for immigrants to move to the community. This assignment may be given as an individual project or to groups. Potential information sources include state or local historical societies, reference librarians at local libraries, tourist information bureaus, chambers of commerce, local historians, and longtime residents of the community. Students can compile the information in a written or oral presentation form. The following questions can guide their research:

   a. What ethnic background/countries are represented in your community?

   b. From what ethnic backgrounds/countries are the majority of the people in your community?

   c. What were some of the reasons people from different ethnic backgrounds/countries came to your community?

   d. How did the people from these different ethnic backgrounds/cultures influence the community?

   e. Is there any visible evidence of the cultures these people came from in the community today (celebrations, traditions, architecture)?

   f. Were there large groups of people from other ethnic backgrounds/countries who came to the community and have since left? Why did they come and go?

4. *Video Assignment:* Students may select a video to watch that depicts the experiences of immigration to the United States for a particular ethnic group or individual. After they have watched the video, have them describe the immigration experience using these questions as a guide:

   a. What factors influenced the group/individual to move to the United States?

   b. What were the primary challenges this group/individual faced in trying to get along in the United States?

   c. How did the group/individual react to these challenges?

   d. Were there any people or events that aided the group/individual?

   Suggested Videos

Far and Away	*El Norte*
Lone Star	*Blue Collar and Buddha*
The Joy Luck Club	

5. *Assessing Cultural Behavior/Ethics Exercise:* This activity is designed to help students begin to explore their personal ethics and the challenges created by viewing intercultural communication in a relativistic rather than a universalistic manner. Be prepared to discuss difficult issues that may arise during this activity and to help students view ethics within a more complex framework by applying the guidelines in this chapter. For this exercise, ask students to find an ethical issue they feel strongly about from a news broadcast, a newspaper article, or the Internet. Instruct them to come prepared to describe the issue and the ethical challenge or dilemma it poses. Challenge students to describe the position a relativist and then a universalist would take on this issue. After all the students have presented their issues (in a large class they could do this in dyads or small groups), ask

them to describe ways in which ethical intercultural communicators would handle these dilemmas using the guidelines in this chapter. Reinforce to students that many ethical issues are difficult and that the guidelines for ethical communication are challenging to use. Therefore, it is important to listen patiently to each other and then help each other sort out the issues by asking questions like the ones suggested in the following hypothetical example.

Example: Suppose a student chose the debate over teaching Ebonics versus standard English in California schools. The ethical issues raised in this debate may include whether Ebonics is a "real" language, whether students of Ebonics will be disadvantaged by not learning standard English, and what message is being communicated to African Americans and speakers of other languages in the United States. You might then encourage students to apply the ethical guidelines in their thinking by asking questions such as:

  a. How can teaching both Ebonics and standard English help us to respect others?

  b. Can we practice self-reflexivity by striving to "see" the value of Ebonics (or standard English) from our own and another's point of view?

  c. What can we learn about others by listening to those who have a viewpoint different from our own?

6. *Early Experiences with Cultural Differences:* This introductory activity is useful for helping students explore their initial experiences with diversity. Ask students to write a one-page essay about their recollection of the first time they were aware of meeting someone who was different from themselves. The difference could have been based on culture, ethnicity, physical disability, religion, or economic class. In their essays students should answer these questions:

  a. How did they meet the person? What were the circumstances?

  b. What made them aware that this person was different?

  c. How did they react?

  d. Was the interaction positive, negative, or neutral?

  e. Did they tell anyone about the interaction, and how did that person react?

  f. How has this first interaction affected future interactions with persons from the same group?

7. *Cultural Artifacts Exercise:* To encourage students to become more aware of their own cultural backgrounds and to emphasize the "hidden" nature of culture, ask them to bring to class an article or object from home that they believe exemplifies their cultural background and its values. During class, the students (if a large class, have them do this in small groups) can "show and tell" their object and explain how the article is representative of their culture's values and beliefs.

8. *Cultural Bingo Warm-Up:* This is a fun and active way for students to meet and begin to develop relationships with one another. Provide each student with a list or a grid with boxes next to 10–15 statements (the number will depend on how many students are participating and the amount of time you want to use). You may want to choose questions that will help identify some of the diversity existing among the students. For example, find someone who:

a. Speaks a language other than English.

b. Is in love.

c. Wants to be a rock star.

d. Was born in a country other than the United States.

e. Has parents who speak more than one language.

f. Saw a movie last week.

g. Has a pet.

Have students move around the room asking each other these questions until they find someone who can answer one affirmatively. That person puts his or her initials in the box or next to the question. The "game" continues until a student gets all the questions answered or until the instructor determines the game is over. The student who gets the most questions initialed "wins." This activity can be debriefed with questions like these:

a. How did the winner (or others) get so many questions answered?

b. What assumptions did you make about the others so as not to waste time asking questions a person could not answer "yes" to?

c. Did you learn anything surprising while doing this activity?

d. What types of diversity exist among the members of this class?

Note: If time is limited or it is not feasible for students to move around the room, you can use this exercise with the entire class at the same time. Simply read statements, and have students raise their hand or stand if the item describs them. This approach will still give students an opportunity to learn about one another.

SUGGESTED VIDEOS

1. *The Amish: Not to Be Modern.* Produced by V. Larimore & M. Taylor and Filmakers Library: distributed by Modern Educational Video Network, 1992. This video shows aspects of the Amish community and examines how their religious beliefs provide the background for their lifestyle choices. (57 minutes)

2. *The Asianization of America.* Produced by WNET/Thirteen; Films for the Humanities, Princeton, 1993. This video depicts the role of Asians in American business and society. (26 minutes)

3. *Becoming American.* Produced by WNET/Thirteen, IRIS Films, and K. Levine & I. W. Levine; distributed by New Day Films, Franklin Lakes, NJ, 1983. This video relates the immigration experience of a Hmong refugee family to the United States and shows some of the obstacles they encountered. (30 minutes)

4. *The Immigrant Experience: 1900–1940.* Distributed by Films for the Humanities, Princeton, 2000. This ABC News program anchored by Peter Jennings tells the dramatic story of the transformation of America into a truly multicultural nation, from the ethnic neighborhoods of New York to the black migration to northern cities during the Great Depression. Also discussed are incidents of racism spurred by the terror tactics of the Ku Klux Klan and the World War II fears that prompted the forced internment of 120,000 Japanese Americans. (29 minutes)

5. *Immigration: Who Has Access to the American Dream?* Distributed by Films for the Humanities, Princeton. This program examines the hard-core questions surrounding current U.S. immigration. All of the issues are examined through the eyes of those seeking entry and the organizations assisting them. Those interviewed include an immigration judge, an immigrant from Kenya, and the owner of a New York City deli from Korea. (28 minutes)

CHAPTER 2

Intercultural Communication: Building Blocks and Barriers

LEARNING OBJECTIVES

After studying the material in this chapter, students should be able to:

Understand various ways to think about culture.

Identify characteristics important to defining communication.

Explain the relationship between communication and culture.

Understand the role of values in intercultural communication.

Describe the relationship between communication and context.

Discuss the role of power in communication interactions.

Identify and explain four barriers to intercultural communication.

KEY TERMS

communication	intercultural communication	prejudice
context	masculinity/femininity	stereotyping
culture	perception	uncertainty avoidance
discrimination	power	values
ethnocentrism	power distance	worldview
individualism		

DETAILED CHAPTER OUTLINE

I. Intercultural Communication: Four Building Blocks
Intercultural communication occurs when people from different cultural backgrounds interact. Communication always happens within a particular situation or context. Power is a part of every intercultural interaction.

II. Building Block 1: Culture. Culture is the core concept in intercultural communication. Culture is defined as learned patterns of perception, values, and behaviors, shared by a group of people. It is also dynamic and heterogeneous.
   A. Culture Is Learned
   1. While all humans share some universal habits (such as eating and sleeping), these are not aspects of culture.
   2. Culture is the unique way we have learned to eat, sleep, and so on, because we are American or Japanese, male or female, and so on.
   3. Other members of our cultural groups taught us slowly and subconsciously how to be members of our culture.

    B. Culture Involves Perception and Values
1. Members of cultural groups share perceptions or a way of looking at the world.
2. We select, evaluate, and organize information (stimuli) from the external environment through perception.
3. Learning and perception are related to the values of the cultural groups we belong to.
4. Values have to do with what is judged good or bad, right or wrong in a culture.
5. We all see the world in particular ways because of the cultural groups to which we belong.

    C. Culture Is Shared
1. Cultural patterns of perception and beliefs are shared by groups of people.
2. These patterns are developed through interactions with different groups—with family and neighbors, at school, in youth groups, at college, and so on.
3. So, our perceptions are similar to those who belong to the same cultural groups. For example:
    a. Men and women share many similar perceptions about being male or female and many attitudes toward each other.
    b. White Americans seem to share a perception that things are getting better for African Americans and that racial attitudes and interactions are improving. In contrast, many African Americans share a perception that, while equality between races has improved, there is still a long way to go.
4. Membership in cultural groups ranges from involuntary to voluntary.
    a. Involuntary associations are groups we belong to with little choice regarding membership (age, race, gender, physical ability, sexual orientation, family groups).
    b. Voluntary associations are groups we choose to belong to (nationality, profession, political associations).
    c. Some groups may be involuntary when we are young (religion, nationality, socioeconomic class) but become voluntary associations later on.

    D. Culture Is Expressed as Behavior
1. Our cultural "lens" or "computer program" also influences our behaviors.
2. We belong to many different cultural groups that collectively determine our perceptions, beliefs, and behaviors.
3. These patterns endure over time and are passed from person to person.

    E. Culture Is Dynamic and Heterogeneous
1. Culture is dynamic or changing and can often be the object of conflict.
2. Cultural patterns are also dynamic and heterogeneous.
3. Sometimes there is conflict over cultural patterns and meanings, such as the debate over definitions of what "Native American" means.
4. Viewing culture as dynamic is important to understand the struggles of various groups as they try to negotiate their relationships and well being in U.S. society.
5. Seeing culture as dynamic and heterogeneous opens up new ways of thinking about intercultural communication, because people from a particular culture are not identical, and any culture has numerous cultural struggles.
6. Yet, cultures are not heterogeneous in the same way everywhere. How sexuality, race, gender, and class function in other cultures is not the same as or even similar to their function in the United States.
7. By viewing any culture as heterogeneous, we can understand the complexities of that culture and become more sensitive to how people in that culture live.

III. Building Block 2: Communication
    A. Communication is defined as a symbolic process whereby meaning is shared and negotiated. In other words, communication occurs whenever someone attributes meaning to another's words or actions.

1. Communication is symbolic.
   a. Words and gestures have no meaning in themselves but are only significant because people agree (to some extent) on their meaning.
   b. When we use symbols (words, gestures) we assume that the other person shares our symbol system.
   c. Symbolic meanings are conveyed both verbally and nonverbally, and thousands of nonverbal behaviors involve shared meanings.
2. Communication is a process.
   a. Communication involves people who are communicating, a message that is being communicated (verbal or nonverbal), a channel (the way communication takes place), and a context.
   b. People can be thought of as senders and receivers as they are sending and receiving messages.
3. Communication is sharing and negotiating meaning.
   a. People have to agree on the meaning of a particular message.
   b. Messages often have more than one meaning, and we assume that the other person takes the meaning we intend.
   c. When we communicate with people from different cultural backgrounds and experiences, it may lead to misunderstandings if we assume the person takes the meaning we intended.
   d. We may have to try harder in intercultural communication to make sure that meaning is truly shared.
4. Communication is dynamic.
   a. It is not a single event but is ongoing—so communicators are both senders and receivers at the same time.
   b. We take in messages through the senses of sight, smell, and hearing, not one at a time but simultaneously.
   c. When we are communicating, we are creating, maintaining, or sharing meanings, implying that people are actively involved in the communication process.
   d. Technically, then, one person cannot communicate alone.
5. Communication does not have to be intentional.
   a. Some of the most important (and disastrous) communication occurs without the sender knowing a particular message has been sent.
   b. For example, an American businessman in Saudi Arabia showed his Saudi host the soles of his feet (an insult in Saudi society), inquired about his wife's health (considered an inappropriate topic), and turned down an offer of tea (considered rude). The business deal fell through, and the American wondered what had gone wrong.
6. Communication is receiver-oriented.
   a. The person who assigns meaning determines the outcome of the communication situation.
   b. If another person interprets a message as prejudicial, sexist, or negative, this interpretation has much more influence over future interactions than does the sender's intended meaning.
   c. By realizing that there is a possibility (particularly in intercultural encounters) that we will be misunderstood, we can paraphrase, ask questions, or watch to see if we get nonverbal clues that indicate misunderstanding.

IV. Culture and Communication
   A. Communication, Cultural Worldviews, and Values: Members of a culture create a worldview (a particular way of looking at the world) made up of the values of a culture. Values have to do with what is judged good or bad, or right or wrong. They are deeply felt beliefs and reflect a perception of what ought to be, not what is.

1. Kluckhohn and Strodtbeck's value orientation
   a. These anthropologists suggested that members of all cultural groups must answer a series of questions.
      i.   What is human nature?
      ii. What is the relationship between humans and nature?
      iii. What is the relationship among humans?
      iv. What is the preferred form of activity?
      v.   What is the orientation toward time?
   b. There are three possible responses for each question, and each cultural group has one or possibly two preferred responses.
   c. The questions and responses are a way to understand broad cultural differences among various cultural groups.
2. The nature of human nature
   a. Basic goodness: This value is seen in societies that emphasize rehabilitating lawbreakers. Religions such as Buddhism and Confucianism focus on improving on the natural goodness of humans.
   b. Combination of goodness and evil: Many groups in the United States hold this perspective, though it has been shifting, and there is less talk now about rehabilitation and reform, and more about punishment. In religious beliefs, there is less emphasis on the fundamental evil of humanity.
   c. Essentially evil: Societies with this value are interested not in rehabilitation, but in punishment. This orientation may be related to the Christian view that humans are essentially evil and born with sin.
3. Relationships between humans and nature
   a. Humans dominate over nature: Evidence of this is found in the United States where scientists attempt to modify or control nature to accommodate human needs or desires.
   b. Nature dominates over humans: In cultures with this perspective, people are more willing to accept what nature brings.
   c. Harmony between humans and nature: In cultures (for example, Japan and Native Americans) with this perspective, people believe that nature plays a vital role in the spiritual and religious life of the community. Some societies (such as many Arab cultural groups) emphasize aspects of both harmony with and the domination of nature.
4. Relationships among humans
   a. Individual (individualism): More emphasis is placed on the individual than on the family, work teams, or other groups. Some claim that this is the most important European American (and Canadian and Australian) value.
   b. Group-oriented (collectivism): More emphasis is placed on the family (particularly extended families), work teams, or other groups.
   c. These values have a strong influence on how people communicate.
   d. People may belong to cultural groups that hold contradictory values. They may live "between" two cultures and find that they try to meet the demands of both cultures.
5. Preferred form of activity
   a. Doing: This orientation emphasizes productivity and is the most common perspective in the United States. Higher status is accorded to those who do rather than to those who think.
   b. Growing: Importance is placed on the spiritual aspects of life. Few cultures practice this value, but some cultures, like Japan, may practice a combination of the doing and growing orientations.

    c. Being: Emphasis is placed on a kind of self-actualization, in which the person is fused with the experience. This value is found in some Central and South American societies and in Greece and Spain.

6. Orientation to time
    a. Future: This value is typical of most U.S. cultural communities. Examples of this orientation include saving money for the future and keeping appointment books of future commitments.
    b. Present: Typical in Spain and Greece, the emphasis is on the here-and-now and the value of living in and realizing the potential of the present moment.
    c. Past: European and Asian societies typically emphasize the past, believing that history has something to contribute to our understanding of the present.

7. Hofstede's value dimensions: Social psychologist Geert Hofstede has identified several additional cultural values that impact communication.
    a. Power distance: This refers to the extent to which less powerful members of institutions and organizations expect and accept that power is distributed unequally. In low power distance cultures (Denmark, Israel, New Zealand), people believe that less hierarchy is better and that power should be used only for legitimate reasons. High power distance societies (Mexico, the Philippines, India) value social hierarchies, and decision making and relationships between people with different statuses are more formalized.
    b. Masculinity/femininity: This two-dimensional value refers to both the degree to which gender roles are valued and the emphasis placed on so-called masculine versus feminine values. People in Japan, Austria, and Mexico seem to prefer a masculine orientation, expressing a general preference for gender-specific roles. People in northern Europe seem to prefer a feminine value orientation, reflecting more gender equality and a stronger belief in the importance of quality of life for all.
    c. Uncertainty avoidance: This value relates to how threatened people feel in ambiguous situations and how they choose to deal with them. Cultures with low uncertainty avoidance (Great Britain, Sweden, Ireland, Hong Kong, the United States) have fewer rules, accept dissent, and are comfortable taking risks. Cultures with high uncertainty avoidance (Greece, Portugal, Japan) prefer more extensive rules and regulations in organized settings and seek consensus about goals.
    d. Long-term (Confucian) versus short-term orientation to life: This dimension was added to Hofstede's original three by Asian researchers. It has to do with a society's search for virtue versus truth. Cultures with a short-term orientation (Western religions of Judaism, Christianity, and Islam) are concerned with possessing the truth, look for quick results in endeavors, and exert social pressure to conform. Cultures with a long-term orientation (China, Hong Kong, Taiwan, Japan, South Korea, Brazil, India) respect the demands of virtue and focus more on thrift, perseverance, and tenacity in one's activities.

8. Intercultural conflicts are often the result of differences in value orientations.

9. Limitations of value frameworks
    a. While identifying cultural values helps us understand broad cultural differences, we must remember that not everyone in a given society holds the dominant value.
    b. Cultural frameworks tend to "essentialize" people. That is, people tend to assume that a particular group characteristic is the essential characteristic of a given person at all times and in all contexts.
    c. People may differ on specific value orientations, yet they may also hold other value orientations in common.
    d. There aren't easy lists of behaviors that are key to successful intercultural interactions.
    e. Value orientations should be used as general guidelines, not rigid rules.

   B. Communication and Cultural Rituals
       1. The way we communicate in cultural contexts strengthens our sense of cultural identity. For example, participating in communication rituals such as prayers may strengthen one's religious identity and sense of belonging to a religious community.
       2. The griping ritual among middle-class Israelis usually concerns something in public life, and the purpose is not to solve the problem, but to vent pent-up tensions. By participating in this ritual, Israelis feel more "Israeli."
       3. Other examples of how people's communication behavior reinforces their cultural identity and worldviews include the way white working-class men in the United States express their gender roles, and differences in the way people in the United States and Colombia persuade others to do something for them.
   C. Communication and Resistance to the Dominant Culture
       1. People may use their own space to resist dominant culture.
       2. Workers often find ways to resist extreme individualism and competition in the workplace.
 V. Building Block 3: Context
   A. Context consists of the physical, social, political, and historical structures in which the communication occurs. People communicate differently depending on the context.
       1. The controversy over the Calvin Klein ads that use young adolescents takes place in a social context that says pedophilia is perverse or immoral.
       2. Pedophilia is not considered wrong in all societies or in all periods of history.
       3. To really understand the meanings of the ads, we have to understand the current meanings attached to pedophilia wherever the ads are displayed.
   B. The political context includes those forces that attempt to change or retain existing social structures and relations.
       1. For example, the political context is important to an understanding of the acts of protesters who throw blood or red paint on people who wear fur coats.
       2. The political context is the ongoing informal debates about animal rights and cruelty to animals.
       3. In other countries or in other times, the protesters' act would not make sense or would be interpreted differently.
   C. The historical context is also important as it may influence interactions in the present.
       1. For example, African Americans and Whites in the United States have more trouble communicating than do Whites and Blacks in Europe.
       2. It's possible that the history of slavery influences African American and White interactions in the United States even today.
VI. Building Block 4: Power
   A. Power is always present during communication although it is not always evident or obvious.
       1. Communication between two people is rarely equal because in every society there exists a social hierarchy that gives some groups more power and privilege than others.
       2. This is true in intercultural communication because straight people often have more power than gays or lesbians, males more power than females, and the able-bodied more access to public facilities than those with disabilities.
       3. Those in power (consciously or unconsciously) create and maintain communication systems that reflect, reinforce, and promote their own way of thinking and communicating.
   B. There are two levels of group-related power.
       1. The primary and involuntary dimensions are more permanent in nature.
       2. The secondary and voluntary dimensions are more changeable.
       3. The dominant communication systems ultimately impede people who do not have the same ways of communicating.

C. Power also comes from social institutions and the roles people occupy in those institutions.
   1. For example, in a college classroom, there is temporary inequality, with the instructor having more power by setting the course requirements, giving grades, and determining who speaks.
   2. Power rests not with the individual instructor, but the role he or she is enacting.
D. Power is dynamic.
   1. It is not a simple one-way proposition.
   2. For example, students are not powerless, as they may assert and negotiate their power.
   3. One cannot teach without students, and the typical power relationship between instructor and student is not perpetuated beyond the classroom.
E. There are also issues of power in the broader societal context.
   1. For example, cosmetic companies have a vested interest in a particular image of female beauty that involves buying and using makeup. Advertising encourages women to feel compelled to accept this cultural definition.
   2. Whatever the reasons women have for deciding not to accept this definition of female beauty, other people are likely to interpret these women's choice in ways that may not match their own reasons.
   3. The message a woman's unadorned face communicates is understood in the context of society's definitions, which are developed by the cosmetics industry.
F. Power should be thought of in broad terms.
   1. Dominant cultural groups attempt to perpetuate their positions of privilege in many ways, and subordinate groups can resist this domination in many ways.
   2. Cultural groups use political and legal means to maintain or resist domination.
   3. The disempowered may negotiate power in many ways.
G. Power is complex, especially in relation to institutions or social structures.
   1. Some inequities (gender, class, race) are more rigid than those created by temporary roles.
   2. We can't really understand intercultural communication without considering the power dynamics in the interaction.
VII. Barriers to Intercultural Communication
   A. Ethnocentrism
      1. This is the belief that one's own cultural group (usually nationality) is superior to all other cultural groups.
      2. It's difficult to see our own ethnocentrism, and we may see it best when we spend extended time in another cultural group.
   B. Stereotyping
      1. Stereotypes are widely held beliefs about a group of people and are a form of generalization.
      2. To make sense out of the barrage of information we receive every day, we categorize and generalize from this information.
      3. Stereotypes may be harmful when they are held rigidly and are applied to all people.
      4. One reason we hold stereotypes is because they help us know what to expect from and how to react to others.
      5. Once stereotypes are adopted, they are difficult to discard because people remember stereotypic information but fail to retain information that contradicts the stereotype.
      6. We learn stereotypes in many different ways.
         a. The media tend to portray identity groups in stereotypic ways.
         b. Our family teaches us stereotypes.
         c. Stereotypes develop out of negative experiences. If we've had unpleasant contacts with people, we may generalize the unpleasantness to include all members of that particular group.

7. Stereotypes can be consciously rejected by recognizing we all hold negative stereotypes and by working at getting individual information that can counteract the stereotype.

C. Prejudice

1. Prejudice (a prejudgment) is a negative attitude toward a cultural group, based on little or no experience.

2. Stereotypes tell us what a group is like; prejudice tells us how we are likely to feel about that group.

3. Being prejudiced fills social functions.

    a. The adjustment function: People want to be accepted and liked by members of their cultural groups, and if they need to reject members of another group to be liked, then prejudice serves as a social reward.

    b. The ego-defensive function: People may hold certain prejudices because they don't want to admit certain things about themselves.

    c. The value-expressive function: People hold some prejudices because they help to reinforce certain beliefs or values.

4. Prejudice arises from the personal need to feel positive about one's own groups and negative about others or the need to feel safe from perceived or real threats.

    a. The threats may be realistic ones that challenge a group's existence or economic/political power.

    b. The threats may be symbolic threats like intergroup value conflicts. Intergroup threats involve the anxiety that results from intergroup contact.

5. Prejudice may also develop if one has had negative previous contact and is anxious about future contact, particularly if there are inequalities and perceived threats.

6. There are different kinds of prejudice.

    a. The most blatant prejudice is easy to see but is not as common anymore.

    b. Other forms of prejudice are less obvious but more difficult to pinpoint.

    c. Those who do not want to admit they are prejudiced show "tokenism."

        i. They go out of their way to engage in unimportant but positive intergroup behaviors.

        ii. They may show support for programs or say things like "I'm not prejudiced" to persuade themselves they are not prejudiced.

    d. Arm's-length prejudice occurs when people engage in friendly, positive behavior toward members of another group in public and semiformal situations (work, large social gatherings, lectures) but avoid intimate contact (dating, or small, intimate social gatherings).

D. Discrimination

1. Discrimination can be defined as behaviors that result from stereotypes or prejudice.

2. Discrimination may be based on race (racism) or any of the other "isms" related to belonging to different cultural groups.

3. If one belongs to a more powerful group and holds prejudices toward a less powerful group, actions toward members of that group are based on an "ism" and can be called discrimination.

4. Discriminatory acts range from subtle nonverbal jabs to verbal insults, to exclusion from jobs or other economic opportunities, to physical violence and even genocide.

5. Alport showed that, if no one objects, prejudice can develop into scapegoating, which can escalate into systematic elimination of a people (ethnic cleansing).

6. Discrimination may be interpersonal, collective, and/or institutional.

DISCUSSION QUESTIONS

1. What are some barriers to positive intercultural communication?

2. Can you think of similar communication rituals you and members of other cultures might participate in?

3. Why do we hold stereotypes?

4. Why are people prejudiced against a particular group of people?

5. How do the values of a cultural group influence communication with members of other cultural groups?

6. What do people do to assert power in communication interactions?

7. What do we mean by the statement, "Trying to understand one's own culture is like trying to explain to a fish that it lives in water"?

8. How do we learn our culture?

9. What is meant by the statement, "Culture is the filter or the lens (like prescription glasses), and each group has a different prescription"?

10. What cultural patterns do you share with members of your cultural group?

11. In what ways is culture dynamic (ever changing)?

12. How can cultural value frameworks "essentialize" people?

13. What is the relationship between the power dynamics in an interaction and in intercultural communication?

14. What is the difference between stereotypes and generalizations?

15. Where do we learn stereotypes about different groups?

16. What are some of the functions of being prejudiced?

17. What might be an example of interpersonal discrimination?

18. What might be an example of institutionalized racism?

19. Why is it important to speak up and resist racism?

CLASSROOM EXERCISES AND CHAPTER ACTIVITIES

1. *Defining Communication Exercise:* Divide students into groups of four to six, and ask them to come up with the best definition they can for "communication." Suggest that as part of this discussion they create a list of the different characteristics of communication. After 10 minutes, have students share their lists and their definitions of communication. This could be followed by a discussion of the characteristics of communication and the reasons there are so many different definitions for communication. At the conclusion of the discussion, you might ask, "How would you define intercultural communication?" and lead a discussion about how the definition might be modified to apply to communication. You may also want to discuss how the characteristics of communication they have listed would influence the process of intercultural communication.

2. *Building Communication Models Exercise:* At the beginning of this exercise, explain to the students that sometimes when we talk about processes we use models to illustrate the process. Show students a communication model. Basic communication, public speaking, and interpersonal communication textbooks are all good sources for such models. Discuss the model with the class. Identify the characteristics of communication shown in the model, and have students suggest aspects of communication they feel are missing from the model. Then divide the class into small groups and challenge them to create an original model that they feel adequately illustrates the communication process. Give them about 15 minutes to complete their models. One or two students from each group should be designated by the group to draw the model on the board and explain the rationale behind its design.

3. *Cultural Artifacts Exercise:* To encourage students to become more aware of their own cultural backgrounds and to emphasize the "hidden" nature of culture, ask students to bring to class an article or object from home that they believe exemplifies their cultural background and its values. During class, the students (if a large class, have them do this in small groups) can "show and tell" their object or article and explain how it is representative of their culture's values and beliefs

4. *Perception Exercise:* This exercise is designed to demonstrate how differing perceptions can affect communication. Have students write (or tell a dyad partner) about a situation in which they and another person were in an interaction together, but their perceptions of the interaction were different from each other's. Students should first present the "facts" of the situation and then describe the situation from their point of view. Next, have students switch perspectives and attempt to describe the situation from the other person's point of view, even if they disagree with that person's perspective. If this exercise is done verbally in dyads, each student takes a turn describing his or her situation. The dyad partner needs to listen carefully to make sure the storyteller is presenting the other persons' perspective as fully and as nonjudgmentally as possible.

5. *Values Exercise:* The goal of this powerful exercise is to enable students to experience first-hand how deeply we hold certain values. Be aware that this may be upsetting for some students, particularly immigrants who may have lost something they value. Allow students to opt out of the process at any time if they find the exercise too disturbing. The exercise will probably work better with a class that is willing to be self-reflective. First, give students 5–10 pieces of paper (determine the number by class size and time constraints). Then follow these steps:

    a. Ask the students to write one of their values on each of the pieces of paper.

    b. Instruct them to organize the pieces of paper according to how important each value is to them, with the most important value at the top and the least important at the bottom.

    c. Invite students to throw away (literally into the middle of the room) the value they think is the least important one to them.

    d. Discuss how it felt to throw away that value, even considering it was their least important one.

    e. Instruct them to throw away their most important value.

    f. Discuss how it felt to even figuratively throw away their most significant value.

    g. (Optional) Ask students to take one of the values from the person on their left and throw it away.

    h. Discuss how this felt.

After the exercise, use the following questions to debrief the exercise.

a. How do you feel about the values you have in front of you?

b. How did it feel to lose values? To keep values?

c. What does this say about the power and the meaning our values have for us?

d. Did you feel differently when another person threw away one of your values than when you did it?

e. Can you think of a situation in which people have lost values?

f. Are there examples of situations in which people have taken other people's values away from them?

g. How did they react? How might you react in a similar situation?

h. What impact has this had on these people?

Invite students to retrieve "tossed" values at the conclusion of this exercise.

6. *Power and Privilege Exercise—"Stand Up"*: This exercise allows students to identify themselves as belonging to a particular group or groups by standing up when a particular statement pertains to them. It is designed to bring into awareness the types of privilege we all have depending on the context. Read each statement to the class, and allow time for students to "stand up" in response to the statement (students need to stand up only if they are comfortable doing so and all the students should remain silent.) You can create statements to fit a particular topic or context: the list that follows merely contains suggestions. You may want to begin with statements that are not very personal and move gradually to those that require more intimate self-disclosure. This list of statements is designed to highlight class issues.

Stand up if:

a. You were born in the United States.

b. You are an only child.

c. You moved more than two times while growing up.

d. You were raised in the country (rural setting).

e. You grew up in an apartment.

f. Your family had few resources (students determine what "few" means).

g. Your family had more than enough resources.

h. Your parents are divorced.

i. You have more resources than your parents.

j. You are working your way through school.

After the exercise, examine each of the statements with the class, and ask students how being a part of the group identified in the statement would affect their ability to communicate with people from other groups. Which groups would be most comfortable communicating with them? Which groups would be least comfortable communicating with them?

7. *Simulation Exercise:* One of the most effective ways to help students identify with the challenges faced by immigrants is to involve them in a simulation in which they must interact without knowing the proper rules for communicating and accomplishing tasks. Two popular simulations that have been used in a variety of orientation programs, intercultural communication classes, and cross-cultural training sessions are "BaFa BaFa" and "Barnga."

   a. "Barnga." Created by Sivasailam Thiagarajan; distributed by Intercultural Press. P.O. Box 700, Yarmouth, ME 04096; (800) 370-2665; fax (207) 846-5181.

   b. "BaFa BaFa: A Cross Culture Simulation." Created by R. Garry Shirts; distributed by Simulation Training Systems, P.O. Box 910, Del Mar, CA 92014; (800) 942-2900; fax (619) 792-9743.

SUGGESTED VIDEOS

1. *Still Killing Us Softly: Advertising's Image of Women.* Produced by Jean Kilbourne; distributed by Cambridge Documentary Films, Cambridge, MA, 1987. The director, Margaret Lazarus, describes the portrayal of women in advertising and the way this portrayal influences women, men, and children. It also suggests ways that advertising's portrayal of women affects the images men and women form of themselves. (32 minutes)

2. *Black View of Discrimination.* Produced by the Educational Film Center for NYT Educational Media; distributed by Filmic Archives, New York, 1995. This video has four modules that deal with Black Americans' views of racial discrimination. (17 minutes)

3. *Eye of the Storm.* Distributed by PBS Video, Washington, DC, 1986. This video reports on the exercise in racism conducted by a third-grade teacher in her classroom. It is a good illustration of some of the effects of racism and some of the strategies people use to adapt to being victims of racist attitudes and actions. (25 minutes)

4. *Skin Deep: College Students Confront Racism.* Distributed by Iris Films, Ho-Ho-Kus, NJ, 1995. This film by Francis Reid documents the thoughts and feelings of several college students spending a weekend retreat together. It addresses issues of racism, prejudice, and cultural difference as seen through the eyes of this very diverse group. (60 minutes)

5. *True Colors.* Produced by MTI/Film and Video, North Brook, IL, 1991. This video questions our accomplishments in the fight for equality since the 1960s by testing various levels of prejudice. (19 minutes)

6. *Overcoming Prejudice.* Distributed by Insight Media, New York, 1996. This documentary examines the origins of prejudice, discussing how it can be learned at home, can be a result of fear or ignorance, or can be a reaction to mistreatment. People who have successfully overcome their own prejudices share their experiences and offer suggestions for finding common ground. (59 minutes)

7. *How Beliefs and Values Define a Culture.* Distributed by Insight Media, New York, 1997. This video considers how the arts, history, religion, and other elements shape cultural beliefs and values. It considers cross-cultural interactions and explores how technology is changing cultures. (24 minutes)

CHAPTER 3

History and Intercultural Communication

LEARNING OBJECTIVES

After studying the material in this chapter, students should be able to:

Understand the role of histories in intercultural communication interactions.

Describe some of the histories that influence our communication.

Explain why it is necessary to recover "hidden" histories.

Explain how we can negotiate histories in interactions.

Understand and identify the various forms of historical contexts that influence intercultural communication.

Explain the connections between histories, identities, and intercultural communication.

KEY TERMS

colonial histories	grand narrative	postcolonialism
cultural group histories	hidden histories	racial histories
diaspora	*Homo narrans*	religious histories
diasporic histories	intellectual histories	sexual orientation histories
ethnic histories	national histories	social histories
family histories	political histories	socioeconomic class histories
gender histories		

DETAILED CHAPTER OUTLINE

I. Introduction: Our cultural background influences our knowledge of history and how we feel about it.
   A. In intercultural encounters, differences may become hidden barriers to communication, and the influence of history on our interactions is frequently overlooked.
   B. Some people want to de-emphasize history, but others believe it is impossible to understand themselves without understanding the history of their cultural group.
   C. How we think about the past influences how we think about ourselves and others, because our identities are rooted in different histories.
   D. Culture and cultural identities are intimately tied to history, as they have no meaning without history.
   E. There is no single version of history; the past has been written in many different ways.

II. From History to Histories: Identifying the various forms of historical contexts is the first step in understanding how history affects communication.
   A. Political, Intellectual, and Social Histories
      1. Political histories are written histories that focus on political events.
      2. Intellectual histories are written histories that focus on the transmission and development of ideas or ways of thinking.
      3. Social histories are accounts of the everyday life experiences of various groups in the past.
      4. Absent histories are historical events that was never recorded.
      5. An absent history does not mean the people never existed, that their experiences did not matter, or that their history was insignificant. But acknowledging absent histories requires more complex ways of thinking about the past and the ways it influences the present and the future.
   B. Family Histories
      1. These occur at the same time as other histories, but on a more personal level.
      2. Often they are not written down, but rather passed along orally from one generation to the next.
      3. Some people do not know which countries or cities their families emigrated from or what tribes they belonged to or where they lived in the United States.
      4. Other people place great emphasis on knowing their family histories.
      5. Many family histories are deeply intertwined with ethnic group and religious histories, and family histories identify the family's participation in these events.
   C. National Histories
      1. The history of any nation is important to its people.
      2. This history is taught formally in school, and we are expected to recognize certain historical events and people.
      3. National history gives us a shared notion of who we are and solidifies our sense of nationhood.
      4. Even if people do not fit into their national history, they are expected to know it in order to understand references to it.
      5. We rarely receive much information about the histories of other nations unless we study other languages.
   D. Cultural Group Histories
      1. Each cultural group may have its own history.
      2. These histories may be hidden even though they are related to the national history.
      3. These histories are not always part of the national history, though they are important in the development of group identities, family histories, and the contemporary lives of these cocultures.
      4. The authors prefer to view these histories as the many stories told about the past, rather than one story on a singular time continuum.
      5. Ignorance of others' histories makes intercultural communication more difficult and may lead to potential misunderstandings.
   E. The Power of Other Histories
      1. At one time a unified story of humankind—the "grand narrative"—dominated how people thought of the past, present, and future.
      2. This is no longer the case, as there are now many competing stories of the past.
      3. In place of the "grand narrative" are revised and restored histories that had been suppressed, hidden, or erased.
      4. This restoration of history enables us to examine what cultural identities mean and to rethink the dominant cultural identity.
      5. While it may seem daunting to confront the many histories of the world, the more we know, the better we will be able to engage in successful intercultural interactions.

III. History and Identity
    A. Histories as Stories
        1. It may be tempting to ignore the many levels of history rather than make sense of them all, yet to do so would belie the substantial influence that history has on our own identities.
        2. Communication scholar Walter Fisher refers to *Homo sapiens* as *Homo narrans* because the label highlights the importance of narratives or story telling in human life.
        3. Histories are stories that we use to make sense of who we are and whom we think others are.
        4. A strong element in our cultural attitudes encourages us at times to forget history.
        5. The desire to escape history tells us about the ways that our culture negotiates its relationship to the past and the ways we view the relationship of other nations and cultures to their pasts.
        6. By ignoring history, we may come to wrongheaded conclusions that reinforce stereotypes.
        7. We really cannot escape history even if we fail to recognize it or try to suppress it.
    B. Nonmainstream Histories: For those with hidden histories, listening to their stories helps us understand how they have negotiated the cultural attitudes of the past that have relevance for the present.
        1. Religious histories
            a. Different religious groups have had very different experiences throughout history.
            b. Understanding the history of a religious group may be central to understanding a group's identity, as is the case with the Jewish or the Mormon history of persecution.
            c. Remembering the Holocaust is crucial to Jewish peoples' identity.
            d. There have been recent attempts by revisionists to deny that the Holocaust happened or to downplay its scope, but these have been met with fierce opposition and a renewed effort to document the Holocaust in great detail.
            e. Religious histories are never isolated, but crisscross other cultural trajectories in that we may feel placed in the position of victim and victimizer at the same time by distant historical events.
            f. For example, during World War II, German American Mennonites were punished as pacifists and yet were also seen as aggressors by U.S. Jews.
            g. It is important to see the ways that these histories make religious differences significant.
        2. Gender histories
            a. Feminist scholars insist that women's history has been obliterated, marginalized, or erased.
            b. While gender histories are important in understanding how we live today, they are often ignored.
            c. Although there is interest in women's history today, it is difficult to write that history due to the restrictions on access to public forums, documents, and records.
        3. Sexual orientation histories
            a. Much of the sexual orientation history of homosexuals has been suppressed.
            b. Martin Duberman wrote a book that reconstructs a partial history of gays and lesbians to correct the view that the "official image of the typical American was hysterically suburban: Anglo-Saxon, monogamous, heterosexual parents pair-bonded with two children and two cars."
            c. Another writer, Guy Hocquenghem, was concerned that people, including homosexuals, were forgetting that gays and lesbians were also victims of the Holocaust.
            d. If we do not or cannot listen to the voices of others, we will miss significant historical lessons, creating misunderstandings about who we are.

4. Racial and ethnic histories
   a. People from nonmainstream cultural groups often struggle to retain their histories.
   b. These histories are not learned in school, yet they are vital to understanding how others are perceived and why.
   c. Mainstream history has neither the time nor the space to include all ethnic and racial histories, and sometimes the racial and ethnic histories seem to question the celebratory nature of a national history.
   d. The injustices done by any nation are often swept under the carpet, as in China, Africa, South America, and the United States.
   e. The internment of Japanese Americans during World War II is often not discussed as it demonstrates the fragility of the constitutional system and its guarantees in the face of prejudice.

5. Diasporic histories
   a. Also overlooked in intercultural communication are the international relationships many racial and ethnic groups have with people who share their heritage and history.
   b. Because most people do not think about the diverse ways that people are connected to other nations and cultures, these histories are hidden.
   c. A massive migration caused by war, famine, slavery, or persecution that results in the dispersal of a unified group is called a diaspora.
   d. Diasporic migrations often cause people to cling more strongly to their group's identity although people become acculturated to some degree in their new homelands.
   e. History helps us understand the cultural connections among people affected by disaporas and other transnational migrations.
   f. We must be careful when recognizing the relationships and making the connections, as they may be helpful or hurtful to intercultural communication.
   g. For example, many Japanese look down on Japanese Canadians, Japanese Americans, Japanese Brazilians, Japanese Mexicans, and Japanese Peruvians. In contrast, the Irish do not look down on Irish Americans or Irish Canadians.

6. Colonial histories
   a. Due to overpopulation, limited resources, notions of grandeur, or other factors, people left their homelands to colonize territories outside their own borders.
   b. By recognizing these colonial histories, we can better understand the dynamics of intercultural communication today.
   c. Colonialism has determined language usage. For example, English is spoken in many regions of the world, as are French, Spanish, Portuguese, Dutch, and other languages.
   d. The languages we speak are not freely chosen by us, and we must learn the languages of the societies into which we are born.
   e. The imposition of language is but one aspect of cultural invasion, as much colonial history is characterized by oppression and brutality.
   f. As a result, many people have looked toward postcolonialism, an intellectual, political, and cultural movement that calls for the independence of colonized states and liberation from colonialist ways of thinking.

7. Socioeconomic class histories
   a. Though frequently forgotten, class issues and economics motivated many people to immigrate to the United States.
   b. People who are socioeconomically well off also emigrate.
   c. These histories are helpful in understanding interactions and class differences among different groups.

IV. Intercultural Communication and History
    A. We are uncomfortable dealing with the past because we do not know how we should feel about or deal with many of the ugly things that have happened.
        1. For example, indigenous peoples in the United States were exterminated or removed to settlements, but many states have few Native Americans and few, if any, reservations.
        2. Contemporary residents had nothing to do with the events in their state's history, but they are the beneficiaries through ownership of farms and other land.
        3. Maurice Blanchot makes an important distinction between the position of fault and the position of responsibility.
    B. There are various ways we might think about history and intercultural communication.
        1. History helps us understand who we are—with all of our identities—and the ways we are constrained by those identities.
            a. History has determined what languages are spoken and not spoken.
            b. Many U.S. Americans no longer speak the language(s) of their forebears.
            c. It is important to recognize our identities—as a member of a racial/ethnic group, a nationality, a language speaker, and so on—do not have the same meaning for us as for someone with differing identities.
            d. Conversely, what others' identities mean to us may not be the same as what they mean for them.
    C. Various histories are negotiated in intercultural interaction in different ways.
        1. We each bring our histories (some known, others hidden) to interactions.
        2. We can try to evaluate the role that history plays for those with whom we interact.
        3. We need to recognize our own historical blinders and assumptions.
        4. Whom we think we are today is very much influenced by how we understand the past, as well as the ways we live and the culture we believe to be our own.

DISCUSSION QUESTIONS

1. How do the differing viewpoints about history affect communication?

2. Where are you from, and what does that mean to you? What does it mean to be a midwesterner, a southerner, a Californian, and a New Yorker?

3. How do you know what other regional identities mean?

4. Think about your family's history—in what ways has your family history been influenced by your family's membership in certain cultural groups but not others?

5. How does your family history tie into the larger story of U.S. history?

6. Is it possible to escape from the history of your family? Why would someone want to do so?

7. What historical events have been ignored in the national history of the United States?

8. What historical forces led you to speak your language and not others?

9. What are some examples of political histories, intellectual histories, and social histories?

10. What are some examples of "hidden" histories, and why are they hidden?

11. What did the French writer Jean Baudrillard mean when she stated, "America was created in the hope of escaping from history . . . [it] has in part succeeded in that project, a project it is still pursuing today"?

12. Do you agree with the phrase "Everybody loves Americans"? Why or why not?

13. Why is it unwise to ask people where they are "really from"?

14. What dangers are there in ignoring history?

15. What makes diasporic histories different from other types of histories?

CLASSROOM EXERCISES AND CHAPTER ACTIVITIES

1. *Defining History Exercise:* Ask students what the term "history" means to them. Have them explain their answers (in a culturally diverse class, students will probably give a variety of answers; in a monocultural class, answers might be more unified, suggesting that history is not very important). This exercise should be used as an introduction before students have read the chapter. You can list the various responses on the board and ask students to think about them as they read the chapter, have the students respond in a journal entry, or use the responses to start a lecture and a discussion about the different histories.

2. *Family/Local History Assignment:* The goal of this assignment is to help students become more familiar with their own personal family history or the history of their community. Have students interview an elderly (at least 70 years old) family member or member of their community (preferably someone who has spent the majority of his or her life in the community). Students should prepare questions that invite the interviewees to talk about what they remember about growing up; what changes they have witnessed (social, technological, economic, and so on), and how they feel these have affected the family/community; what they know about the origin of the family/community; how they think growing up today is different from when they grew up; and whether they feel that values in society have changed, and what effect this change has had on life today. Students should take notes or ask permission to record the interview. After completing the interview, they should write a paper that addresses questions such as these:

   a. How do you think growing up in your family/community is different today than it was for your interviewee?

   b. What are some of the changes that have occurred in the United States during the lifetime of your interviewee, and how do you think those changes have affected your family/community?

   c. What new information did you learn about your family/community?

   d. What did you learn about the origins of your family/community in the United States?

   e. Of the information you gained, what was the most interesting/meaningful to you?

3. *Negotiating History Exercise:* This exercise is designed to encourage students to investigate an event in U.S. history from different cultural perspectives. Have students research videos, magazine articles, and so on that reported events surrounding the 500th anniversary of Christopher Columbus's "discovery" of America from a pre-assigned cultural viewpoint such as Native American, European American, African American, Asian, Latino, European, or Spanish. It is likely that students will need to look at a variety of nonacademic resources for this assignment. In addition, students may want to interview cultural informants asking for their opinions of this event. During class, have students present this event from their assigned perspective. Encourage them to defend/support why the group perceived the situation the way it did. (This could also be a small-group assignment.)

4. *Variation to Negotiating History Exercise:* Pick a recent event with an intercultural focus that has been in the news, such as the Elian Gonzales case, and have students investigate the event following the guidelines above.

5. *History Assignment:* This assignment is designed to encourage students to learn about someone whose culture is different from theirs by reading about that person's life. Have students read an autobiography of or essay about a person whose culture, religion, gender, sexual orientation, or social class status is different from their own. The person may be famous, but this is not necessary to meet the goals of the assignment. Students can either make verbal presentations to the class or write a two- to three-page report about the person's life. Ask them to point out how events in the person's cultural, gender, socioeconomic, or other histories influenced her or his life.

6. *Ethnicity and Communication Assignment:* This assignment is designed to motivate students to think about their own ethnic histories and the extent to which their histories influence their communication. Instruct students to research their own family background to gain a sense of their ethnic identity. They should talk with parents and other family members to find out where each generation of their ancestors was raised. With this information, they should address the following questions:

   a. What is your ethnic background?

   b. To what extent do you feel your ethnic background influences who you are?

   c. If you think your ethnic background has little influence on you today, what other variables do you feel have a significant influence on your behavior?

   d. To what extent do you think people are aware of your ethnic background? Do you think this influences the way they communicate with you?

7. *Guest Lecture Exercise:* Invite two nonmainstream individuals from the college or the community who are comfortable discussing the hidden histories of the group to which they belong to lecture. Be sure to allow enough time for students to ask questions of the guest lecturers about their group's histories.

8. *Guest Lecture Exercise Variation:* After the students have listened to the guests lecture about their nonmainstream histories, have them write a one- to two-page essay on their reaction to one of the guest lecturer's stories, answering the following questions:

   a. What is the history of the guest lecturer you are writing about?

   b. What is your personal history? (That is, if the guest discussed a religious history different from the student's, the student should discuss his or her own religious history.)

   c. How does your history and the guest lecturer's history differ?

   d. What factors might contribute to the success or failure of an intercultural interaction between the two of you?

SUGGESTED VIDEOS

1. *Awakenings.* Distributed by PBS Video, Alexandria, VA, 1986. This video is the first episode of the Eyes on the Prize series. It reviews the history of the segregation of Blacks in the south. (60 minutes)

2. *Eyes on the Prize II.* Distributed by PBS Video, Alexandria, VA, 1986. This series of videos looks at the civil rights movement from 1965 to 1985. There are eight episodes in this series, beginning with "Ain't Gonna Shuffle No More."

3. *Before Stonewall: The Making of Gay and Lesbian Community.* Distributed by MPI Home Video. This video looks at the emotionally charged origins of today's gay rights movement, focusing on events that led to the 1969 riots at a New York City gay bar (Stonewall Inn) and many other milestones in the gays' struggle for acceptance.

4. *Reexamining U.S. History from a Multicultural Perspective.* Distributed by Insight Media, New York, 1998. This series of three videos offers a multicultural look at U.S. history from the pre-European era to the present. This reexamination presents a perspective on U.S. society that enables students to gain a more accurate understanding of the nation's past. (75 minutes total)

5. *Multicultural Influences on the Founding Fathers.* Distributed by Insight Media, New York, 1998. Analyzing little-known documents, this video examines the impact of African Americans, Hispanic Americans, and Native Americans on the early history of the nation. (22 minutes)

CHAPTER 4

Identity and Intercultural Communication

LEARNING OBJECTIVES

After studying the material in this chapter, students should be able to:

Understand the multiple nature of identities.

Explain how identities are developed through our communicative interaction with others.

Identify some of the ways in which people communicate their identity.

Explain how societal influences contribute to the formation of identity.

Identify some of the major social and cultural identities that are manifest in our communication.

Explain differences in how identities are developed for minority versus majority group members in the United States.

Discuss the ways in which one's own identity and perception of other's identities influence communication.

Understand the process of cultural adjustment and the identity development of multiracial and multicultural people.

Discuss the three common characteristics shared by White people in the United States.

Understand how identities are expressed through core symbols, labels, and norms.

KEY TERMS

age identity	global nomads	personal identity
class identity	hyphenated Americans	physical ability identity
constructive identity	identity labels	racial identity
core symbols	majority identity development	regional identity
culture shock	minority identity development	religious identity
encapsulated identity	multiracial identity	U-curve theory
ethnic identity	national identity	Whiteness
gender identity	norms	

DETAILED CHAPTER OUTLINE

I. Understanding Identity: Identity is our self-concept, who we think we are as a person.
   A. Identities Are Created Through Communication
      1. Identities emerge when communication messages are exchanged between persons and are negotiated, cocreated, reinforced, and challenged through communication.

   2. In other words, when people communicate with each other, different identities are
      emphasized depending on the individuals they are communicating with and the
      topic of conversation.
   3. Communication is most successful when each person involved confirms the identity
      of the other.
B. Identities Are Created in Spurts
   1. Identities are created not in one smooth, orderly process, but in spurts, with long
      periods when we do not think much about ourselves or our identities. At other times,
      events may provide insights into who we are, causing us to focus on identity issues.
   2. For example, sometimes we may feel that we know exactly who we are and what our
      place in the world is, and other times we may feel rather confused.
C. Identities Are Multiple
   1. We belong to various groups and develop multiple identities.
   2. These multiple identities come into play at different times depending on the context.
      For example, when we go to church, our religious identity is highlighted; when we
      are at a club or bar, our sexual orientation is highlighted.
D. Identities Are Influenced by Society
   1. Societal forces such as history, economics, and politics also influence identities.
   2. People can be pigeonholed into identity categories, or contexts, even before they are
      born.
   3. Categorization and stereotyping are often based on identity groups. Where one is
      positioned—by language, by society—influences how and what is seen and, most
      importantly, what it means.
   4. People may assign identities to others that are socially and politically determined and
      that are not created by the self alone.
   5. Socially and politically determined identities are created by popular culture. For
      example, the label "heterosexual" is less than 100 years old.
   6. People may try to resist assigned identities and the position that the identities put
      them in, and to assign other identities to themselves.
   7. Often, the process of resistance requires that people start with the position that the
      stereotype places on them.
   8. The implications for intercultural communication are that societal influences establish
      the foundations from which interactions occur.
E. Identities Are Dynamic
   1. The societal forces that give rise to particular identities are always changing.
   2. The political and cultural identity of being a woman in the United States has changed
      over the years, as have the identity labels for ethnic groups—for example, "colored,"
      to "Negro," to "Black," to "Afro-American," to "African American."
F. Identities Are Developed in Different Ways in Different Cultures
   1. Identity development does not occur in the same way in every society.
   2. In the United States, young people are often encouraged to develop a strong sense of
      identity, which stems from the value of individualism.
   3. In other societies, such as African, Asian, or Latino societies, childhood and
      adolescent experiences revolve around the family, which emphasizes dependency
      and interdependency.
II. Social and Cultural Identities: People identify with many groups based on gender, age,
    ethnicity, occupational interests, sports, leisure activities, and special abilities. Belonging to
    these groups helps shape identities and affects communication to some degree.
    A. Gender Identity
       1. The formation of gender identity begins in infancy.
       2. Gender is not the same as biological sex.

      3. Gender identity is communicated to others, and popular culture defines what it means to be a man or a woman.

      4. The implication for intercultural communication is that gender means different things in different cultures.

B. Age Identity

      1. Age identity is influenced by cultural notions of how people of a particular age should look and act.

      2. Notions of age and youth are based on cultural conventions.

      3. As people age, their thoughts about age change. Yet the relative nature of age is only one part of the identity process. Social constructions of age are also part of the process.

        a. Different generations have different philosophies, values, and ways of speaking.

        b. Slang creates ingroups within generations.

      4. Although not all people in any generation are alike, the attempt to find trends across generations reflects our interest in understanding age identity.

      5. Cultures differ in their views on aging, and these different views have implications for intercultural communication. For example, in the United States old age is demeaned; in other societies, it is revered.

C. Racial and Ethnic Identity

      1. Racial identity

        a. Racial identity in the United States today is both a sensitive and a pervasive issue, although many people feel uncomfortable about discussing it.

        b. In the 15th and 16th centuries, the debates on race centered on religious questions about whether there was "one family of man" and what rights those who were different should have.

        c. Views about which groups were "human" or "animal" provided the rationale for slavery.

        d. In the 18th and 19th centuries, scientists tried unsuccessfully to classify races according to genetics and brain size.

        e. Scientists now believe that there are more physical similarities than differences among so-called races and have abandoned a strict biological basis for classifying racial groups.

        f. There are several arguments against the physiological basis for race.

          i. Racial categories vary widely throughout the world.

          ii. A variety of definitions are used in U.S. law to determine racial categories.

          iii. Racial categories are fluid and have shifted over time in the United States.

        g. Racial categories are based to some extent on physical characteristics, but they are also constructed in fluid social contexts.

        h. How people construct these meanings and think about race influences the ways in which they communicate with others.

      2. Ethnic identity

        a. Ethnic identity is a set of ideas about one's own ethnic group membership.

        b. Dimensions of ethnic identity include self-identification, knowledge about the ethnic culture, and feelings about belonging to a particular ethnic group.

        c. Ethnic identity often involves a common sense of origin and history linking people to distant cultures in Asia, Europe, Latin America, or other locations.

        d. Some U.S. residents see ethnicity as a specific and relevant concept, and themselves as connected to an origin outside the United States—as "hyphenated Americans" (Mexican-American, Japanese-American, and so on)—or the region prior to its being part of the United States (Navajo, Hopi, and so on).

        e. For others, ethnicity is a vague concept. They see themselves as "American" and reject the notion of hyphenated Americans.

    3. Racial versus ethnic identity
       a. Scholars have differing views on whether racial and ethnic identity are similar or different and which should be emphasized. Others reject that interpretation.
          i. On the one hand, discussions about ethnicity tend to reflect a "melting pot" perspective on U.S. society.
          ii. On the other hand, discussions about race as shaped by U.S. history allow for racism.
       b. Most White people comprehend the sense of belonging to an ethnic group, but what it means to belong to the dominant White culture is more difficult.
       c. Racial or ethnic identity develops over time, in stages, and through communication with others.
          i. Stages of development seem to reflect phases in the development of an understanding of who people are and depend to some extent on the type of groups to which people belong.
          ii. Many ethnic or racial groups experience oppression, which may generate attitudes and behaviors consistent with a struggle to develop a strong sense of self and group identity. For many cultural groups, these strong identities have ensured the survival of the group.
D. Physical Ability Identity
    1. People have physical ability identities based on their height, weight, sex, age, capabilities, and so on.
    2. Physical ability, like age, changes over time. Some people will experience a temporary disability (breaking a bone or recovering from a serious surgery) while others are born with a permanent disability, experience an incremental disability, or have a sudden-onset disability.
    3. Physical abilities/disabilities are only one of many characteristics of a person.
    4. The number of people with disabilities is growing (7% of the population), and in certain states, people with disabilities constitute the largest minority group.
    5. Adjusting to disability involves changing the definitions of how people see themselves and how others see them, and this understanding of identity often happens in stages or phases.
       a. The first stage involves a focus on rehabilitation and physical changes.
       b. The second phase involves adjusting to the disability and the effects the disability may have on relationships.
       c. The final phase is stigma incorporation, when people begin to integrate being disabled into their own definitions of self.
    6. People with disabilities see themselves as a cultural group.
       a. Many persons with disabilities share similar perceptions and communication patterns.
       b. As is true with many majority identities, nondisabled people are not as aware of this aspect of physical ability identity.
    7. People who are able-bodied and those with disabilities often have difficulty communicating with each other.
       a. Able-bodied people often restrict their communication with people with disabilities and do not make eye contact.
       b. People with disabilities struggle to communicate a positive identity; their physical ability is only one of many identities.
E. Religious Identity
    1. Religious identity can be an important dimension of many people's identities, as well as a source of intercultural conflict.

2. Often, religious identity is confused with racial/ethnic identity, and drawing distinct lines between various identities—such as racial, class, national, and regional—can be problematic.
3. Historically, intercultural communication among religious groups has often been difficult. For instance, religious differences have caused a number of conflicts, from the Middle East, to Northern Ireland, to India/Pakistan and Bosnia-Herzegovina.
4. Some people take religion very seriously and some are willing to fight and die for their beliefs.
5. Conflicts arise when religious beliefs are imposed on individuals who do not share them.
6. Some people communicate their religious beliefs by the clothes they wear.
7. Other religions do not mark their members through their clothes, and so their everyday interactions may not communicate their religious identity.
8. In the United States religious beliefs are considered private, yet they still have implications for intercultural communication.

F. Class Identity
1. People rarely think about socioeconomic class as part of their identity, especially if they are members of the middle class.
2. Class identity is communicated by the words people use, the magazines they read, the kinds of drinks they consume, and so on.
3. Because people feel it is impolite to ask about others' class backgrounds, they use communication strategies to place others in a class hierarchy.
4. These strategies do not always elicit accurate information.
5. People assume that with enough work and persistence they can move up in the class hierarchy, but research has proven otherwise.
6. Poor people are generally blamed for their poverty—a classic example of blaming the victim.
7. Working-class people who aren't upwardly mobile are often portrayed in movies and television as not very smart, non-law-abiding, or unwilling to do what it takes to raise their class status.
8. Race and class, and sometimes gender identity, are interrelated, but race and class are not synonymous. So, these multiple identities are interrelated but not identical.
9. The implications for intercultural communication are that the lack of understanding about class differences and the stereotypes perpetuated in the media often makes meaningful communication between classes very difficult.

G. National Identity
1. Among the many identities we may have, we have a national identity that is different from our racial or ethnic identity.
2. Nationality is one's legal status in relation to a nation.
3. Our national identity influences the way we look at the world and the way we communicate with people of other nationalities.
4. In many instances, people have identified themselves with a nation that may or may not have emerged (for example, the Confederate States of America).
5. Sometimes nations have disappeared permanently or temporarily, but in all instances, citizens have various ways of thinking about nationality.

H. Regional Identity
1. Many regions of the world have separate but vital cultural or regional identities.
2. In the United States, regional identities are important, but decreasingly so as the nation becomes more homogeneous.

    3. Regional identities that lead to national independence movements often reflect cultures that are affirmed by distinct cuisine, dress, manners, and languages.

    4. Understanding regional identities may be important in intercultural communication, particularly if inhabitants of different regions speak different dialects.

I. Personal Identity

    1. Identity issues are closely tied to one's notion of self.

    2. Each person has a personal identity, but it may not be unified or coherent.

    3. We are whom we think we are, but at the same time, outside influences constrain and influence whom we think we are.

    4. We have many identities, and they can conflict—as is sometimes the case with gender and ethnic identities.

    5. Whom we think we are is important to us, and we try to communicate that to others.

III. Identity Development

    A. Minority Identity Development: U.S. minority group members tend to develop a sense of racial and ethnic identity much earlier than majority group members. The following stages of minority identity development may apply to other majority/minority identities (for example, class, gender, and sexual orientation). It is important to remember that not everyone experiences these stages in the same way. Some people may spend more time in one stage than others do, may experience the stages in different ways, and may remain in one of the previous stages.

      1. Stage 1: Unexamined identity.

        a. This stage is characterized by a lack of exploration of ethnicity.

        b. Minority group members may accept the values and attitudes of the majority group, including negative views of their own group.

        c. They may have a desire to assimilate into the dominant culture and express positive attitudes toward it.

        d. Ideas about identity may come from parents or friends, or the individuals may simply be disinterested in or not concerned with their ethnicity.

      2. Stage 2: Conformity

        a. At this stage, individuals internalize the values and norms of the dominant group and have a strong desire to assimilate into the dominant culture.

        b. Minority group members may have negative attitudes toward themselves and their group.

        c. People who criticize other members of their own group may be given negative labels such as "Uncle Toms" or "oreos" for African Americans, "bananas" for Asian Americans, "apples" for Native Americans, and "tio tacos" for Chicanos.

        d. This stage may continue until the individuals encounter situations that cause them to question their pro–dominant culture attitudes.

      3. Stage 3: Resistance and separatism

        a. Movement to this stage may be triggered by events, including negative ones such as encountering discrimination or name-calling, leading to a growing awareness that not all dominant group values are beneficial to minorities.

        b. This may motivate the individuals to learn about their heritage and to join clubs and groups in which they can discuss common interests and experiences and find support.

        c. It may also be characterized by a blanket endorsement of one's group and it's accompanying values and attitudes, and a subsequent rejection of the values and norms of the dominant group.

      4. Stage 4: Integration

        a. The ideal outcome of the identity process is an achieved identity.

  b. Persons who reach this stage have a strong sense of their own group identity (based on gender, race, ethnicity, sexual orientation, and so on) and an appreciation of other cultural groups.
  c. Individuals realize that racism and other forms of oppression occur, but any anger is redirected toward positive ends.
  d. The result is a confident and secure individual who desires to eliminate all forms of injustice, not just oppression aimed at his or her own group.

B. Majority Identity Development
  1. Stage 1: Unexamined identity
    a. This stage is the same as for minority individuals.
    b. People may have an awareness of differences, but they do not fear other groups or feel superior to them.
    c. Communication and relationships are not based on racial differences.
  2. Stage 2: Acceptance
    a. This stage represents the internalization and acceptance of the basic racial inequities in society.
    b. Individuals have no conscious identification with being White; however, some assumptions based on an acceptance of inequities in society are subtly racist. For example, minority groups are culturally deprived and need help to assimilate; White culture—music, art, literature—is "classical" while works of art by people of color are folk art or "crafts."
    c. Either communication with minorities is avoided, or a patronizing stance is taken—or both.
    d. Some people never move beyond this stage, and if they do it is a result of a number of events, such as becoming good friends with people of color or taking a class or workshop that deals with issues of racism or White privilege.
  3. Stage 3: Resistance
    a. Movement to this stage represents a major shift.
    b. Individuals move from blaming minority group members to blaming their own group for racial or ethnic problems.
    c. The resistance may take the form of passive resistance, with little behavior change, or active resistance—an ownership of racism.
    d. Individuals may feel embarrassed or ashamed and may avoid or minimize their communication with Whites and seek out interactions with people of color.
  4. Stage 4: Redefinition and Reintegration
    a. As in the minority development model's fourth stage, people begin to refocus their energy on redefining Whiteness in nonracist terms and are able to integrate being White into other facets of their identity.
    b. Individuals realize that they do not have to accept the definition of White that society placed on them and can see positive aspects of being European American.
    c. People not only recognize their identity as White but also appreciate other groups.
    d. There is no defensiveness about racism, but a recognition that prejudice and racism exist in society, and that blame, guilt, or denial doesn't help eliminate racism.
    e. Individuals are aware of the importance of understanding Whiteness and White identity.

C. Characteristics of Whiteness
  1. It is difficult for most White people to describe the cultural patterns that are uniquely White.
  2. There are at least three common characteristics shared by White people in the United States:
    a. An advantage of race privilege

      i.   Some advantages are economic in that, overall, Whites still have higher incomes than minority group members.

     ii.   Some are social—for example, Whites can shop without worrying about being followed, they aren't asked to speak for their entire race, and they see people like themselves most places they go.

   iii.   All Whites do not have power and do not have equal access to power. Some White communities were not privileged and were viewed as separate or different at various times in U.S. history.

    iv.   Many White people in the United States are poor and do not have economic power.

     v.   There is an emerging perception that being White is not automatically equated with privilege, particularly as demographics change in the United States and as some Whites come to perceive themselves to be in the minority.

    vi.   Some White students from working-class families feel that being White is a liability—that they are prejudged as racist, blamed for social conditions they did not cause, and denied opportunities that are unfairly given to minority students.

  vii.   Due to corporate downsizing and the relocation of U.S. jobs overseas, many middle-aged White men have not achieved the degree of economic or professional success they had hoped for and may blame it on immigrants, women, and minorities in the workplace.

 viii.   Although many of these perceptions are inaccurate, the point is that identities are negotiated and challenged through communication, and people act on their perceptions, not on some external reality.

   b. A "standpoint" or perspective from which White people look at themselves, others, and society

      i.   Something about being White versus Black influences how people view the world and communicate with others.

     ii.   For example, a majority of Whites believe that race relations in the United States are generally good, but Blacks have a different perception.

   iii.   White women have different views about whether being White is a positive or negative thing.

   c. A set of cultural practices largely unrecognized by White people

      i.   Other groups do not necessarily share views held consistently by Whites.

     ii.   Some cultural practices and values are expressed primarily by Whites and significantly less by members of minority groups.

   iii.   These cultural practices are most clearly visible to those who are not White and to those who are excluded.

IV. Multicultural Identity

  A. Multiracial People

    1. There are approximately 2 million multiracial people in the United States. Racial identity development for biracial children is different from that for others, and they don't fit into a neat racial category.

      a. The first stage of identity development for biracial children is "awareness of differentness." In this stage, these children discover that they are different from their peers, who may be people of color but belong to a single racial group, unlike themselves.

      b. The second stage is the "struggle for acceptance," in which the children experiment with and explore both cultures to which they belong. They may feel they live in cultural margins, struggling with two sets of cultural realities, and they are sometimes asked to choose one racial identity over the other.

        c. The final stage is "self-acceptance and assertion," in which the children develop a more secure sense of self. The exposure to more than one culture's norms and values leads to a flexible and adaptable sense of identity—a multicultural identity.

  B. Identity and Adaptation

    1. Global nomads are people who grew up in many different cultural contexts because their parents moved around a lot (for example, children of missionaries, military personnel, or international business employees).

    2. Multicultural identity may form as a result of cultural adaptation after living in a new culture for a long time. The U-curve theory of adaptation outlines a common pattern.

        a. In the first phase, migrants experience excitement and anticipation, especially if the move to the new culture is voluntary.

        b. The second phase, culture shock (the bottom of the U-curve), happens to almost everyone in intercultural transitions.

           i. Culture shock is a relatively short-term feeling of disorientation and discomfort due to the unfamiliarity of the surroundings and the lack of familiar cues in the environment.

           ii. In addition to disorientation, some people experience a crisis of identity.

        c. Adaptation is the third phase, in which individuals gradually learn the rules and customs of the new cultural context. They may learn a new language, decide to change some aspects of behavior and not others, and determine to what degree to adapt.

        d. The U-curve model may seem simplistic, and it may be more accurate to think of long-term adaptation as a series of U-curves.

        e. Culture shock occurs to almost all migrants who cross cultural boundaries, whether voluntarily or involuntarily.

        f. Most migrants eventually more or less adapt to the new culture; for others, the process is not so easy.

        g. Some migrants actively resist assimilation in the short term while others resist it in the long term.

        h. Some people would like to assimilate but are not welcome in the new culture, as is the case with many immigrants to the United States from Latin America.

        i. Other people adapt to some aspects of the new culture but not others.

  C. Living "on the border"

    1. Encapsulated multicultural people feel torn between different cultural identities. They may have trouble making decisions, be troubled by ambiguity, and feel pressure from both groups to which they belong.

    2. In contrast, constructive multicultural people thrive living on the margins of two cultures. They see themselves (rather than others) as choice makers and recognize the significance of being "in between," as many multicultural people do.

V. Identity, Language, and Intercultural Communication: Identities are expressed to others through communication in core symbols, labels, and norms.

  A. Core symbols are about fundamental beliefs, which are the central concepts that define a particular identity.

  B. Labels are a category of core symbols and are the terms used to refer to particular aspects of identities (African American, Latina/Latino, White, European American).

  C. Some norms of behavior are associated with particular identities. For example, women may express their gender identity by being more concerned about safety than men, taking more precautions when they go out at night. Or people might express their religious identity by participating in activities such as going to church or Bible study meetings.

DISCUSSION QUESTIONS

1. What are some of the ways in which we express our identities?

2. How do you feel when someone does not recognize the identity that is most important to you?

3. How and why do people identify with particular groups and not others? What choices are available to them?

4. How does popular culture create certain identities?

5. How does being White affect people's experiences in the United States?

6. What are some of the ways members of minority cultures and members of majority cultures develop their cultural identities?

7. If we never talk about race, but only about ethnicity, can we consider the effects and influences of racism?

8. What does it mean to be "middle class" in U.S. society? Or "working class"?

9. Why does culture shock occur to people who make cultural transitions?

10. Why are some adaptations to cultures difficult for some people and easier for others?

11. What do we mean when we say that our identities are formed through communication?

12. Can you think of a time when you have resisted a negative identity that was assigned to you? What did you do or say? Were you successful?

13. Are people comfortable talking about race? Why or why not?

14. What are some terms that you hear in everyday interactions that mark class differences?

15. If you were biracial, which culture would you put down on your college registration form? Which one would you leave off? Why? How would you make that decision?

16. Can you think of a time when you have gone through a major change in your life? Did you go through any of the stages outlined in the U-curve model?

17. Have you ever been in a situation in which you felt that you were living "on the border"?

18. What labels do you use to describe yourself?

CLASSROOM EXERCISES AND CHAPTER ACTIVITIES

1. *Multiple Identities Exercise:* Have students list labels they would use to identify who they are to others. Ask several students to read their lists, and ask the class what they notice about those lists. Explain to students that these labels represent multiple identities they have. In which contexts are some identities more important to students than others? (You might ask them what happens to their identities when they go back home to visit their parents.)

2. *Race and Ethnicity Exercise:* Ask the students to write down a definition of race, and then have them read their definitions to the class. As they read them, write each different definition on the board and explain that "race" does not have a fixed meaning but is a socially constructed term that people use to refer to a variety of things, such as skin color, nationality, ethnicity, region of origin, and biological differences.

3. *Identity Model Exercise:* This exercise is designed to help students gain a clearer understanding of identities. Ask students to draw a picture or create a model that depicts their various identities. Students may think of a particular situation when they develop their model to help place them within a context. Let the students know that the models will be posted on the classroom walls and that they will be asked to describe them to the class. Allow ample time for presentations and discussion.

4. *Socially and Politically Assigned Identities and Self-Assigned Identities Exercise:* This exercise will help students understand the difference between socially and politically assigned identities and self-assigned identities, and the ways people resist socially and politically assigned identities. Invite students to compile a list of their self-assigned identities and another list of their socially and politically assigned identities. Then have them indicate on their lists from which individuals or groups they got their socially and politically assigned identities, and under what circumstances they acquired them. Finally, ask students to indicate any actions they or others may have taken to resist any of their socially and politically assigned identities.

5. *Video Identity Exercise:* The goal of this exercise is to have students think about and explore their identities by showing the video *Skin Deep,* which is about college students who spend a weekend exploring racial and ethnic identity issues. Have students write an essay on or discuss in dyads the character in the video whom they most identified with, and why. You may also want to have students discuss how their chosen person communicated his or her identities during interactions with the other students.

6. *Identity Awareness Activity:* This activity is designed to help students think about situations in which they become conscious of their identities. You can choose which identity or identities you want to work with in this exercise. Instruct students to write down the answers to the following questions, but tell them that they will not be required to hand them in or show them to anyone. These questions focus on racial identity, but other identities (gender, regional, and so forth) could be substituted.

    a. What is your racial identity?

    b. How did you learn that having your racial identity was different from having another racial identity?

    c. When you learned this, how did you feel?

    d. What are the advantages and disadvantages of having this racial identity for you personally?

    e. How does this racial identity influence you in school or at work?

    f. How does your racial identity influence the way you communicate with people from your own and other races?

    When the students are finished, invite them to share general observations about when they feel people learn what it means to have a racial identity, how that identity influences them in different situations, and how people feel about their racial identities.

7. *Power and Privilege Exercise—"Stand Up":* This exercise allows students to identify themselves as belonging to a particular group or groups by standing up when a particular statement pertains to them. It is designed to bring into awareness the types of privilege we all have depending on the context. Read each statement to the class, and allow time for students to "stand up" in response to the statement. (Students need to stand up only if they are comfortable doing so, and all the students should remain silent.) You can create

statements to fit a particular topic or context; the list that follows merely contains suggestions. You may want to begin with statements that are not very personal and move gradually to those that require more intimate self-disclosure. This list of statements is designed to highlight class issues:

Stand up if:

a. You were born in the United States.

b. You are an only child.

c. You moved more than two times while growing up.

d. You were raised in the country (rural setting).

e. You grew up in an apartment.

f. Your family had few resources (students determine what "few" means).

g. Your family had more than enough resources.

h. Your parents are divorced.

i. You have more resources than your parents.

j. You are working your way through school.

After the exercise, examine each of the statements with the class and ask them how being a part of the group identified in the statement would affect their ability to communicate with people from other groups. Which groups would be most comfortable communicating with them? Which groups would be least comfortable communicating with them?

8. *Guest Lecture Exercise:* Invite two individuals from the college or the community who are immigrants to the United States or who are from the United States but have lived abroad to share their experiences of adapting to another culture. During the class period prior to their lectures, ask students to spend 5 minutes writing down questions about the cultural adaptation process. Have them save these for the guest lecturers.

9. *Simulation Exercise:* One of the most effective ways to help students identify with the challenges faced by immigrants is to involve them in a simulation in which they must interact without knowing the proper rules for communicating and accomplishing tasks. Two popular simulations that have been used in a variety of orientation programs, intercultural communication classes, and cross-cultural training sessions are "BaFa BaFa" and "Barnga."

   a. "Barnga." Created by Sivasailam Thiagarajan; distributed by Intercultural Press, P.O. Box 700, Yarmouth, ME 04096; (800) 370-2665; fax (207) 846-5181.

   b. "BaFa BaFa: A Cross Culture Simulation." Created by R. Garry Shirts; distributed by Simulation Training Systems, P.O. Box 910, Del Mar, CA 92014; (800) 942-2900; fax (619) 792-9743.

SUGGESTED VIDEOS

1. *Still Killing Us Softly: Advertising's Image of Women.* Produced by Jean Kilbourne; distributed by Cambridge Documentary Films, Cambridge, MA, 1987. The director, Margaret Lazarus, describes the portrayal of women in advertising and the way this portrayal influences women, men, and children. It also suggests ways that advertising's portrayal of women affects the images men and women form of themselves. (32 minutes)

2. *Eye of the Storm.* Distributed by PBS Video, Washington, DC, 1986. This video reports on the exercise in racism conducted by a third-grade teacher in her classroom. It is a good illustration of some of the effects of racism and some of the strategies people use to adapt to being victims of racist attitudes and actions. (25 minutes)

3. *When Billy Broke His Head . . . and Other Tales of Wonder.* Distributed by Fanlight Productions. This video by Billy Golfus and David Simpson is about Billy Golfus, an award-winning journalist who sustained a brain injury. Golfus meets disabled people around the country and witnesses firsthand the strength and anger that is forging a new civil rights movement for disabled Americans. (57 minutes)

4. *Color Adjustment.* Distributed by California Newsreel, San Francisco, 1991. This two-part video explores race relations in the United States as portrayed on television. (Part I, 48 minutes; Part II, 39 minutes)

5. *My America . . . or Honk if You Love Buddha.* Distributed by Sai Communications, Ho-Ho-Kus, NJ, 1999. This video documents the experiences and history of the diverse Asian American cultural groups in the United States. (87 minutes)

6. *Skin Deep: College Students Confront Racism.* Distributed by Iris Films, Ho-Ho-Kus, NJ, 1995. This film by Francis Reid documents the thoughts and feelings of several college students spending a weekend retreat together. It addresses issues of racism, prejudice, and cultural difference as seen through the eyes of this very diverse group. (60 minutes)

7. *True Colors.* Produced and distributed by MTI/Film and Video, North Brook, IL, 1991. This video questions our accomplishments in the fight for equality since the 1960s by testing various levels of prejudice. (19 minutes)

8. *The Way of the Willow.* Produced by Beacon Films; distributed by Modern Educational Video Network, New York, 1992. This video tells the story of a Vietnamese boat family that immigrated to Canada. It shows some of the challenges the family faced and the ways it worked to adapt to and overcome them. (29 minutes)

CHAPTER 5

Verbal Issues in Intercultural Communication

LEARNING OBJECTIVES

After studying the material in this chapter, students should be able to:

Identify and explain the components of language.

Discuss the connections between language and perception.

Describe some cultural variations in communication style.

Discuss the role of context in cultural variations in communication style.

Understand the connections among language, power, and social relationships.

Describe assimilation, accommodation, and separation strategies used by cocultural groups when communicating with the dominant group.

List some of the power effects of labels.

Identify some communication challenges faced by bilingual and multilingual communicators.

Define translation and interpretation, and describe the equivalency challenges.

Discuss language politics and policies, and the difficulties created for intercultural communication.

KEY TERMS

bilingual	interpretation	pragmatics
bilingualism	language	semantics
cocultural groups	language acquisition	social positions
code switching	language policies	source text
communication style	low-context communication	syntactics
equivalency	multilingual	target text
high-context communication	phonology	translation

DETAILED CHAPTER OUTLINE

 I. Introduction: Language plays a central role in communication, and it can be one of the most frustrating aspects of intercultural communication, as well as one of the most rewarding. There are about 6,000 languages spoken in the world today, and the top 10 languages (Chinese-Mandarin, English, Spanish, Bengali, Hindi, Portuguese, Russian, Japanese, German, and Chinese-Wu) are spoken by nearly half of the world's population.

 II. The Study of Language

    A. The Components of Language: Linguistics (study of language) answers important questions such as, Are there any universal aspects shared by all languages? and, Can the same concept be expressed in any language?

1. Phonology is the study of the sound system of language.
   a. Phonology looks at how words are pronounced, which units of sound (phonemes) are meaningful, and which sounds are universal.
   b. Because different languages use different sounds, it is often difficult for nonnative speakers to learn how to pronounce some sounds.
2. Semantics is the study of meaning.
   a. Semantics describes how words communicate the meaning we intend to get across. For example, a person may understand individual words but not the meaning of the phrase when the words are put togther.
   b. Sometimes semantics focuses on the meaning of a single word. Different languages have different words for the same object. Even cultures that share a language (the United States and Britain) have different words for the same object.
3. Syntactics is the study of the structure of a language or the rules for combining words into meaningful sentences.
   a. The word order in a sentence creates a particular meaning.
   b. Languages have rules concerning the structure and expression of plural, possessive, and gender forms; subject, verb, and object arrangement; and so on.
   c. Learning a language is not merely learning words and their meanings. One must also learn the rules that govern the language.
4. Pragmatics is the study of how language is actually used in particular contexts, with the focus on specific purposes of language use.
   a. There are five specific functions or ways we use language.
      i.   Language is used to give information.
      ii.   Language is used to control others' behavior.
      iii. Language communicates feeling.
      iv.   Language is used to participate in rituals.
      v.   Language is used to execute plans.
   b. The meaning of language depends on the context and the persons who are communicating, which makes pragmatics different from semantics (which focuses solely on the meaning of the words spoken).
   c. The meaning does not come from the words or the word order alone. Meaning also depends on other things like nonverbal communication.
B. Language and Perception
1. Edward Sapir and Benjamin Whorf developed the Sapir-Whorf hypothesis based on their research of Native American languages.
   a. They propose that language not only expresses ideas but also shapes ideas and perceptions of the world. In other words, language defines our experience.
      i.   The concept of possession is one way languages differ. For example, the Navajo language does not contain possessives (his/her/our/your), and so we might conclude that the Navajos think in a particular way about the concept of possession.
      ii. Another difference is in verb forms, suggesting that different language speakers may think differently about movement or action.
      iii. A third difference is variation in color vocabulary. Navajos use one word for blue and green, two for two different shades of black, and one for red; these form the primary colors in Navajo language. This suggests that English and Navajo speakers perceive colors differently.
      iv. Various languages express formality and informality differently. In Japanese, formality is part of the entire language system; nouns take the honorific "o" before them, and verbs take more formal and polite forms.

   b. The relationship between language and perception may not be as close as suggested by the Sapir-Whorf hypothesis.
   c. It may be more accurate to view language as a tool rather than a mirror of perception.
   d. However, the languages we speak have a tremendous impact on what and how we communicate, which has huge implications for intercultural communication.
   e. It may mean that members of cultural groups really experience the world very differently and in a sense live in very different perceptual worlds. Thus, perhaps it's not just languages that differ.

III. Cultural Variations in Language
   A. Attitudes Toward Speech and Silence
      1. In some cultural groups, including many in the United States, speech is highly valued, and it is important to be articulate in interpersonal, small-group, and public settings.
      2. Being a good listener is a secondary or less important mode of communication for many people in the United States.
      3. In the United States, silence is sometimes seen as embarrassing, and it may also be associated with isolation or a lack of knowledge.
      4. In contrast, many cultural groups place a primary emphasis on silence and harmony and a secondary emphasis on speech.
      5. Speech is sometimes distrusted, particularly public speech, as is the case with the Amish, Native Americans, and many Japanese and Asian cultures.
   B. Variations in Communication Style
      1. Communication style combines both verbal and nonverbal communication and refers to the way people use language. An understanding of communication style differences helps listeners understand how to interpret verbal messages.
         a. High-context/low-context: This is a primary way cultural groups differ in their communication style.
            i. High-context style is rather indirect, with most of the information residing in the context or internalized in the person, rather than in the spoken verbal message.
            ii. Low-context communication style is demonstrated when the bulk of the meaning and information of the message resides in the spoken words. The emphasis is on verbally explicit communication.
         b. Direct/indirect: This dimension is closely related to high/low-context communication.
            i. A direct style is one in which verbal messages reveal the speaker's true intentions, needs, wants, and desires. The emphasis is on low-context communication. Many people in the United States hold the direct style as most appropriate in most contexts, valuing honesty, openness, individualism, and forthrightness, especially in business contexts.
            ii. An indirect style is one in which communication is often designed to hide or minimize the speaker's true intentions, needs, wants, and desires. The emphasis is on high-context communication. Some cultural groups prefer the indirect style, preferring to preserve the harmony of the relationship rather than being totally honest. A speaker may look for a "soft" way to communicate that there is a problem, providing many contextual cues.
            iii. Many intercultural communication problems arise from these differences in style, particularly different priorities regarding truth, honesty, harmony, and conflict avoidance in relationships.

      c. Elaborate/exact/succinct: This refers to the quantity of talk that is valued and is related to attitudes toward speech and silence.
          i. The elaborate style involves the use of rich, expressive language in everyday talk.
          ii. The succinct style features understatement, simple assertions, and silence.
          iii. The exact style (valued in most U.S. contexts) falls between the elaborate and the succinct. The emphasis is on cooperative communication and sincerity as a basis for interaction.
          iv. These different uses of language communicate different things to culturally different audiences.
      d. Personal/contextual: This dimension refers to the extent to which the speaker emphasizes the self, as opposed to his or her role.
          i. The personal style enhances the sense of "I," and the language emphasizes personhood, informality, and symmetrical power relationships.
          ii. In the contextual style, the emphasis is on prescribed roles, status, and formality.
      e. Instrumental/affective: This dimension of communication styles is closely related to direct/indirect styles.
          i. An instrumental style is receiver- and process-oriented. The burden is on the sender to make the message clear, and assertiveness and persuasion are valued.
          ii. An affective style encourages the listener to sense the message before the speaker actually expresses him- or herself verbally, so the burden is on the receiver. Information is viewed as a complex indicator of fluid human relationships.
   C. Variations in Contextual Rules
      1. While there are differences in communication style, it is important not to stereotype specific groups in terms of communication style.
      2. We should not expect any group to use a particular communication style all the time, and the style used may vary from context to context.
      3. Understanding the dynamics of various speech communities helps us see the range of communication styles. We might use code switching (changing our communication style) for another cultural group to fit its contextual rules.
IV. Language and Power: All language is social and powerful, The language, words, and the meanings used depend on the context and the social relations that are part of the interaction.
   A. Language and Social Position
      1. Individuals occupy social positions, and recognizing differences in social positions is central to understanding communication.
      2. Power is a central element of this focus on social position.
      3. When we communicate, we note (however consciously) the group membership and positions of those with whom we are communicating.
      4. Groups with the most power use a communication system that supports members' perception of the world.
      5. Cocultural groups (nondominant groups such as ethnic minorities, women, and gays) have to function in communication systems that often do not represent members' lived experiences.
      6. Nondominant groups find themselves struggling to either adapt to dominant forms of communication or maintain members' own styles.
      7. Cocultural groups may employ three communication strategies or postures when communicating with more powerful (dominant) groups: nonassertive, assertive, or aggressive.

8. Within each type of posture, cocultural individuals may emphasize assimilation, accommodation, or separation strategies.
   a. Assimilation strategies involve trying to become like the dominant group.
      i. Nonassertive assimilation strategies might emphasize commonalities, self-monitoring, and avoidance of controversy. These strategies may help some people keep their jobs, but these people may also experience a lowering of self-esteem because they feel as if they cannot be authentic. These strategies can foster an unhealthy communication climate, which reinforces the dominant group's social and political power.
      ii. Assertive assimilation strategies seek to downplay cocultural difference, but in a more forceful manner that does not privilege anyone's needs. These strategies may promote an us-versus-them mentality, and people find it difficult to sustain these strategies for long.
      iii. Aggressive assimilation strategies emphasize fitting in, resulting in cocultural members going to great lengths to prove that they are like members of the dominant group. Some strategies are dissociating (showing that one is not like other cocultural group members), mirroring (dressing and behaving like the dominant group), and self-ridiculing. A benefit of these strategies is that individuals may not be seen as "typical" cocultural group members, but a cost can be ridicule from other cocultural members.
   b. Accommodation strategies involve adapting to the dominant group.
      i. Nonassertive accommodation involves blending in while at the same time "delicately" challenging the dominant structure to recognize cocultural practices. This strategy may involve increasing visibility and dispelling stereotypes. Benefits to both groups are obvious. But some people might criticize individuals who use these strategies for not being more aggressive in trying to change the dominant structures. In fact, these strategies don't really promote major change.
      ii. Assertive accommodation involves trying to strike a balance between the cocultural and dominant group members. These strategies include communicating self, doing intragroup networking, using liaisons, and educating others.
      iii. Aggressive accommodation strategies involve becoming a part of the dominant structures and then working from within to promote significant change. Those who use these strategies may be seen as confrontative and self-promoting, yet they may have a genuine desire to work with dominant group members. Some members may also use assertive accommodation strategies so that they are perceived as committed to the larger group's good. But those who employ these strategies may be seen as too confrontative, which may alienate them from cocultural members and dominant group colleagues.
   c. Separation strategies involve trying to remain separate from the dominant group.
      i. Nonassertive separation strategies are used by those who assume that some segregation is part of everyday life in the United States. Some cocultural members use subtle communication practices to maintain separation and simply avoid interacting with dominant group members whenever possible.
      ii. Assertive separation strategies resflect a conscious choice to maintain space. They include practices such as stressing strengths and embracing stereotypes. Assertive accommodation strategies such as communicating self and doing intragroup networking are employed to assert separation. While these strategies promote cocultural unity and self-determination, they must be implemented without access to dominant group–controlled resources.

          iii. Aggressive separation strategies are used by those for whom cocultural segregation is an important priority. These strategies include attacking and sabotaging others. These people may criticize others for using assimilation or accommodation strategies. While cocultural members don't have the power base of the dominant group, these strategies enable them to confront the discriminatory structures. However, they risk retaliation from the dominant group.

    9. Each strategy has benefits and costs, so it is important to think about when it is effective to use them.

  B. The "Power" Effects of Labels

    1. Another way of looking at power and language is to think about the labels we use to refer to others and ourselves.

    2. Labels acknowledge and communicate aspects of our social identity.

    3. The context in which a label is used may determine how strongly we feel about the label.

    4. We agree with some labels and do not have trouble with them, but if we don't like a label or feel it inaccurately describes us, then we have trouble with it.

    5. Labels communicate many levels of meaning and establish particular kinds of relationships between speaker and listener. Some labels, like "friend," "lover," and "partner," communicate equality. Others, like "dumb bitch," "gook," and "camel jockey," intentionally communicate inequality.

    6. At times people unintentionally use labels that are offensive, which demonstrates their ignorance, lack of cultural sensitivity, and real connection to the other group.

    7. Other labels communicate negative characteristics about the speaker and establish distance between speaker and listener.

    8. Language use is closely tied to social structure, so the messages communicated through labels depend on the social position of the speaker.

    9. If the speaker has a powerful social position, then her or his use of labels will have an even greater impact.

    10. Individuals from the powerful groups do the labeling of others; they themselves do not get labeled.

V. Moving Between Languages: Sometimes entire nations are bilingual or multilingual. Switzerland, for example, has four official languages and the United States has many bilingual speakers of English and Spanish.

  A. Multilingualism

    1. Bilinguals are people who speak two languages.

      a. Rarely do they speak both languages with the same level of fluency, preferring one language over another, depending on the context and topic.

      b. Bilingualism results from people's need to communicate interculturally or to escape from the history of oppression reflected in their own language.

    2. Multilinguals are those who speak more than two languages.

      a. Multilinguals must engage in language negotiation, working out, explicitly or implicitly, which language to use in any given situation.

      b. The choice of language is sometimes clearly embedded in power relations, or it may be based on courtesy to others.

    3. Language acquisition

      a. Studies of language acquisition indicate that it is nearly impossible for people to learn the language of a group they dislike.

      b. Learning another language can lead to respect for another culture.

  B. Translation and Interpretation: We rely on translators and interpreters because we cannot learn every language in the world.

1. Translation generally involves the process of producing a written text that refers to something said or written in another language.
   a. The original language text is the source text.
   b. The text into which it is translated is the target text.
   c. Languages are entire systems of meaning and consciousness that are not easily translated in a word-for-word equivalence.
2. Interpretation is the process of verbally expressing what is said or written in another language.
   a. It can be simultaneous, with the interpreter speaking at the same time as the original speaker.
   b. It can be consecutive, with the interpreter speaking only during the breaks provided by the original speaker.
3. Issues of equivalency and accuracy
   a. The tradition of translation studies has tended to emphasize issues of equivalency and accuracy. That is, the focus has been on comparing the translated meaning to the original meaning.
   b. For those interested in the intercultural communication process, the emphasis is on the bridges people construct to cross from one language to another, rather than on equivalency issues.
4. The role of the translator or interpreter
   a. We assume that translators and interpreters are "invisible," but they are intermediaries who often regulate what is said.
   b. We also assume that anyone who knows two languages can be a translator or interpreter, but research shows that high levels of fluency in two languages does not necessarily make someone a good translator or interpreter.
   c. Because of the complex relationships between people, particularly in intercultural situations, translation and interpretation involve more than the traditional focus on linguistic equivalence.
C. Language Politics and Policies
   1. Some nations have multiple official languages.
   2. In the United States there is no official, legal language although English is the de facto national language.
   3. When laws or customs determine which language is spoken where and when, these are referred to as language policies, which often emerge from the politics of language use.
   4. Language politics are connected to politics of class, culture, ethnicity, and economics, and have nothing to do with the supposed "quality" of the language itself.
   5. Economic and social contexts, and the power of various linguistic groups influence attitudes toward a given language and those who speak that language.
   6. People have various opinions about language "battles," with some embracing bilingualism and others embracing monolingualism.
   7. These differences make intercultural communication more difficult.

DISCUSSION QUESTIONS

1. Is it possible for two people to communicate effectively if they don't speak the same language?
2. Should everyone learn a second language?
3. How do you feel when someone describes you with a label you like? A label you don't like?
4. What is the relationship between the language you speak and the way you perceive reality?

5. What are some cross-cultural variations in language use and communication style?

6. What does a translator or an interpreter need to know to be effective?

7. Why do some people say that we should not use labels to refer to people but should treat everybody as individuals? Do you agree?

8. Why do people have such strong reactions to language policies, as in the "English only" movement?

9. What is your communication style? Are you a high-context or low-context communicator?

10. What are some of the functions or ways we use language?

11. What are your cultural rules concerning silence and public forms of speech?

12. What is the Sapir-Whorf hypothesis, and what does it have to do with language and perception?

13. Why do people use labels when referring to themselves or others?

14. What are some advantages to being bilingual or multilingual?

15. What are some of the challenges to speaking more than one language?

16. What are some of the ways cocultures adapt to dominant group communication styles?

17. When might it be appropriate to use code switching?

CLASSROOM EXERCISES AND CHAPTER ACTIVITIES

1. *Nuts and Bolts of Second Language Acquisition Assignment:* The purpose of this assignment is to familiarize students who have not experienced learning a second language with the challenges and benefits of this process. Have students select someone they know who has learned to speak another language fluently (this could be someone who has lived in another country or someone from another country who is living here). Instruct them to interview the person about what it was like to learn the second language, why he or she was motivated to learn it, and what process he or she went through. Students should then write a brief report about what they learned, answering the question, What should you know about learning _____?

2. *Current Language Issues Assignment:* This assignment is designed to increase students' awareness of current debates over language usage. Choose a language-related issue (for example, English only or bilingual education), and assign four-member teams to play certain roles associated with the topic. For example, if you chose the English-only debate, one student team could represent the group of non-English-speaking immigrants, another the police department or health care system, and another English-speaking taxpayers. Instruct each team to split into two pairs. One pair should present the positive benefits of the proposed language issue, and the other pair should present its drawbacks for people in their role. In pairs, students can research their side of the issue. You can give them 2 weeks to prepare for the class debate on the issue. Students will probably need part of the class period before the scheduled debate to coordinate efforts with their partners. On the day you split the students into teams, you should briefly discuss the history of the issue with the class and describe the format for the debate. On the day of the debate, arrange the desks in a large circle, and instruct the student teams to sit together. You may want to make place cards for each team so that the other teams will be able to remember from which perspective they are speaking. Start the debate by choosing one team to present the issue from their role perspective. Give each pair 3 minutes to present their

side of the issue. After each team is finished, allow all the students to question the teams or to challenge their positions in a 5-minute cross-examination. This process continues until all of the teams have presented on the issue.

To debrief the debate, you could raise the following questions:

a. What do you know about this issue that you did not know before the debate?

b. Is it easier for you to take a stand on this issue now than it was before the debate? Why?

c. What do you think will have to happen in society for the conflict over this issue to be resolved?

d. What are the possible solutions?

e. What will be the outcomes for intercultural communication and relationships between cultural groups?

f. How does the debate over this issue in society affect intercultural communication and intercultural relationships today?

g. What is the role of power in the debates over this issue?

3. *Variations in Language Style Assignment:* This assignment will help students differentiate between the three communication styles of elaborate, exact, and succinct. Assign or have students locate a speech written in one of the three styles. During class, have students read an excerpt from their speech that they believe best exemplifies that communication style. After all of the speech excerpts have been read, ask the students the following questions:

a. Which style did you prefer to read/listen to? Why?

b. What can you say that is positive about each style?

c. What can you say that is negative about each style?

d. Are your opinions based on your cultural preferences?

e. Is one style better than the other?

f. Can all three styles be equally valid?

4. *Regional Language Variations Activity:* Show students the video *American Tongues.* Then, in small groups, have them discuss the many examples of regional variations in language portrayed in this video. You might ask the students to discuss their answers to the preceeding questions in their small groups.

5. *Power of Labels Exercise:* This exercise is designed to demonstrate the power that labels have for students and the way labels are used to describe negative and positive characteristics of entire groups of people. On the chalkboard, list a few broad terms such as "man," "woman," "lawyer," and "doctor." Ask the students to quickly write down as many labels as they can think of for each term. Do not give the students much time to do this, as they may begin to edit out those labels that are least favorable. The students' first thoughts will yield the best and most honest labels. Once they have completed their lists, have students share their answers while charting them under the appropriate term on the blackboard. You can either collect all the answers for all the terms at one time or start with one term, gather the labels, discuss them, and then go on to the next term. Suggested debriefing questions include these:

   a. Which of the labels communicate positive characteristics, and which negative?

   b. Which labels would you use to describe yourself?

   c. Which labels would you not like others to use when describing you?

   d. Are there some labels only your close friends, relatives, or others can call you? Why?

   e. What role do status and power play in labeling?

6. *Exploring Labels Assignment:* The purpose of this assignment is to encourage students to recognize the labels they have been exposed to for other cultural groups and the way these labels may influence communication between members of different cultural groups. Instruct student to choose one cultural group represented in the United States and to write a report that addresses the following issues:

   a. Identify and describe the culture, using the labels you can remember. Write honestly; your identification and description of the labels is not an indication that you agree with them.

   b. Discuss how you think you learned these labels and from what sources.

   c. Describe how these labels may hypothetically influence communication with an individual from the culture you are discussing.

7. *Communication Style Activity:* This exercise is designed to make students more aware of their own preferred communication style by asking them to play a role that may contain verbal and nonverbal behaviors that are different from their own. Divide the students into pairs, and have them decide who is person A and who is person B. Distribute a set of behaviors to one member of each pair, which they are to act out without revealing it to the other person. They can talk about whatever they like during the 5 or so minutes they will be acting out their roles as long as they do not reveal their behaviors explicitly to their partner. When you have called "time," ask the students to share their roles with each other. Next, debrief the exercise asking the following questions:

   a. What behaviors were you asked to perform?

   b. How did it feel to do that particular behavior?

   c. Is that behavior your preferred way of communicating? Why or why not?

   d. How did it feel to have the other person acting out his or her behaviors?

   e. What did you learn about your own communication style?

Scripts

Person A
You prefer sitting quite close to the other person, and you touch him or her frequently on the arm while talking. You avoid eye contact, and you are reluctant to disagree with anything the other person says to you. When you answer the other person's questions, you do it very indirectly, maybe through the use of long stories with elaborate language.

Person B
You are very direct and forthright with your opinions and your body language. This means you make and keep direct eye contact, and "tell it like it is." You like a lot of space around you and avoid touching others or being touched. When others are avoiding being direct, you make an effort to get them to be more open.

SUGGESTED VIDEOS

1. *American Tongues.* Distributed by Facets Multimedia, 1988. This video examines the regional diversity of American accents, dialects, and slang, as well as attitudes toward language use (specifically southern and Black English dialects). (56 minutes)

2. *Bilingual Americans.* Distributed by Video Knowledge, New York, 1990. This two-part video explores language issues and the impact of culture on U.S. society. (55 minutes)

3. *Dialects.* Distributed by Indiana University, 1959. This video demonstrates some of the different dialects found in the United States and describes the geographical areas where the dialects are found. (29 minutes)

4. *Language and Communication.* Distributed by Insight Media, New York, 1983. This video vividly conveys how the feelings and aspirations of a culture are expressed through its language. Keith and Claudia Kernan discuss the structure of language and its relationship to thought and dialect, and raises the question of whether language reflects or influences culture. (30 minutes)

5. *Gender and Communication: She Talks, He Talks.* Distributed by Insight Media, New York, 1994. Examining the communication gap between men and women, this video explores the different ways in which men and women converse, and considers what may have created these differences. Among the topics explored are why some males emphasize the literal meanings of words, why some women weaken their speech patterns, and what motivations each has for asking questions. (22 minutes)

CHAPTER 6

Nonverbal Issues in Intercultural Communication

LEARNING OBJECTIVES

After studying the material in this chapter, students should be able to:

Understand how verbal and nonverbal communication differ.

Discuss the types of messages that are communicated nonverbally.

Identify cultural universals in nonverbal communication.

Define and give an example of cross-cultural differences in proxemics, eye contact, facial expressions, time, and silence.

Define cultural space.

Explain why it is important to understand cultural spaces in intercultural communication.

KEY TERMS

adaptors	home	polychronic
contact cultures	illustrators	regionalism
cultural spaces	migrating	regulators
deception	monochronic	relational messages
emblems	neighborhood	silence
eye contact	noncontact cultures	status
facial expressions	nonverbal communication	traveling
gestures	personal space	

DETAILED CHAPTER OUTLINE

I. Defining Nonverbal Communication: Two forms of nonverbal communication are discussed: nonverbal codes (facial expression, personal space, eye contact, use of time, and conversational silence) and cultural spaces (contexts that form our identity—the cultural meanings created in places such as where we grew up and where we live).

    A. Comparing Verbal and Nonverbal Communication: Both are symbolic, communicate meaning, and are patterned. Different societies have different nonverbal languages, and the rules for nonverbal communication vary among cultures and contexts.

        1. Learning nonverbal behavior

           a. Nonverbal behavior and its meanings are learned unconsciously, unlike verbal behavior.

           b. Some strategies for nonverbal communication are learned as part of being socialized about appropriate behavior.

       2. Coordinating nonverbal and verbal behaviors
         a. Nonverbal behaviors can reinforce, substitute for, or contradict verbal behavior.
         b. When the nonverbal and the verbal message contradict each other, we tend to believe the nonverbal behavior as it operates on a more unconscious level.
  B. What Nonverbal Behavior Communicates: Relationship, status and power, and deception
       1. Nonverbal behavior communicates the relationship aspect of messages such as how we really feel about someone. These messages, however, can be easily misinterpreted unless the context of the situation and the person's other nonverbal behaviors are taken into account.
       2. Nonverbal behavior communicates status and power. For example, a supervisor may be able to touch subordinates, but it may be unacceptable the other way around. Some positions, gestures, and use of space may also communicate status and power.
       3. Deception is communicated through nonverbal means.
         a. Earlier researchers believed that certain nonverbal behaviors indicated lying.
         b. Now researchers believe that verbal and nonverbal behaviors that are idiosyncratic to a particular person communicate deception.
         c. Only a few nonverbal behaviors seem consistently indicative of deception (pupil dilation, blinking, higher pitch).
II. Cultural Variations in Nonverbal Behavior: Some behaviors seem to be very basic, perhaps universal (particularly facial expressions), and innate (not learned). These include the eyebrow flash, nose wrinkling (slight social distancing), and the "disgust face." In addition, at least six basic emotions are communicated in much the same way in most societies: happiness, sadness, disgust, fear, anger, and surprise. However, what causes the nonverbal behavior may vary from culture to culture. There are also variations in the rules for nonverbal behavior and in the contexts it takes place in.
  A. Nonverbal Codes
       1. Personal space is the "bubble" that surrounds people, marking the territory between them.
         a. The size of a person's bubble depends on his or her cultural background.
         b. Differences in bubbles can create misunderstanding and even discomfort.
         c. Some cultural groups are identified as contact cultures, and others as noncontact cultures. In contact cultures, people stand closer together while talking, make more direct eye contact, touch more frequently, and speak in louder voices.
         d. Other factors also influence personal space decisions, including gender, age, ethnicity, the context of the interaction, and the topic of discussion.
       2. Eye contact is often included as part of personal space because it regulates interpersonal distance.
         a. Eye contact communicates respect and status, and often regulates turn taking.
         b. Patterns of eye contact vary by culture.
       3. Facial expressions also vary by culture although some are expressed very similarly all over the world.
         a. There is a lot of variation in what causes people to smile or frown.
         b. Cultural rules often regulate facial expressions.
       4. There are at least four different kinds of gestures.
         a. Emblems have a specific verbal translation, such as waving a hand to say goodbye, but they may vary across cultures.
         b. Illustrators accompany speech and the amount of "talking with one's hands" may vary from one culture to another.
         c. Regulators control and direct many aspects of conversation, including turn taking, greeting, and leave-taking. Each culture has its own, somewhat unique set of regulators.

        d. Adaptors are gestures that are related to managing our emotions, such as tapping our feet or fingers when we are nervous, or rubbing our eyes when we feel like crying, or clenching our fists when we're angry. The types of adaptors used to manage/reflect emotions will depend on one's cultural upbringing.

    5. Cultures vary in the use of time. One way to understand these variations is to look at the differences between monochronic and polychronic time orientations. These differences can cause significant problems for businesspeople, students, and others.

        a. In monochronic time orientation, time is a commodity. Time is linear, with one event happening at a time. Being punctual, completing tasks, and keeping schedules are valued, sometimes regardless of any relational emergency.

        b. In polychronic orientation, time is more holistic and circular. Many events can happen at once, and things get done because of personal relationships, not in spite of them.

        c. Many academic endeavors and international business negotiations can be challenged because of differences in time orientations.

    6. Cultural groups may also vary in the emphasis placed on speaking and silence.

        a. In the United States, silence is not highly valued. Particularly in developing relationships, silence is awkward and uncomfortable, and people may use active uncertainty reduction strategies, such as asking questions.

        b. In other cultures, people may reduce uncertainty by being silent, observing, and asking a third party about someone's behavior.

        c. In Japan, for instance, silence may be used to show respect for the person who has just spoken or to unify people.

        d. Keith Basso identified five contexts for appropriate uses of silence among the Western Apache in Arizona: meeting strangers, courting someone, seeing friends after a long absence, being with people who are grieving, and getting cussed out.

  B. Cultural Variation or Stereotype?

    1. The cultural patterns in nonverbal codes should be used not as stereotypes for all members of cultures, but as tentative guidelines and, more important, as examples to help people understand the great variation in nonverbal behavior.

    2. Prejudice is often based on nonverbal aspects of behavior such as physical appearance or physical behavior.

III. Defining Cultural Space: Understanding cultural spaces is important in understanding our identities. The meanings of cultural spaces are dynamic and ever-changing, and the relations between those cultural spaces and our identities are negotiated in complex ways.

  A. Cultural Identity and Cultural Space

    1. One of the earliest cultural spaces we experience is home.

        a. Home often communicates social class nonverbally through its furnishings, landscaping, and so on.

        b. Home can be a source of tremendous identification, and we often model our own lives on the ways things were done in our childhood homes.

        c. Home may signify a place of safety and security.

        d. Home is not the same as the physical location it occupies or the building on that location. Home can be defined as specific addresses, cities, states, regions, and even nations.

        e. People vary in their feelings about home. Some are very fond of the home, and others may feel negative about it.

    2. Ethnic or racial neighborhoods emerged as one significant type of cultural space in U.S. cities over the last 50 years.

        a. Segregated neighborhoods and "Whites-only" areas have been very common in U.S. history.

    b. Through legal means and by harassment, certain cultural groups in segregated neighborhoods define who gets to live where and dictate the rules by which other groups must live.
    c. These types of neighborhoods are good examples of how power influences intercultural contact.
    d. Historical forces and power relations have led to different settlement patterns of other cultural groups in ethnic enclaves in the United States. For example, in Iowa, Germans settled in Amana, Dutch in Pella, and Czechs and Slovaks in Cedar Rapids.
  3. Many people identify quite strongly with particular regions.
    a. Regionalism can be expressed in many different ways, from symbolic expressions of identification to armed conflict.
    b. In the United States, people may identify themselves or others as southerners, midwesterners, and so on; others may identify more strongly with a province rather than a nation.
    c. People may demonstrate their regionalism by flying regional flags, wearing particular kinds of clothes, celebrating regional holidays and participating in other cultural activities.
B. Changing Cultural Space: There are two ways that people change cultural spaces: traveling and migration.
  1. Traveling is more than a leisure activity. Traveling changes cultural spaces in a way that often transforms the traveler.
    a. In terms of intercultural communication, traveling requires that we change who we are and how we interact with others.
    b. Traveling raises important issues related to altering communication styles.
  2. People change cultural space when they migrate.
    a. Migration involves a different kind of change in cultural space than traveling, which is temporary and usually desirable. People who migrate do not always do so willingly—for example, the people who were forced from their homelands in Rwanda and Bosnia.
    b. Many people immigrate so that they can survive, but they often find it difficult to adjust to the change, especially if the language and customs of the new cultural space are unfamiliar.
C. The Dynamic Nature of Cultural Spaces
  1. Cultural spaces may be fluid in place and time, and those using the space may create the meaning of that space.
  2. This notion of fluid cultural space is in sharp contrast to the previous notions of space, which promoted land ownership, surveys, borders, colonies, and territories.
  3. Cultural space exists only as long as those using the space need it.
  4. People may frequent one location to express ethnic cultural identity and another location to express other aspects of their identities. Thus, contemporary urban space is dynamic and allows people to participate in the communication of identity in new ways.

DISCUSSION QUESTIONS

  1. How is nonverbal communication different from verbal communication?

  2. What are some of the messages that we communicate through our nonverbal behaviors?

  3. Which nonverbal behaviors, if any, are universal?

4. What is the difference between contact and noncontact cultures?

5. How does our sense of space in terms of land ownership, borders, and territories differ from the notion of cultural space as dynamic and responsive to changing cultural needs?

6. How do our cultural spaces affect our identities?

7. What is the importance of cultural spaces in intercultural communication?

CLASSROOM EXERCISES AND CHAPTER ASSIGNMENTS

1. *Ambiguity of Nonverbal Messages Assignment:* This assignment is designed to help students see the ease with which nonverbal messages can be misinterpreted. Have the students write a one- to two-page essay about an interpersonal situation in which they misread or misinterpreted someone's nonverbal message. Students should describe what the nonverbal message was, how it was misinterpreted, and what happened as a result of the misinterpretation. You can allow them to choose any interaction for this assignment or ask them to focus on an intercultural interaction that caused the misinterpretation.

2. *Proxemics Exercise:* This exercise illustrates the various distances people use in everyday interactions and helps students find their "bubble" or comfort zone. The exercise also points out how our bubbles vary depending on our culture and personal preferences. Have students pair off and stand facing each other at a variety of distances while conversing. Instruct them to pay attention to their own and the other person's posture while doing this exercise. Specifically:

   a. Have students stand with toes touching.

   b. Have students stand one arm's length away from each other.

   c. Have one person move to his or her comfortable conversational distance while the other does not move.

   d. Have the person who did not move find his or her comfortable conversational distance while the other person does not move.

   Debrief this exercise by asking students which of the distances they were most comfortable with. Did they notice any differences between their own and their partner's bubble? When they were uncomfortable, what did they do with their bodies to "create" distance (such as not look at each other, bend backward as far as they could go, or turn should to shoulder rather than face each other). What did this exercise reveal to them about personal space and cultural differences?

3. *Role of Nonverbal Communication Exercise:* This exercise will help students understand that nonverbal communication is present in all of our communication interactions and will help them recognize some of the functions of nonverbal communication. Ask for four student volunteers to participate in a class contest. Have them each choose an experience to tell the class that was either very funny, scary, exciting, or infuriating. The object of the contest is to tell the story without using any nonverbal communication. As such, the only movement they can make is with their mouths, to formulate the words coherently. Give the four volunteers a few minutes to think of their stories. Meanwhile, instruct the rest of the class that they will be the judges of the contest. As soon as they notice any nonverbal behaviors, they should shout, "Stop." Assign one student to keep time. Ask the four volunteers to come to the front of the class. Instruct them to take turns telling their stories and to stop

when they hear the word "Stop." You may want to sit where you can see the faces of the volunteers, because students are sometimes hesitant to speak up at the first one or two violations, so you will probably have to do so. Halt the story as soon as you see even the slightest changes in facial expressions, eye movement, swaying, and so forth. Students seldom last more than 4–6 seconds. After the student is stopped, tell the student what movement he or she made, and ask him or her to remain standing in front of the class. When all four students have finished, ask the class whether it is possible to communicate without using nonverbal behaviors.

Then invite the students to relax and tell the stories as they normally would, using whatever nonverbal behaviors they like. After they finish, let them sit down, and ask the class whether the stories were more or less interesting with the nonverbal communication behaviors. Also ask the class what functions the nonverbal behaviors of these students played in the telling of their stories. Elicit specific examples.

4. *Nonverbal Variations Assignment I:* This assignment focuses on nonverbal differences in other cultures. Instruct students to choose a culture and research it to discover differences in nonverbal behaviors. Have them write a brief paper outlining the differences as compared with general behaviors typically found in the United States.

5. *Nonverbal Variations Assignment II:* A variation to the previous assignment is to have the students research the nonverbal behaviors of another culture in small groups and present their findings in role-play form instead of as a written report.

6. *Cultural Space Assignment:* Have students choose a cultural space they are interested in studying. Then instruct them to visit it on four different occasions to observe and take notes on how the people interact. When their observations are complete, they should write a brief paper summarizing their observations about proper nonverbal behavior in this cultural space. Remind them to be careful about generalizing or overestimating the influence of culture.

7. *Time Activity:* This exercise is designed to help students think about their cultural norms for time. Ask students to help you create a list on the chalkboard of the different places they have to go during the week (church, a party, dinner with a friend, study groups). Then suggest a meeting time for each event, and ask the students to write on a piece of paper the time that they would most likely arrive. After students have finished, have them share the times they would arrive, and keep track of these on the board. Then examine these times with the class to identify behavioral patterns using the following questions:

    a. For which activities are we most likely to arrive nearest the suggested meeting time?

    b. For which activities are we most likely to arrive late?

    c. For which activities do the arrival times vary the most?

    d. For which activities is it most socially acceptable to be late? Why?

    e. What is the acceptable time to be late for each of these activities? (Note: If there is a lot of variation between students' responses, ask them why they think they have different ideas about when it is acceptable to be late.)

    f. How do we learn these rules for being late?

    g. What does this exercise tell us about the relationship between culture and time?

SUGGESTED VIDEOS

1. *Communication: The Nonverbal Agenda.* Distributed by CRM Films, Carlsbad, CA, 1988. This video provides a general introduction to nonverbal communication. The relationship between verbal and nonverbal communication is explored, and some elements of nonverbal communication that are important in contemporary business environments are discussed. (20 minutes)

2. *Without Words: An Introduction to Nonverbal Communication.* Distributed by Prentice-Hall Publishing Company, Englewood Cliffs, NJ, 1977. This video gives several examples of nonverbal communication and discusses clothing as nonverbal communication. There is also a discussion of contrasts in nonverbal communication between Arab and U.S. American cultures. (23 minutes)

3. *Architecture: Why Man Builds.* Distributed by McGraw-Hill Publishing Company, New York, 1971. This video describes how architecture communicates about forces influencing civilizations and the people who design and use buildings. The video posits that architecture should be thought of as "a part of, rather than a backdrop for, life." (18 minutes)

4. *A World of Gestures: Culture and Nonverbal Communication.* Distributed by University of California Extension Media Center, Berkeley, 1991. This video shows some of the cultural variations in gestures and explores the origins and functions of gestures. (27 minutes)

5. *Nonverbal Communication.* Distributed by the Intercultural Communication Institute, 1989. This video by Dr. Milton Bennett presents a lively introduction to the topic of nonverbal behavior across cultures, with a review of primary nonverbal categories and illustrative anecdotes. Designed for individuals who will be interacting across cultures, the video makes the topic of nonverbal communication accessible to all audiences.

CHAPTER 7

Popular Culture and Intercultural Communication

LEARNING OBJECTIVES

After studying the material in this chapter, students should be able to:

Define popular culture.

Identify some types of popular culture.

Describe characteristics of popular culture.

Explain why it is important to understand popular culture in intercultural communication.

Discuss how and why people consume or resist specific cultural texts.

Understand how cultural texts influence cultural identities.

KEY TERMS

cultural identities	electronic colonialism	media imperialism
cultural imperialism	high culture	popular culture
cultural texts	low culture	reader profiles
culture industries		

DETAILED CHAPTER OUTLINE

I. Popular Culture and Intercultural Communication
   A. Much of what we know about places we've never been to probably comes from popular culture—the media experience of television, music, videos, and magazines.
   B. The complexity of popular culture is often overlooked in our society.
   C. People express concerns about the social effects of popular culture, yet most people think of popular culture as insignificant. This contradiction makes it difficult to investigate and discuss popular culture.
   D. Many U.S. film, music, and television stars are popular outside the United States, and products of U.S. popular culture are well known and circulate widely in the international marketplace. In contrast, U.S. Americans are rarely exposed to popular culture from outside the United States except for rock stars who sing in English.
   E. The apparent imbalance of cultural texts globally not only renders U.S. Americans more dependent on U.S.-produced popular culture but also leads to cultural imperialism.
II. What Is "Popular Culture"?
   A. Chapter 2 discussed how "low culture" has been reconceptualized as "popular culture."
   B. Brumment offers the following definition: "Popular culture refers to those systems or artifacts that most people share and that most people know about."
      1. Using this definition, television, music videos, and popular magazines are systems of popular culture, but not the symphony or the ballet, because most people would not be able to identify with them.

2. Popular culture is seen as populist, including forms of contemporary culture that are made popular by and for the people.
3. Lipsitz states: "The popular speaks to—and resonates from—the people, but it speaks to them through a multiplicity of cultural voices."

C. There are four characteristics of popular culture.
1. It is produced by culture industries.
2. It is different from folk culture.
3. It is everywhere.
4. It fills a social function.

D. Popular culture is nearly always produced within a capitalist system by culture industries that see the products of popular culture as commodities that can be economically profitable.

E. Popular culture is everywhere; we are bombarded with it every day, which makes it difficult to avoid.

F. Popular culture also serves an important social function—especially television, which provides a cultural forum for discussing and working out ideas on a variety of topics.

G. People negotiate their relationships to popular culture in complex ways, which makes it difficult to understand the roles of popular culture in intercultural communication.

H. We are not passive receivers of popular culture; in fact, we are quite active in our consumption of or resistance to it.

III. Consuming and Resisting Popular Culture: To maintain and reshape our identities, we often turn to popular culture. At times, we seek it out; at other times, we try to avoid certain texts.

A. Consuming Popular Culture
1. Popular culture texts do not have to win over the majority of the people to be considered "popular."
2. People seek out or avoid specific forms of popular culture that serve their needs.
3. Often people in our social groups participate in particular forms of popular culture, and we feel that we should participate as well.
4. While there is some unpredictability in the ways people navigate through popular culture, there are some patterns, such as those portrayed in reader profiles, that emerge.
5. Popular culture serves important cultural functions that are connected to cultural identities.
   a. We participate in those texts that address issues relevant to our cultural groups.
   b. They tend to affirm cultural identities that are sometimes invisible or are silenced by the mainstream culture.
6. Readers choose from among all of the available texts, consuming those that fulfill important cultural needs and resisting those that do not.
   a. Not all popular culture texts are easily correlated to particular cultural groups.
   b. The reasons some people enjoy some texts and not others cannot easily be determined.

B. Resisting Popular Culture
1. People resist particular forms of popular culture by refusing to engage in them.
2. Conscious decisions to resist some forms of popular culture are based on concerns about cultural politics.
3. Resistance can also be related to social roles and stems mainly from concerns about the representation of various social groups.
4. Popular culture plays a powerful role in how we think about and understand other groups.

IV. Representing Cultural Groups: Popular culture is a lens for viewing other cultural groups, and it does so in more intimate ways than tourists experience because it permits us to see the private lives of people. Because some people use popular culture forms as a source of information about a particular culture, the question of how the cultural groups are portrayed becomes important. And some groups are less often portrayed than others, so it is easier to stereotype those groups.

A. Migrant's Perceptions of Mainstream Culture
1. People use popular culture to learn about other cultures.
2. Sometimes people use U.S. popular culture to learn about U.S. Americans and watch shows about their own culture to affirm their cultural identities.
3. Migrants both resist and consume U.S. popular culture.

B. Popular Culture and Stereotyping: Our knowledge of places, even those we have been to, is largely influenced by popular culture.
1. For people with limited experience with other cultures, the impact of popular culture may be greater.
2. There are many familiar stereotypes of ethnic groups represented in the media, including Arabs, Mexicans, and African American women.
3. It appears from Manusov and Hegda's study that having some cultural information and positive expectations may lead to more in-depth conversations and positive outcomes than having no information.
4. A study involving Whites interviewing Black and White job candidates showed that negative racial stereotypes appeared to constrain the behavior of both Blacks and Whites.

V. U.S. Popular Culture and Power: It is important to consider the power relationships that are embedded in popular culture.

A. Global Circulation of Images/Commodities
1. A high percentage of international circulation of popular culture originates in the United States.
2. Many U.S. films make more money outside of the United States, which ensures that Hollywood will continue to export them.
3. Other forms of popular culture are also exported.

B. Popular Culture from Other Cultures
1. Although U.S. popular culture dominates the world market, not all popular culture comes from the United States.
2. Some popular culture is limited to particular cultures while other forms of popular culture cross into an international market.
3. The appropriation of James Bond into the U.S. ideological and economic terrain complicates arguments about popular culture and intercultural communication.

C. Cultural Imperialism: It is important to think about the impact of the U.S. media on the rest of the world.
1. In the 1920s, U.S. media was exported to boost sales of U.S. products.
2. Tomlinson identifies five ways to think about cultural imperialism.
    a. As cultural domination
    b. As media imperialism
    c. As nationalist discourse
    d. As a critique of global capitalism
    e. As a critique of modernity
3. Tomlinson's analysis demonstrates the interrelatedness of issues of ethnicity, culture, and nationalism in the context of economics, technology, and capitalism.
4. There is no easy way to measure the impact of popular culture, but we need to be sensitive to its influences on intercultural communication.

DISCUSSION QUESTIONS

1. What do we know about places we have never been and how do we know it?

2. Why do people select some popular culture forms over others?

3. How do the choices we make about what forms of popular culture to consume influence the formation of our cultural identity?

4. What strategies can people use to resist popular culture?

5. What types of consumers might be interested in Pokémon as opposed to MTV's *Road Rules*?

6. What are some examples of high culture?

7. What are some examples of low culture?

CLASSROOM EXERCISES AND CHAPTER ACTIVITIES

1. *Cultural Perceptions Exercise:* This exercise is designed to encourage students to think about the information they receive about other cultures from different forms of print media. Prior to class, collect examples from the U.S. media portraying people from other cultures (for example, the babushka as a representation of Polish people/women) and images of the United States in foreign newspapers and magazines (most libraries have an international section). You might ask students:

   a. Do they tend to accept images of other cultures in the U.S. media as true representations?

   b. Do they want other people to accept images of the United States in foreign media as representative of the whole country? Why?

   c. Why do the media choose to portray people the way they do?

   d. What effect do particular portrayals have on intercultural communication?

2. *Defining "Popular" Exercise:* The purpose of this class discussion is to explore with students the notion of what popular is. To do so, you might ask students the following questions:

   a. What is popular today in movies, magazines, and music?

   b. What makes a film, video, or magazine popular?

   c. Who decides what is and is not popular?

   d. Why do people differ in their perceptions of what is popular?

   e. How does popular culture influence us today?

3. *Video Assignment:* This project is designed to encourage students to explore how popular culture provides us with information about other cultures. Instruct students to pick a video that portrays a specific cultural group or interactions between two cultural groups; a few suggestions follow. Have students view the video and write a brief report on it. In the report, they could address these questions:

   a. What did you learn about the culture(s) portrayed in this video?

   b. How accurately do you think the directors portrayed the cultures? Why?

   c. Do you think people would perceive this cultural group in a negative or positive manner after watching this video?

d. If people saw this cultural group on this video and then met with a member of the cultural group, how might watching the video affect their communication with the person?

Suggested Videos

Rising Sun	*The Joy Luck Club*
Dances with Wolves	*The Color Purple*
Schindler's List	*Mi Familia*
Do the Right Thing	*Witness*

4. *Exported Popular Culture Assignment:* Identify for students examples of television programs that are popular exports in other countries. Assign students to watch one of them and write a critique addressing the following ideas:

   a. How are U.S. Americans portrayed in this show?

   b. Which cultural groups are portrayed?

   c. If this show were your first introduction to the culture of the people in the United States, what would you think about them?

   d. How might the portrayal of U.S. Americans in this show influence intercultural communication with the people who have seen the show but had no other experience with U.S. Americans?

5. *Consuming Pop Culture Assignment:* This exercise will help students clarify their relationship with pop culture and help them determine to what extent they are influenced by pop culture. Ask the students to be detectives in their own homes by examining the labels on their clothes, the product labels on their home decorations (for example, a poster of a movie, or a candy dish with Mickey Mouse on it), and the magazines and newspapers they buy. In a one- to two-page paper, students should identify those items they believe are examples of pop culture. Then they should discuss the level of influence these items hold for them and whether they could resist any of these items. For instance, if most of the clothes the student owns display the Nike swoosh, the student may feel highly influenced by this form of pop culture. However, the student may also write that he or she could easily live without Nike products, thereby indicating that this is a form of pop culture that he or she could resist but instead chooses to consume.

6. *Alternative to Consuming Pop Culture Assignment:* Instead of asking students to write a paper, have them bring to class at least one item from their home that they consider to be representative of pop culture. In small groups, ask students to share their item, answering the questions in assignment 5.

SUGGESTED VIDEOS

1. *Still Killing Us Softly: Advertising's Image of Women.* Produced by Jean Kilbourne and Cambridge Documentary Films, Cambridge, MA, 1987. The director, Margaret Lazarus, describes the portrayal of women in advertising and the way this portrayal influences women, men, and children. The video also suggests ways that advertising's portrayal of women affects the images men and women form of themselves. (32 minutes)

2. *True Colors.* Produced by Prime Time Live; distributed by Coronet/MTI Film and Video. This powerful collection of scenes, recorded with a hidden camera by Prime Time Live, graphically demonstrates the costs—both financial and psychological—of racism in America. The video illustrates the "grinding down" of the human spirit as it shows an African American investigator being variously followed, ignored, overcharged, and excluded. Observers of this video are moved to recognize the impact of bias and to internalize that such bias exists in their own communities. (60 minutes)

CHAPTER 8

Culture, Communication, and Conflict

LEARNING OBJECTIVES

After studying the material in this chapter, students should be able to:

Describe what is meant by conflict as opportunity and conflict as destructive.

List the basic principles of nonviolence.

Suggest some ways in which cultures differ in their views toward conflict.

Identify five different types of conflict.

Understand how people learn their default conflict strategies.

Discuss the role ethnicity and gender play in conflict.

Describe how conflict styles vary in individualistic and collectivist societies.

Define social movements.

Explain why it is important to understand the role of the social and historical contexts in intercultural conflicts.

List the characteristics of intercultural conflict.

KEY TERMS

avoiding style	incompatibility	mediation
compromising style	integrating style	obliging style
conflict	intercultural conflict	pacifism
confrontation	interdependent	social conflict
dominating style	intermediary	social movements

DETAILED CHAPTER OUTLINE

I. Introduction: Conflict is unavoidable. Conflicts are happening all around the world, at the personal, societal, and international levels. Conflicts may also arise from mediated communication, such as U.S. television, film, and other media.

II. Characteristics of Intercultural Conflict: Conflict is usually defined as a perceived or real incompatibility of goals, values, expectations, processes, or outcomes between two or more interdependent individuals or groups. Intercultural conflicts are often characterized by more ambiguity, language issues, and contradictory conflict styles than intracultural conflict.
   A. Ambiguity: This is often present in intercultural conflicts.
      1. We may be confused about or unsure of how to handle conflict.
      2. We may be unsure if we both see the conflict the same way.
      3. When we encounter ambiguity, we may quickly resort to our default style of handling conflict (the style we learned in our family).

4. The conflict may become worse if the preferred styles of handling conflict are different for the people involved in the conflict.

B. Language Issues: These can lead to intercultural conflict and can also contribute to solving the conflict.
    1. When people don't know each other's languages very well, it may be difficult to handle conflict effectively.
    2. Remaining silent, which can provide a "cooling off" period, may be effective in some situations.

C. Contradictory Conflict Styles: These can lead to more conflict.

III. Conflict Types, Strategies, and Contexts

A. Types of Conflict
    1. Affective conflict occurs when individuals become aware that their feelings and emotions are incompatible.
    2. A conflict of interest arises when people have incompatible preferences for a course of action or plan to pursue.
    3. Value conflict, a more serious type of conflict, occurs when people differ in ideologies on specific issues.
    4. Cognitive conflict describes a situation in which two or more people become aware that their thought processes or perceptions are in conflict.
    5. Goal conflict occurs when people disagree about a preferred outcome or end state.

B. Strategies and Tactics in Conflict Situations: Although we may have a general predisposition to deal with conflict in particular ways, we may choose different tactics in different situations rather than be locked into a particular conflict strategy. Sometimes people try very hard to reject the conflict styles modeled by their parents.
    1. Dominating style
        a. This style reflects a high concern for the self and a low concern for others.
        b. This may be thought of as a win-lose orientation whereby individuals may use forceful behavior to win their position.
        c. This style is often associated with loud and forceful expressiveness, which may be counterproductive to conflict resolution.
    2. Integrating style
        a. This style reflects high concern for both the self and the other person.
        b. It involves an open and direct exchange of information in an attempt to reach a solution that is acceptable to both parties.
        c. It is seen as the most effective strategy to use in conflicts because it attempts to be fair and equitable.
        d. It involves collaboration, empathy, objectivity, recognition of feelings, and creative solutions.
        e. It requires a lot of time and energy.
    3. Compromising style
        a. This style reflects a moderate degree of concern for the self and others.
        b. It involves sharing and exchanging information in such a way that both parties give up something to find a mutually acceptable solution.
        c. Sometimes this style is less effective than the integrating approach because people feel forced to give up something they value and so have less commitment to the solution.
    4. Obliging style
        a. One person in the conflict plays down the differences and incompatibilities, and emphasizes commonalities that satisfy the concerns of the other person.
        b. This style may be most appropriate when one person is more concerned with the future of the relationship than with the issues.

      c. This style is common in hierarchical relationships in which one person has more status or power than the other. The person with lower status may use an obliging style in conflicts.

    5. Avoiding style

      a. In the dominant U.S. cultural contexts, a person who uses this style attempts to withdraw, sidestep, deny, and bypass the conflict.

      b. In some cultural contexts, if both parties use this style, it may be an appropriate strategy resulting in more harmonious relationships.

C. The Importance of Context

    1. The choice of how to manage conflict may depend on the context or situation.

    2. The conflict context can be viewed in two ways:

      a. As the situation in which the conflict happens

      b. As a larger societal context

IV. Cultural Influences on Conflict Management: One's cultural background may influence whether one thinks conflict is good or bad, whether conflict strengthens or leads to problems for relationships and groups, and what are the best ways to handle conflict.

A. Two Approaches to Conflict

    1. In many Western cultures, conflict is seen as fundamentally a good thing, offering an opportunity for strengthening relationships.

      a. There are benefits for groups working through conflict.

      b. Members can gain new information about people or other groups.

      c. Groups are able to diffuse more serious conflict.

      d. They can increase cohesiveness when engaging in conflict with other groups.

      e. There is value in direct confrontation and conciliation by recognizing conflict and working through it in an open, productive way.

      f. Conflict is seen as necessary to the redistribution of opportunity, release of tensions, and renewal of relationships.

    2. Many cultural groups (including many Asian cultures and some religious groups in the United States) view conflict as ultimately destructive for relationships.

      a. Conflict is seen as disturbing the peace.

      b. The Amish and others maintain the spiritual value of pacifism, so when conflict arises they respond in a nonresistant manner—often avoidance.

      c. These groups think that when members disagree, they should adapt to the consensus of the group rather than engage in conflict. Members who undermine group harmony may be sanctioned.

      d. Confrontations are seen as destructive and ineffective, and silence and avoidance are often used to manage conflict.

      e. Individuals from these groups also use intermediaries (a friend or colleague) to act on their behalf in dealing with conflict. This is also true for people in the Western world; however, they tend to be professionals, such as a lawyer, counselor, or therapist used in formal settings.

    3. The basic principle of nonviolence involves "peacemaking." People who approach conflict with this orientation do three things:

      a. They strongly value the other person and encourage his or her growth.

      b. They attempt to de-escalate conflicts or to keep them from escalating once they start.

      c. They attempt to use creative negotiation to resolve conflicts when they arise.

    4. These two approaches have different underlying cultural values involving identity and face saving.

      a. The more individualistic approach sees conflict as good and is concerned with preserving people's personal dignity.

       b. The more communal approach (Amish, Japanese, and others) is concerned with maintaining harmony in interpersonal relationships and preserving the dignity of others.

B. Gender, Ethnicity, and Conflict
1. Men and women in the United States seem to have different communication styles, which sometimes lead to conflict and can influence how they handle it.
    a. When showing support, women sometimes make sympathetic noises while men may say nothing to show respect for independence. But women may interpret men's silence as indifference.
    b. Men and women differ in their "troubles talk" and in story telling.
    c. Women discuss the relationship process to feel better while men see little point in discussing something if nothing is identified as needing fixing.
2. Ethnic background affects the way people deal with conflict.
    a. When African Americans, Asian Americans, White Americans, and Mexican Americans were asked how they dealt with a conflict involving a close friend, they gave different kinds of answers.
       i. African Americans said they used a problem-solving approach (integration style).
      ii. Asian Americans reported using more conflict-avoiding styles than did White Americans.
     iii. Whites seemed to focus on the importance of taking responsibility for their behavior. Males emphasized being direct, and females talked about being concerned with the other person, the relationship, and situational flexibility.
     iv. Mexican American males reported talking to reach a mutual understanding, while females said that they focused on reinforcement of the relationship.
     v. In general, males and females in all groups described females as more compassionate and concerned for feelings, and males as more concerned with winning the conflict and being "right."
3. It is important to remember that, whereas ethnicity and gender may be related to ways of dealing with conflict, it is inappropriate and inaccurate to assume that any one person will behave in a particular way because of his or her ethnicity or gender.

C. Value Differences and Conflict Styles
1. Cultural values in individualistic societies differ from those in collectivist societies.
    a. Individualistic societies place greater importance on the individual than on groups. Individualism is often cited as the most important value for European Americans and is encouraged in children.
    b. Collectivist societies often emphasize extended families and loyalty to groups.
2. These contrasting values may influence communication patterns during conflict.
    a. People in individualistic societies share several characteristics.
       i. They tend to be more concerned with saving their own self-esteem during conflict.
      ii. They are more direct in their communication.
     iii. They use more controlling, confrontational, and solution-oriented conflict styles.
    b. People in collectivist societies share several characteristics.
       i. They tend to be more concerned with preserving group harmony and with saving the other person's dignity during conflict.
      ii. They use a less direct conversational style.
     iii. They may use avoiding and obliging conflict styles instead.
3. How individuals choose to deal with conflict in any situation depends on the type of conflict and their relationship with the other person.

V. Managing Intercultural Conflict
  A. Productive Versus Destructive Conflict
    1. Productive conflict
      a. Individuals carefully narrow the conflict to try to understand the specific problem.
      b. Individuals limit conflict to the original issue.
      c. Individuals or groups direct their efforts toward cooperative problem solving.
      d. Individuals or groups trust leaders who stress mutually satisfactory outcomes.
    2. Destructive conflict
      a. Individuals or groups escalate the issues and negative attitudes.
      b. Individuals escalate the conflict from the original issues, and anything in the relationship is open for reexamination.
      c. Threats, coercion, and deception are used.
      d. People polarize behind single-minded and militant leaders.
  B. Competitive Versus Cooperative Conflict
    1. Destructive conflict features competitive escalation, such that the conflicting parties set up a self-perpetuating, mutually confirming expectation.
    2. A competitive atmosphere promotes coercion, deception, suspicion, rigidity, and poor communication.
    3. A cooperative atmosphere promotes perceived similarity, trust, flexibility, and open communication.
    4. At the beginning stages of relationships or group interaction, a cooperative atmosphere needs to be fostered, as it is difficult to turn a competitive relationship into a cooperative one once a conflict has started to escalate.
    5. Exploration is essential to setting a cooperative atmosphere.
      a. Both parties must put the issue in conflict on hold.
      b. Both parties must investigate other options or delegate the problem to a third party.
      c. Both parties must suspend blame so it's possible to come up with new ideas or positions.
      d. If all parties are committed to the process, there is a sense of joint ownership of the recommended solution.
VI. Understanding Conflict and Society: Many intercultural conflicts can be better understood by looking at the underlying social, economic, historical, and political forces.
  A. Social and Economic Forces
    1. Social conflict arises from unequal or unjust social relationships between groups.
    2. In social movements, people work together to bring about social change using confrontation as a strategy to highlight the injustices of the present system.
    3. Social movements involve conflicts such as movements against racism, sexism, and homophobia, or in support of animal rights, the environment, and free speech.
    4. Although nonviolence is not the only form of confrontation employed by social movements, it has a long history.
    5. Some social movements have also used violent forms of confrontation. The use of violence tends to stigmatize these groups as terrorists rather than protesters.
    6. Many conflicts are fueled by economic problems, which find their expression in blaming and pointing fingers at immigrants, people of color, and Jews. Blaming marginalized or less powerful groups diverts attention from the people who actually wield the power and own the wealth.
    7. As the economic contexts change, more cultural conflict takes place. Prejudice and stereotyping that lead to conflict often result from perceived economic threats and competition.

B. Historical and Political Forces
   1. Derogatory words derive power from their historical usage and the history of oppression that they reference.
   2. It is only through understanding the past that we can understand what it means to be a member of a particular cultural group.
   3. Sometimes identities are constructed in opposition to or in conflict with other identities, so when people identify as members of particular cultural groups, they are marking their difference from others.
   4. When these differences are infused with historical antagonism, it can lead to future conflicts.
   5. All around the world, historical antagonisms become part of cultural identities and cultural practices that place people in positions of conflict.
   6. The danger in viewing conflict only as an interpersonal issue is that we lose sight of the larger social and political forces that contextualize these conflicts.

DISCUSSION QUESTIONS

1. Why is it important to understand the context in which an intercultural conflict occurs?
2. How are conflict strategies used in social movements?
3. What makes intercultural conflict different from other kinds of conflict?
4. Should conflict be welcomed or avoided?
5. What are some gender and ethnic group conflict style differences?
6. How did your family handle conflicts? Is that the way you handle conflict?
7. Why is it important to understand your own conflict style preference?
8. Can you think of a conflict that escalated due to differences in the way you and the other person handle conflict?
9. What are some of the differences between constructive and destructive conflict?
10. How can language differences cause conflict?
11. Is there a best way to handle conflict? What is it, and why?
12. How can we set up a cooperative and not a competitive atmosphere?
13. In what ways does the economic context influence conflict?
14. How do value differences influence intercultural conflict?

CLASSROOM EXERCISES AND CHAPTER ACTIVITIES

1. *Guest Lecture on Cultures in Conflict Exercise:* The purpose of this exercise is to acquaint students with a cultural conflict and the history of that conflict. You should invite a speaker who has studied a particular cultural conflict between national or local cultural groups and who can not only provide students with an update of the current situation but can also explain the history of the conflict and relations between the two groups. For example, you might invite a professor from the political science department who has studied the political conflict in Kosovo. Instruct your students to take notes during the

lecture and to ask questions at the end. Then have them write a two- to three-paragraph analysis describing what each side will need to do to resolve the conflict.

2. *Intercultural Conflict Role-Plays:* This exercise encourages students to practice various strategies for managing or resolving intercultural conflicts. Form students into groups of four to five members. Have each group develop a scenario that depicts an intercultural conflict, which they should then resolve using one of the strategies discussed in the textbook. Each group can then perform their role-play in front of the class, and the class can try to "guess" which conflict strategy the group enacted. After each role-play, the actors should remain at the front of the class to answer any questions or offer any comments they may have about their role-play.

3. *Alternative to Intercultural Conflict Role-Plays:* Have the students enact their role-plays without offering a strategy or resolution to their scenario. The class can then try to answer questions about the scenario such as these:

    a. Is this productive or destructive conflict?

    b. Is this competitive or cooperative conflict?

    c. What strategies could the persons in the role-play employ to manage the conflict? (Students could even "try out" the suggested strategy to test its appropriateness.)

4. *Identifying One's Preferred Style of Managing Conflict Exercise:* Often people's preferred style of dealing with conflicts is based (perhaps unconsciously) on the style they saw modeled as children. This exercise is designed to help students identify their preferred style of dealing with conflict by reflecting on the style(s) they grew up with or the style that stands out for them. Begin the exercise by asking students to reflect on the style of conflict they were most exposed to as children. You may need to suggest that they think about specific instances in which a conflict in their family arose and the way the conflict was handled. For instance, in one family, every time there was a conflict, a loud shouting match ensued, and then everybody went to their rooms for a nap. When they all awoke, the family members acted as if the conflict had never happened.

    After the students identify the style(s) of handling conflict that they were exposed to, ask them to reflect on whether this is their preferred style as adults or whether they have consciously or unconsciously changed their preferred style of managing conflict. Debrief this exercise by asking students to share their answers, which will expose the class to various styles. The discussion that follows should be respectful of the different styles of dealing with conflict that emerge, and you should urge students to think more about the implications of the styles, rather than dichotomizing them in terms of right or wrong.

5. *Attitudes Toward Conflict Exercise:* As a first step to understanding and managing conflict, students need to become aware of their personal feelings toward conflict. In this simple exercise, ask students to write down the first words that come into their minds when they think of "conflict." Then ask them to share some of their words with the class, and record them on the board. After a few minutes, ask the students to reflect on the words you've recorded and to share any of their thoughts. One of the most powerful observations that comes out of this exercise is the negative feeling people have about conflict. Another important observation is that often the behaviors for managing conflict are negative or destructive behaviors, such as hating, yelling, or hitting. Once students have had an opportunity to explore their attitudes toward conflict, you can introduce alternate and more positive views of conflict.

6. *Draw a House Exercise:* For this fun and instructive exercise, pairs of students are forced to cooperate with each other. Pair the students and tell them that they will be drawing a picture of a house together. The catch is that they have to make the drawing while both are holding the same pencil. After the students have had an opportunity to draw their picture, have them discuss in their pairs the following questions:

   a. Was this exercise easy or difficult?

   b. How were decisions made to draw the house?

   c. Were there any struggles or conflicts in any stage of this exercise?

   d. How did you work out conflicts?

   e. Now that you have completed this exercise, is there anything you would do differently if asked to do it again?

   f. How does this exercise relate to studying conflict?

SUGGESTED VIDEOS

1. *Arab and Jew: Wounded Spirits in a Promised Land.* Distributed by PBS Video, Alexandria, VA, 1989. The video explores the cultural tensions between Arabs and Jews in Israeli territories. (118 minutes)

2. *A Conflict of Cultures.* Distributed by Annenberg/CPB Project, 1986. This video shows the conflicts that emerge from the mixing of cultures in Africa. (60 minutes)

3. *Chairy Tale.* Distributed by Film & Video Rental Center, Syracuse University. This is a fairy tale in the modern manner, told without words. The film shows a simple ballet between a youth and a kitchen chair. The young man tries to sit but the chair declines to be sat upon. The ensuing struggle, first for mastery and then for understanding, forms the story. (10 minutes)

CHAPTER 9

Intercultural Relationships in Everyday Life

LEARNING OBJECTIVES

After studying the material in this chapter, students should be able to:

Identify some differences in how intercultural relationships develop.

Discuss how cultural differences influence the initial stages of relational development.

Understand relational differences between gay and heterosexual relationships.

List some of the characteristics of intercultural relationships.

Identify some of the benefits and challenges in intercultural relationships.

Suggest reasons people give for and against intercultural dating and marriage.

Describe some of the approaches partners use in dealing with differences in intercultural marriages.

Understand how to become interpersonal allies.

Explain some of the ways to build coalitions.

KEY TERMS

complementarity	intercultural dating	physical attraction
compromise style	intercultural relationships	romantic relationships
consensus style	interpersonal allies	similarity principle
friendship	intimacy	submission style
gay relationships	obliteration style	

DETAILED CHAPTER OUTLINE

I. Benefits of Intercultural Relationships
   A. Intercultural relationships encompass differences in age, physical ability, gender, ethnicity, class, religion, race, and nationality.
   B. The key to these relationships is the balance of differences and similarities.
   C. Intercultural relationships offer several benefits:
      1. Learning about the world
         a. Participants gain specific information about unfamiliar cultural patterns and language.
         b. Participants gain general information about what it really means to belong to a different culture.
         c. Participants gain history—a kind of "relational learning" that comes from a particular relationship but generalizes to other contexts, which may increase curiosity to learn the history of other ethnic groups.

      2. Breaking stereotypes
      3. Acquiring new skills
II. Challenges in Intercultural Relationships
    A. Differences in Communication Styles, Values, and Perceptions
      1. Dissimilarities are most noticeable in the early stages of relational development—before people get to know each other on a more personal, individual level.
      2. Once commonality is established and the relationship develops, the cultural differences may have less impact.
    B. Negative Stereotypes
    C. Anxiety: There may be more anxiety in the early stages of intercultural relationships compared to intracultural relationships.
      1. Some anxiety always exists in the early stages of a relationship.
      2. Anxiety comes from being worried about possible negative consequences (being afraid of looking stupid or of offending someone due to unfamiliarity with the person's language or culture).
      3. Some differences (physical ability, class, race) cause more discomfort than others (age).
      4. Once a person develops a close intercultural relationship, it acts as a kind of "hurdle," and it becomes much easier to develop other intercultural relationships.
      5. If a person has negative expectations based on a previous interaction or on stereotypes, the level of anxiety may be higher.
    D. The Need for Explanations: Intercultural relationships present the challenge of having to explain several things:
      1. To ourselves (consciously or unconsciously) the meaning of being friends with someone who is different
      2. To each other as we learn to see from the other's perspective—a process of ongoing mutual clarification
      3. To our respective communities the meaning of the relationship
        a. Majority Communities: One of the biggest obstacles to boundary-crossing friendships comes from majority communities.
          i. Those in the majority have the most to gain by maintaining social inequality and are less likely to initiate boundary-crossing friendships.
          ii. Minority groups have more to gain from these friendships, as it can help them survive economically and professionally.
III. Foundations of Intercultural Relationships
    A. Similarities and Differences
      1. Similarity principle
        a. We are attracted to people who hold attitudes similar to ours.
        b. Finding people who agree with our beliefs confirms our own beliefs.
        c. We can better predict others' behavior if they are similar to us.
        d. The similarity principle is self-reinforcing—similarity is based not on whether people actually are similar, but on the recognition or discovery of a similar trait.
        e. When people think they're similar, they have higher expectations about future interaction.
      2. Differences (complementarity)
        a. In intercultural relationships, we are attracted to persons who are somewhat different from ourselves.
        b. We may seek out those who have different personality traits and therefore provide balance or complementarity in a relationship.
        c. Some people are attracted to others simply because they have a different cultural background.

          d. People are attracted to some but not other differences, and society seems to accept some relationships of complementarity better than others.

  B. Cultural Differences in Relationships

    1. Friendships

        a. In the United States, "friend" is a fairly broad term that applies to many different kinds of relationships. In other countries, such as India, a "friend" is defined more narrowly.

        b. What most people in the world consider a friend is what a U.S. American would consider a "close friend."

        c. International students in the United States remark that U.S. American students seem superficial and treat the international students as acquaintances, not"close" friends.

        d. Young people in Japan and the United States seem to be attracted to people who are similar to them in some way, and both groups use the same words to define "friend": trust, respect, understanding, and sincerity.

           i. However, Japanese students listed togetherness, trust, and warmth as the top characteristics, and U.S. students named understanding, respect, and sincerity as the top ones.

          ii. The Japanese list emphasizes relational harmony and collectivism, and the U.S. list reflects the importance of honesty and individuality.

        e. Latino/Latina, Asian American, African American, and Anglo American students' notions about friendship also reveal similarities and differences.

           i. All the groups listed trust and acceptance as the two most important characteristics of close friendships.

          ii. However, Latino, Asian American, and African American students said it took about a year to develop a close friendship, while Anglo-Americans felt it took only a few months.

         iii. Latinos emphasized relational support; Asian Americans, caring, positive exchange of ideas; African Americans, respect and acceptance; and Anglo Americans, recognizing the needs of individuals.

    2. Romantic relationships

        a. In general, most cultures stress the importance of some degree of openness, involvement, shared nonverbal meanings, and relationship assessment.

        b. There are differences, however. U.S. American students emphasize physical attraction, passion, love, and individual autonomy (individualistic orientation).

        c. In contrast, many other cultural groups emphasize the acceptance of the potential partner by family members as more important than romantic or passionate love (collectivist orientation).

        d. An emphasis on individual autonomy can make it very difficult to balance the needs of two "separate" individuals.

        e. Extreme individualism makes it difficult for either partner to justify sacrificing or giving more than he or she is receiving, which creates fundamental conflicts in trying to reconcile personal freedom with marital obligations.

        f. People who hold extremely individualistic orientations may experience less love for, trust in, and physical attraction toward their partners; these problems are less common in more collectivist societies.

    3. Gay relationships: There is much less information available about gay or same-sex relationships than about heterosexual romantic relationships. Homosexuality has existed in every society and in every era, and it may be intracultural and intercultural. Gay relationships differ from straight relationships in several ways:

      a. Same-sex friendships
         i. U.S. males are socialized toward less self-expression and emotional intimacy in same-sex friendships, so they turn to women for emotional support. In contrast, men in gay relationships tend to seek emotional support from same-sex friendships.
        ii. Both gay and straight women seek intimacy more often through same-sex friendships.
      b. Cross-sex friendships
         i. In heterosexual relationships, friendship and sexual involvement are kept separated, as the sex thing always "gets in the way."
        ii. Gay friendships may start with sexual attraction and involvement but endure after sexual involvement is terminated.
      c. Relative importance of friendship
         i. Close friendships may be more important for gay people than for straights due to discrimination and hostility from the straight world and often-strained relationships with families.
        ii. The social support from friends in the gay community plays a special role, and sometimes friends act as family.
      d. Permanent relationships and relational dissolution
         i. In the United States, there is little legal recognition of permanent gay relationships, and the federal government passed the Defense of Marriage Act, which would allow states to refuse to recognize gay marriages in other states.
        ii. Some countries do recognize same-sex relationships and create a different environment for gay and lesbian relationships.
        iii. Some gay relationships may terminate earlier than straight marriages due to family and social pressures, religious beliefs, custody battles, and so on. Although shorter lived, gay relationships may be happier and more mutually productive.

IV. Relationships Across Differences
  A. Communicating in Intercultural Relationships: Some unique themes guide thinking about communicating in intercultural relationships.
    1. Competence: There are four levels of intercultural communication competence.
      a. Unconscious incompetence is the "be yourself" approach in which the person is not conscious of difference and does not feel the need to act in any particular way. This works in interactions with people similar to ourselves but isn't very effective in intercultural interactions.
      b. Conscious incompetence is the level at which we realize things may not be going very well in the interaction, but we're not sure why.
      c. Conscious competence is a level necessary to being a competent communicator, but it is not sufficient. As instructors of intercultural communication, we teach at a conscious, intentional level.
      d. Unconscious competence is the level at which communication goes smoothly, but it is not a conscious process. It requires being well prepared cognitively and attitudinally, but knowing when to "let go" and rely on our holistic cognitive processing.
    2. Similarity: While dissimilarity accounts for the initial attraction, it is important to find and develop some similarity.
    3. Involvement: All relationships take time to develop, but it is especially important in intercultural relationships. Intimacy of interactions is another element of involvement, as are shared friendship networks.

    4. Turning points: These relate to perceived changes in the relationship that move the relationship forward or backward. Points of understanding (self-disclosure) may move the relationship to a new level.

  B. Intercultural Dating.

    1. The reason people give for dating within and outside their own ethnic group is similar: they are attracted to the other person, physically and/or sexually.

    2. The reasons people give for not dating someone within or outside of their own ethnic group are often different.

      a. The reason for not dating someone within the ethnic group is lack of attraction.

      b. The reasons for not dating outside the ethnic group are lack of opportunity and not having thought about it.

    3. These different responses reflect the social and political structure of U.S. American society. People have been taught that it is better to date within their own ethnic and racial group: and they probably have very little opportunity to date interethnically.

    4. Families often pass on negative attitudes regarding interracial friendship or romance to their children.

  C. Intercultural Marriage

    1. Pressure from the family and society and issues involved in raising children are major concerns for spouses in intercultural marriages, more so than for other married couples.

    2. Most couples face similar problems related to friends, politics, finances, sex, in-laws, illness and suffering, and child raising, but certain issues can be more serious in intercultural marriages, including values, eating and drinking habits, gender roles, ethnocentrism, religion, place of residence, stress, and attitudes regarding time.

    3. In every couple, partners have to develop their own way of relating to each other, but intercultural marriages pose consistent challenges. There are four common styles of interaction in intercultural marriages.

      a. Submission (the most common style) occurs when one partner submits to the culture of the other, abandoning or denying his or her own. It may occur only in public, with the relationship more balanced in private life. This style rarely works in the long run, as people cannot erase their core cultural background no matter how hard they try.

      b. Compromise occurs when each partner gives up some parts of his or her culturally bound habits and beliefs to accommodate the other. It seems fair, but it means that both people give up important aspects of their life, and one or both partners may begin to resent the sacrifice.

      c. Obliteration requires that both partners deal with differences by attempting to erase their individual cultures and form a new culture with new beliefs and habits. However, it's difficult to completely cut oneself off from one's own cultural background, so this is not a good long-term solution.

      d. Consensus style (the most desirable) is based on agreement and negotiation. It is a win-win proposition and may incorporate elements of the other models.

    4. Couples considering permanent international relationships should prepare carefully for the commitment. Partners who marry interculturally should consider legal issues like their own and their children's citizenship, finances and taxation, property ownership, women's rights, divorce, and issues regarding death.

V. Society and Intercultural Relationships

  A. It is important to consider how society influences interpersonal relationships.

  B. We must consider the kinds of persecution that intercultural relationships encounter and think about the social institutions that might discourage such relationships.

DISCUSSION QUESTIONS

1. How did you get to know people who are different from you?

2. Are your intercultural relationships any different from those that you have with people similar to you?

3. How do intercultural relationships form?

4. What are the characteristics of a friend?

5. Why do some people marry outside their group?

6. What are some of the benefits of intercultural relationships?

7. What are some challenges for people involved in intercultural relationships?

8. How do your family, friends, and media sources affect decisions about whom you will form relationships with?

9. How are gay relationships different from and similar to heterosexual relationships?

10. What are some reasons for choosing to date interculturally?

11. What are some of the difficulties in becoming interpersonal allies?

12. What are the steps the text offers to begin building coalitions? Can you think of any others?

CLASSROOM EXERCISES AND CHAPTER ACTIVITIES

1. *Relationship Formation Exercise:* The purpose of this exercise is to help students explore how and with whom they tend to form relationships. Form groups of four to six students, and ask them to identify and record responses to the following questions:

   a. Why do we develop relationships with other people?

   b. How do we get to know our friends and romantic partners?

   c. How do we form relationships with people with whom we want to become friends?

   d. How do we get to know people who are different from us? Are these relationships different from those characterized by similarity?

   e. What are some of the criteria we use to determine who we want to form friendships with and with whom we don't want to be associated?

   Students should keep track of their answers; after 15 minutes, instruct each group to report back to the class.

2. *Defining Friendship Exercise:* This exercise helps students explore the characteristics of friendship. Have students form groups of four to six and come up with a definition of friendship. Explain to them that this definition needs to be broad enough to distinguish a friendship from an acquaintanceship. Suggest that before they frame their definition they should identify differences between friendships and acquaintanceships and generate a list of characteristics found in friendships. After the students have completed their definitions, they should share them with other groups. This may stimulate a class discussion on characteristics important to friendships and some cultural differences in how friendships are defined.

3. *Physical Attraction Exercise:* The object of this exercise is to encourage students to explore what characteristics constitute physical attractiveness and where their notions of physical attractiveness come from. You will need six to eight pictures of males and females from magazines or catalogues per group. Divide your students into groups of four to six individuals (mixed males and females). Give each group a set of pictures, and ask them to work as a group to rate the attractiveness of each person on a scale of 1 to 10, and then to explain their rating by listing the characteristics of the person they consider to be attractive/unattractive. Instruct the students to think about these characteristics and where they got the idea that these characteristics are positive/negative. At the end of the activity, lead a class discussion exploring the following questions:

   a. Did everyone in the group agree about what characteristics were considered attractive? If there were differences/similarities, why do you think they existed?

   b. Did male and female members of the group have the same ideas about what characteristics made men/women attractive?

   c. Where do we learn our notions of attractiveness?

4. *Cultural Variations in Relationships Assignment*: The purpose of this assignment is to encourage students to become familiar with relationship differences in a specific culture. The assignment may be modified to serve as a term or chapter assignment depending on the number of issues you assign students to investigate; it could also be given as a group project. Have students choose a national or cultural group they are interested in studying. Then suggest that they investigate the following questions about relationships in the culture:

   a. What constitutes friendship in the culture?

   b. What are the cultural norms and taboos regarding meeting and dating people of the opposite sex?

   c. How are marriage proposals conducted in the culture?

   d. What is a typical wedding like in the culture?

   e. How do members of the culture view divorce?

   f. If divorce occurs, what are the rights of each partner?

   g. What is the general cultural attitude toward homosexuality?

   h. How are the general perspectives of this culture the same as or different from yours regarding gender roles?

5. *Intercultural Relationships Interview Assignment:* This assignment focuses on exploring the challenges of forming intercultural relationships. Assign students to interview someone from their own culture who has lived for an extended period of time (a minimum of 3 months) in a foreign country or someone from another country currently living in the United States. Advise them to follow the suggestions and guidelines below, and to answer the following questions in writing a three- to four-page essay:

   a. How did you feel about meeting members of the culture for the first time?

   b. Before you met members of the culture, what did you expect them to be like?

   c. Did you encounter any surprises when you began interacting with members of the culture?

d. How would you describe the experience of forming relationships with members of this culture? Was your experience different from or similar to that when forming relationships with members of your own culture?

e. Did you notice differences from or similarities to your own culture in how friendships were formed with members of the opposite sex?

f. Did you notice differences from or similarities to your own culture in the expectations and norms for friendships with members of the same sex?

g. What advice would you give to people unfamiliar with the culture about forming relationships with members of this culture?

The following suggestions may help students set up and conduct their interview.

Preparing for the Interview

a. Plan the interview several weeks before the due date.

b. Decide whom you want to interview.

c. Think of an appropriate place to conduct the interview, one in which both you and the interviewee will be comfortable, will be able to hear each other, and will have few distractions.

d. Call or contact the person to set a date for the interview. When you contact the person, be sure to explain the purpose of the interview. Ask if he or she is willing to help. If the person agrees, set the date, time, and place for the interview. Give her or him an idea of how much time it will take, and ask if it's okay to take notes or tape-record the interview.

e. Prepare your question so that you are comfortable with their wording and are sure that they are clear and easy to understand. Short questions work better than detailed questions. Avoid using cliches or slang in the questions.

f. Prepare any note-taking equipment. (Remember to take extra batteries for a tape recorder if you are using one and the interviewee agrees to be tape-recorded.)

During the Interview

a. Be professional. Dress comfortably but nicely to show respect for the interviewee. Ask ethical and thoughtful questions that demonstrate your sensitivity to cultural issues and respect for him or her.

b. Before you begin the interview, establish rapport with your interviewee by spending a few minutes sharing information about yourself, the class, or other issues that will break the ice and create a convivial atmosphere.

c. Start the interview by explaining its purpose and verifying that the person is comfortable with the method you have chosen for recording the information you elicit.

d. As you ask the questions you have prepared, be sure to listen carefully to the answers and to ask follow-up questions if the interviewee does not provide the information you are seeking or gets off track. Be flexible in asking the questions, but try to keep the interviewee from going off on a tangent.

e. Stick to the agreed-upon time limit unless the interviewee seems offended that the time is so short. Avoid being abrupt in ending the interview, but at the same time be respectful of the interviewee's schedule.

f. When the interview is finished, thank the interviewee for his or her time and help. It is also appropriate to send a thank-you note.

6. *Intercultural Relationships Interview Assignment Variation:* This assignment is similar to the previous two in that it focuses on the challenges of intercultural relationships. However, in this assignment, students interview a person who is in an intercultural romantic relationship such as being married, going steady, or experiencing some other form of a committed relationship. Encourage the students to view "intercultural" broadly to include persons of different religions, different social class or economic groups, different ability levels, different sexual orientations, and so on. Have the students summarize the interview data in a two- to three-page paper. Advise them to follow the suggestions and guidelines given previously, and to use the following questions as a basis for the interview:

a. What cultures/religions are they members of?

b. How did they meet?

c. How long have they been in the relationship?

d. What attracted them to each other?

e. What role did culture/religion play in their attraction to each other, if any?

f. What are the strengths of their relationship?

g. What are the challenges of their relationship?

h. Do they see the strengths and challenges as different from those found in same-culture relationships?

i. How have friends and family displayed their support or lack of support for the relationship?

7. *Intercultural Relationships Video Assignment:* The goal of this assignment is to encourage students to explore the unique challenges and rewards of intercultural relationships. The video for this assignment can be shown during class time, or students can choose from a list of popular videos that highlight intercultural relationships. After viewing the video, students should write a one- to two-page essay answering the questions from the previous assignment. Some suggested videos are:

Suggested Videos

Jungle Fever   *Fools Rush In*

Mississippi Masala   *The Joy Luck Club*

SUGGESTED VIDEOS

1. *Halmani.* Distributed by California Newsreel, Chicago, 1988. This video tells the story of a Korean grandmother who comes to the United States to visit her daughter, U.S. American son-in-law, and granddaughter. It recounts the generational and cultural differences she encounters. (30 minutes)

2. *Hot Water: Intercultural Issues Between Women and Men.* Distributed by NAFSA Association of International Educators, Washington, DC, 1996. This video examines cultural differences in the relationships between women and men. Cultural variations discussed include perceptions of dating, intercultural marriage, and homosexual relationships, as well as

nonverbal differences. The video also suggests some safety issues for men and women who sojourn in other countries. (27 minutes)

3. *The Politics of Love in Black and White.* Distributed by California Newsreel, San Francisco, 1993. In this documentary video, college students discuss interracial relationships and their experiences with and feelings about interracial dating and marriage. (32 minutes).

4. *In My Country: Gender Perspectives on Gender.* Distributed by Utah Valley State College, Behavioral Science Department. This two-part video explores dating, marriage, and other relationship issues and cultural influences.

CHAPTER 10

Intercultural Communication and Tourism

LEARNING OBJECTIVES

After studying the material in this chapter, students should be able to:

Describe ways the tourism industry may have a positive or negative impact on host cultures.

Discuss the range of attitudes held by host culture locals toward tourists.

List limitations and challenges of the tourist–host communication encounter.

Describe the relationship between culture shock and the tourist–host interaction.

KEY TERMS

boundary maintenance	host	revitalization
eco-tourism	retreatism	tourist

DETAILED CHAPTER OUTLINE

I. Intercultural Communication and Tourism
   A. Introduction
      1. Travel and tourism is one of the world's largest industries, and by 2010, it is expected to generate $8 trillion dollars of economic activity and 328 million jobs.
      2. Tourism contexts provide rich opportunities for intercultural encounters.
      3. The encounters may be positive, or they may be tinged with resentment and reflect power differentials.
      4. Tourism often involves relatively privileged tourists visiting less wealthy sites, which may lead to negative encounters and to resentment on the part of the locals.
      5. Tourists come from a variety of cultural and socioeconomic backgrounds.
      6. Business/service providers are the people who serve in the tourist industry, such as hotel workers, tour guides, and waiters.
      7. Hosts, or residents of the tourist region, may have varying attitudes toward tourists.
   B. Attitudes of Hosts Toward Tourists
      1. Attitudes of residents toward tourists can range from resistance and retreatism to boundary maintenance, revitalization, and adoption.
      2. Local residents who are very resistant express their hostility overtly and even aggressively.
      3. Community members may practice retreatism avoiding contact with tourists.
         a. This may occur where the economy is dependent on tourism but tourism is not accepted.
         b. Tourists may not be aware of this attitude toward them.
      4. Boundary maintenance is a way to regulate the interaction between hosts and tourists.
         a. It is a common response among certain cultures within the United States that do not desire a lot of interaction with tourists (Amish, Hutterites, Mennonites).
         b. These hosts may interact on a limited level while maintaining a distance from outsiders—for example, turning their backs to cameras.

      c. They base their objection to being photographed on the Bible and learn to ignore or endure the tourists' gaze and the insulting photography, and to go on with their lives.

      d. The Amish and others may maintain their boundaries by offering tourists commercially simulated cultural experiences like "Amish Village" or "Amish Farm and Home," in which actors play Amish characters and educate tourists about Amish culture.

      e. However, due to economic needs, Amish who stay in their community depend on tourism and interact more directly with tourists.

   5. Economic revitalization of communities has occurred because of tourism, and some communities may actively invest money to draw tourists or may passively tolerate tourism while maintaining boundaries.

   6. Towns like Tombstone, Arizona, and seasonal beach or ski towns capitalize on tourism, accepting it as part of their social and cultural fabric.

   7. Development associated with tourism may not bring the desired economic prosperity for most locals, creating job substitution instead of job enrichment. Hawaii is one example.

   8. Within the same community, there may be a variety of responses to tourism, which can cause conflicts among community members.

  C. Characteristics of Tourist-Host Encounters: Most intercultural interactions between hosts and tourists are limited, as they are transitory, have time constraints, lack spontaneity, and are unbalanced.

   1. Many encounters are simply business exchanges and are predictable and ritualistic.

   2. Tourists don't have the time for lengthy interactions, and they have very few opportunities to engage in social interaction with locals.

   3. Tourists are more economically and socially privileged than those with whom they interact (hosts and service providers), thus creating an unbalanced interaction.

   4. An unbalanced interaction can lead to resentment and an unwillingness to communicate on the part of hosts, so tourists may learn less about the host culture than they might otherwise.

  D. Cultural Learning and Tourism

   1. Some tourist–host encounters unexpectedly go beyond a superficial level—for example, when sharing food, holding a long conversation, or participating in a meaningful slice of the local culture.

   2. One can learn something about the local culture even in a short time.

II. Communication Challenges in Tourism Contexts

  A. Social Norms and Expectations: Relevant cultural norms that have implications for intercultural communication between tourists and hosts include norms about public social behavior, shopping, and communication style.

   1. Comportment on the street ranges from very informal, as in the United States, to more formal, as in many countries. These norms may be related to religious beliefs and traditions.

   2. Cultural norms dictate how people interact in public.

      a. In Egypt and many North African countries, there is much more interaction on the streets than in the United States.

      b. In some European countries, there is much less smiling at strangers.

      c. In Japan, there is very little interaction with strangers (verbal or nonverbal) in public.

      d. The size of the community and other factors, such as expectations for male–female relations affect the interaction.

   3. Communication norms for shopping vary from culture to culture.

      a. Touching merchandise is expected in the United States, but in many cultures, people do not touch items, and try on clothing only when they are almost certain to buy it.

        b. Bargaining is another culture-specific norm. In the United States, prices are set and not negotiated, but in some countries, shoppers are expected to bargain. It is through the act of bargaining that people are connected.

  B. Culture Shock

    1. Being in new cultural contexts can often lead to culture shock and feelings of disorientation.

    2. Whether one experiences culture shock, and to what extent, may depend on the degree of difference between the host culture and the tourist's home culture.

    3. The physiological aspects of traveling can be troublesome for tourists. On short trips, the body doesn't have time to adjust to a new climate, exotic foods, or local customs.

    4. It is the tourist who experiences the culture shock; the problem is not with the culture itself.

    5. Often, when tourists experience culture shock, they take it out on the host community. For example, they may get angry with waiters, complain about the smells or sights, or take a prejudicial or patronizing attitude toward the local culture.

    6. Members of the host culture are challenged when tourists behave rudely, and they may have difficulty remembering that the tourists actually may be expressing general frustration, may be suffering from culture shock, or may simply be fatigued.

  C. Language Challenges

    1. Language is often a problem for tourists They cannot learn all the languages of the places they might visit, and it is frustrating not to be able to understand what is being said.

    2. Language difficulties are often part of culture shock.

    3. Various host cultures have different expectations of tourists regarding language.

        a. Sometimes tourists are expected to get along using the host language.

        b. Some cultures provide more language assistance for travelers.

DISCUSSION QUESTIONS

1. Why is it important to study tourism in an intercultural communication class?

2. When you have traveled, what attitudes were expressed by the host culture toward tourists? How do you account for those attitudes?

3. What responses might hosts have toward tourists, and why?

4. Can you think of other examples of boundary maintenance?

5. Do you agree that intercultural interaction between host cultures and tourists is unbalanced? Why or why not?

6. In your travels, have you noticed differences in dress, public interaction, or shopping norms?

7. How might experiencing culture shock affect your interactions with the local culture?

8. How have you dealt with language challenges either as a host member or as a tourist?

CLASSROOM EXERCISES AND CHAPTER ACTIVITIES

1. *Guest Lecture Exercise:* Invite someone from a country that has a high rate of tourism to speak to the class. Ask the person to speak about both the positive and the negative effects of tourism. If possible, also ask the person to discuss ways locals have responded to the increased tourism. Speakers may be found by contacting local chambers of commerce, language clubs on campus, faculty, and so on. The person does not necessarily need to come from a different country; he or she could be from a U.S. community that is considered a tourist destination.

2. *Researching a Destination Exercise:* The purpose of this small-group exercise is for students to consider what they may need to know prior to encountering another culture. Place students in small groups, and ask them to decide on a place they would all like to visit some day. Then have them create a list of things it would be important for them to know about the culture prior to taking their trip. After about 20 minutes, bring the class together and have each group share one thing on its list. Depending on the time, you can continue to have students share their items. The items will be surprisingly similar regardless of where the students chose to visit, and you may want to point this out to the class.

3. *Researching a Destination Assignment:* After they have completed the previous exercise, have students, individually or in small groups, pick a place that they would like to visit. Students should research their chosen destination and write a three-page paper about that place focusing on issues raised in the previous exercise and any others they deem important. Students can gather useful information from tourist bureaus, travel books, books that focus on the relevant culture, history books, and so on. The students may even choose to interview someone from the location itself (a student from that culture, a friend who has been there) if possible. If class size and time allow, have students present what they learned about the culture to the rest of the class.

4. *Simulation Exercise:* One of the most effective ways to help students identify with the experience of being a visitor or a host culture member is to involve them in a simulation in which they must interact without knowing the proper rules for communicating and accomplishing tasks. Two popular simulations that have been used in a variety of orientation programs, intercultural communication classes, and cross-cultural training sessions are "BaFa BaFa" and "Barnga."

   a. "Barnga." Created by Sivasailam Thiagarajan; distributed by Intercultural Press, P.O. Box 700, Yarmouth, ME 04096; (800) 370-2665; fax (207) 846-5181.

   b. "BaFa BaFa: A Cross Culture Simulation." Created by R. Garry Shirts; distributed by Simulation Training Systems, P.O. Box 910, Del Mar, CA 92014; (800) 942-2900; fax (619) 792-9743.

SUGGESTED VIDEOS

1. *Going International.* Produced by Griggs Productions, San Francisco. This series of six films and training guides is designed to assist travelers in developing the cross-cultural skills required for a successful, enjoyable international experience. It also includes a leader's guide and a user's guide as training materials.

2. *Japanese Version.* Distributed by the Center for New American Media, New York. Presented as a personal journey through certain aspects of Japanese society, this video, in a series of "up-close" scenes, tries both to complement already existing films and media portraits of Japan, and to present a side of Japanese culture that has not been widely seen abroad.

3. *Around the World in 80 Days: Outward Bound* (Parts 1 and 2). Produced by Michael Palin; distributed by BBC Enterprises Ltd., London. This video examines intercultural issues in the context of world travel.

CHAPTER 11

Intercultural Communication and Business

LEARNING OBJECTIVES

After studying the material in this chapter, students should be able to:

Make connections between intercultural communication and global and domestic growth.

Describe how power differences may impact communication in intercultural business encounters.

Discuss some of the challenges in business contexts created by cultural differences in work-related values.

Understand how language and communication style differences affect intercultural business interactions.

Explain some of the intercultural differences in business etiquette.

Discuss some of the reasons companies address affirmative action and diversity issues.

Understand the range of attitudes toward affirmative action policies.

KEY TERMS

affirmative action (AA)

Americans with Disabilities Act (ADA)

collectivism

equal employment opportunity (EEO)

multinational

DETAILED CHAPTER OUTLINE

I. The Booming Economy: The business context presents opportunities and challenges for intercultural communication. Cultural differences may contribute to prejudice and discrimination or present challenges in multinational corporate ventures. Many of us already have experience dealing with cultural differences at work.
   A. Domestic Growth
      1. The population of people of color is growing faster than the White population in the United States.
      2. Minorities in the workforce are expected to increase by 51% by 2005, and the number of women by 62%. The number of people with disabilities wanting to work increased from 66% in 1986 to 79% by 1994.
      3. The market is also more diverse.
         a. The annual purchasing power of Asian Americans, Blacks, and Hispanic Americans increased from about $400 billion in 1996 to a projected $650 billion by 2001.
         b. Income for Americans with disabilities increased from $925 million in 1999 to $975 million by 2000.
         c. Women purchase about 46% of all vehicles and influence more than 85% of household purchases.

B. Global Growth
   1. Global markets are also expanding.
   2. The prospects for U.S. workers are tied to the international market.
   3. The international market is especially attractive because communication and transportation costs have plummeted; Internet communication costs are almost zero.
II. Power Issues in Intercultural Business Encounters
   A. Intercultural communication occurs in encounters with superiors, subordinates, and peers, and with customers and clients.
   B. Communication across power divides can be difficult, particularly when there are cultural differences in how power is viewed or how power distance is expressed.
      1. Cultural groups that believe in high power distance feel that organizations function best when differences in power are clearly marked and there is no confusion as to whom is the boss and whom is the worker.
      2. In contrast, cultural groups that believe in low power distance (most U.S. contexts) feel that power differences should be minimized. That is, the best boss acts informally and is called by workers by his or her first name. Power differences exist in U.S. organizations, but they are communicated more subtly.
III. Communication Challenges in Business Contexts
   A. Work-Related Values
      1. Individualism versus collectivism
         a. Many cultures (such as most U.S. cultures) are individualistic. Workers are expected to perform certain functions with clearly defined responsibilities; a clear boundary exists between their own and another person's job.
         b. Others cultures (such as in Asia, and Central and South America) are collectivist. For example, Japanese organizations (as well as many Latin American and southern European cultures) do not necessarily define the precise job responsibilities assigned to each person; rather, it's the job of a work unit, section, or department.
         c. Differences in work-related values can cause intercultural conflicts on the job.
            i. For example, managers who have a collectivist work and communication style may encourage workers to fill in for one another, try to preserve the harmony of the team, and be careful not to criticize workers in front of their peers. They may either talk with them in private or communicate through a third party in a conflict situation.
            ii. This style may clash with that of managers who have a more individualistic orientation and who see the other manager as too lenient with or supportive of their staff.
         d. For some cultural groups (Greeks, for example), individualism in the workplace may be more developed than in the United States.
            i. Most Greeks strongly prefer working for a large company or being self-employed.
            ii. Greeks are not accustomed to working in teams unless it is their family—a concept that extends to the workplace.
      2. Work and material gain
         a. Most U.S. Americans see hard work as a virtue that will eventually pay off.
         b. Other cultures view work as a necessary burden.
            i. Australians admire the "bludger"—the person who appears to work hard while actually doing little.
            ii. Most Mexicans (and some Europeans) consider work a necessary evil. They work to earn enough money to live and to have some left over to enjoy family and friends.

    iii. Cultural groups that place a low priority on work believe that, because work is necessary and takes up most of the daylight hours, a convivial workplace is important.

   c. Different attitudes toward work can lead to intercultural communication conflicts in the workplace.

    i. For example, when U.S. American and Saudi managers went to Japan and met with Japanese engineers, the Saudis stood too close, made intense eye contact, touched the Japanese, and had a leisurely approach toward work.

    ii. The Japanese engineers felt the Saudis weren't serious about the project, and the tension escalated between them.

    iii. The U.S. Americans became the buffers between the Saudis and Japanese.

  3. Task versus relationship priority

   a. In most U.S. work contexts, accomplishing the task is most important, and it's not necessary to like the people one works with.

   b. In many cultures, work gets done because of relationships.

   c. These different priorities can cause frustration in the multicultural work setting.

B. Language Issues

  1. In overseas contexts or in multinational corporations, most people do not speak English.

   a. Outside of the major cities and in most offices, the average staff member does not speak English.

   b. Increasingly, international business travelers have to deal with many languages.

  2. In domestic business situations, there is growing cultural and linguistic diversity.

  3. Several behaviors can make working with a multilingual workforce easier.

   a. Don't assume that people speaking a language other than English are talking about you.

   b. Speak simple, but not simple-minded, English.

   c. Avoid using slang or jargon.

   d. Try not to crowd too much into one sentence, and pause between sentences.

   e. Pronounce words clearly and speak slowly.

   f. Don't be condescending and don't raise your voice.

  4. Another potential language issue involves communication between deaf and hearing people. Sometimes hearing people negatively interpret a person's behavior, not knowing the person may be deaf.

C. Communication Styles: Several elements of communication style are especially relevant in business contexts, including indirect versus direct, and honesty versus harmony.

  1. Indirect versus direct

   a. People with a direct style simply ask for information from the appropriate person.

   b. A person with an indirect style might not feel comfortable giving the information, particularly when a problem exists and there is a need to save face.

   c. One way to obtain information when no one is speaking up is to observe how others get information from one another and how they get it from you.

  2. Honesty versus harmony.

   a. Honesty is not always the best policy in intercultural business contexts; form and social harmony may be more highly valued.

   b. For example, Koreans are careful not to disturb someone's *kibun,* or sense of harmony or wellness, and will hold back, delay, or adjust bad news to avoid doing so.

   c. An experienced businessman said, "Everywhere you go, except in Europe and Australia, people will tell you what they think you want to hear."

        i. If you ask for directions and they don't know, they will give you directions anyway to make you happy.

       ii. This requires asking questions in such a way that the other person can't really figure out what you want to hear—or even better, to engage the other person in a conversation so that the information simply emerges.

D. Business Etiquette
   1. This varies from culture to culture and is related to differences in values and communication styles.
   2. Most cultural groups tend to be more formal in business contexts than are U.S. Americans.
   3. In Latin America, great importance is attached to courtesy.
   4. In many African countries, high-level officials and business executives expect to be treated with solemnity and respect.
   5. When conducting business in most cultures, people should be very careful to avoid excessive familiarity (no slouching, putting one's feet up on a desk, or lounging in general), especially in initial meetings.
   6. An emphasis on formality extends to language use.
   7. In Japan, France, and the People's Republic of China, and in most African business settings, business etiquette is symbolized by properly engraved business cards that give a professional title and academic credentials.

E. Diversity, Prejudice, and Discrimination
   1. The real challenge in workplace communication is knowing how to work with cultural differences in a productive way.
   2. Not all differences are seen as equal, and certain communication styles may be viewed negatively, which can lead to prejudice and discrimination.
   3. The language and communication styles of those holding the most power in the business context often are the desired form of communication.
      a. Until recently in most U.S. organizations, the dominant style was individualistic, and the emphasis was on directness, honesty rather than harmony, and task completion rather than relationship building.
      b. Individuals who held different values and communication styles often didn't fit in or were not hired or promoted.
      c. These traits are sometimes still required, making it difficult for women, minorities, and international workers who do not possess these attributes.
      d. The resulting discrimination and prejudice have led to (among other things) diversity training and affirmation action policies that direct companies to hire a certain percentage of women and minorities.
   4. Some minorities and women are grateful for the emphasis on diversity and affirmative action policies while others are troubled by the question of whether they are viewed as having been given advantages.
   5. Although affirmative action policies originated as a way to address past discrimination, the focus now is on reverse discrimination, with majority members claiming they are being disadvantaged by affirmative action.
   6. Enforcing affirmative action policies poses challenges particularly for minorities in positions of power.
   7. Companies have many reasons for addressing affirmative action and diversity issues.
      a. There may be moral grounds based on a need to address the long history of racism, sexism, and conflictual intergroup relations in the United States.
      b. There may be a feeling that it is the responsibility of those who have benefited from this historical pattern to begin to "level the playing field."

    c. More often it is legal and social pressures (equal employment opportunity laws, affirmative action, and the Americans with Disabilities Act) that cause companies to address affirmative action issues.

    d. They may address issues of multiculturalism and diversity because they think it will have an impact on their bottom line—profit. Studies indicate that companies that value, encourage, and ultimately include the full contributions of all members of society have a much better chance of succeeding and profiting.

DISCUSSION QUESTIONS

1. What are some of the indications in your community of global and domestic changes in the economy?

2. What are some of your daily intercultural interactions in the business world?

3. At your job (now or in the past), how did you refer to your boss, and vice versa? Is this indicative of a low or high power distance value?

4. Can you think of any examples of differences in values related to individualism or collectivism leading to intercultural communication conflicts on the job?

5. How do you view work? Is hard work a virtue or a necessary evil?

6. How might different attitudes toward work lead to intercultural communication conflicts?

7. What strategies have you used when communicating with someone with limited English proficiency at work?

8. What did the authors mean when they said, "To have good intercultural business communication, people need to slow down and sneak up on information"?

9. How do the communication styles of honesty and harmony differ?

10. What are some of the etiquette rules at your place of business?

11. How do you feel about affirmative action policies? Do you think they are helpful or harmful to minorities?

12. What are some of the reasons companies address affirmative action and diversity issues?

CLASSROOM EXERCISES AND CHAPTER ACTIVITIES

1. *Guest Lecture Activity:* Invite a local businessperson who can represent both the domestic and global marketplace to speak to the class. Potential topics include changes brought about by the growing global and domestic diversity in personnel, intercultural communication challenges to doing business internationally and domestically, and global business etiquette. Be sure to allow enough time for students to ask questions of the guest lecturer. You might want to prepare the class prior to the guest lecturer's visit by having students brainstorm questions to ask the lecturer.

2. *Guest Lecture Activity Variation I:* Invite a representative from the local or state Equal Employment Opportunity Commission to speak to the class about EEO, ADEA, ADA, and other employment laws.

3. *Guest Lecture Activity Variation II:* Invite the affirmative action representative from your college or university to present information on admissions guidelines for recruitment of underrepresented minorities.

4. *Business Etiquette Interview Assignment:* This assignment focuses on exploring the intercultural communication challenges faced by organizations doing business overseas. Assign students to interview someone who works for a multinational company. Advise them to follow the suggestions and guidelines below, and to answer the following questions in writing a three- to four-page paper.

   a. Whom did you interview? What company does this person work for, and what is his or her job title?

   b. What country or countries does his or her company do business in?

   c. What does this company do to prepare its representatives for doing business with members of another culture?

   d. What kinds of intercultural communication challenges have arisen related to language, work-related values, attitudes toward work, or business etiquette?

   e. Has this company ever contracted the services of a cross-cultural trainer to prepare its employees for overseas business exchanges? Was this helpful?

   f. As a student of intercultural communication, what skills does the interviewee think you would need to be successful working for a company doing business overseas?

   g. What changes does this company anticipate with regard to its overseas markets in the coming years?

The following suggestions may help students set up and conduct their interview.

Preparing for the Interview

   a. Plan the interview several weeks before the due date.

   b. Decide whom you want to interview.

   c. Call or contact the person to set a date for the interview. When you contact the person, be sure to explain the purpose of the interview. Ask if he or she is willing to help. If so, set the date, time, and place for the interview. Give the person an idea of how much time it will take, and ask if it's okay to take notes or tape-record the interview.

   d. Prepare your questions so that you are comfortable with their wording and are sure that they are clear and easy to understand. Short questions work better than detailed questions.

   e. Prepare any note-taking equipment. (Remember to take extra batteries for a tape recorder if you are using one and the interviewee agrees to be tape-recorded.)

During the Interview

   a. Be professional. Dress comfortably but nicely to show respect for the interviewee. Ask ethical and thoughtful questions that demonstrate your respect for him or her.

   b. Before you begin the interview, establish rapport with your interviewee by spending a few minutes sharing information about yourself, the class, or other issues that will break the ice and create a convivial atmosphere.

   c. Start the interview by explaining its purpose and verifying that the person is comfortable with the method you have chosen for recording the information you elicit.

   d. As you ask the questions you have prepared, be sure to listen carefully to the answers and to ask follow-up questions if the interviewee does not provide the information you are seeking or gets off track. Be flexible in asking the questions, but try to keep the interviewee from going off on a tangent.

e. Stick to the agreed-upon time limit to show respect for the interviewee's schedule.

f. When the interview is finished, thank the interviewee for his or her time and help. It is also appropriate to send a thank-you note.

SUGGESTED VIDEOS

1. *Affirmative Action Versus Reverse Discrimination.* Produced by Annenberg/CPB; distributed by Insight Media, New York, 1984. This video examines the value of affirmative action and the fine line between affirmative action and reverse discrimination. It features a discussion among Ellen Goodman, Eleanor Holmes Norton, William Raspberry, and Albert Shanker. (60 minutes)

2. *Exploring Race and Affirmative Action.* Distributed by Insight Media, New York, 1996. This video features the perspectives of four young U.S. Americans on racism, equality, and affirmative action. It presents the students' interviews of legal, civic, and media experts, showing their reactions when confronted with opinions significantly different from their own, and offers a lively debate on the merits, efficacy, and future of affirmative action. It includes footage of critical moments in the history of U.S. race relations. (27 minutes)

3. *Doing Business in Japan.* Distributed by Vision Associates, New York. Based on a real-life international business negotiation that failed, this video illustrates such fundamental problems as the gulf between verbal and nonverbal communication, modes of expression peculiar to each culture, and misconceptions. (22 minutes)

4. *Land of O's.* Distributed by Goodmeasure, Inc., Cambridge, MA. This follow-up to the video *A Tale of O* links diversity with productivity, competitiveness, and the bottom line. It addresses real-world issues, and in practical, solution-oriented terms, it shows how to take a diverse workforce and leverage its inherent differences to the advantage of both the organization and the individual.

5. *The Multicultural Workplace.* Produced by Jaime Wurzel; distributed by Intercultural Press, Yarmouth, ME. Dramatizations show the difficulties that can result when people from differing backgrounds interact in business. It reveals how, because of misunderstanding and cultural assumptions, many employees are undervalued. It also underscores the need to consider an individual's cultural values and professional style.

CHAPTER 12

Intercultural Communication and Education

LEARNING OBJECTIVES

After studying the material in this chapter, students should be able to:

Understand how educational goals differ depending on the cultural context.

Explain the connection between the educational experience in the United States and the nation's colonial legacy.

Discuss the educational context of international students and the role history plays in their educational experience.

Describe the histories of culturally specific educational institutions.

Understand how intercultural communication affects expectations in the education process.

Describe how roles, grading, and power differ depending on the cultural context.

Explain the link between cultural identity, education, and communication.

Describe how educational systems empower some students and not others.

KEY TERMS

Afrocentric	grading system	learning styles
colonial education system	HBCUs	study-abroad programs
Eurocentric	international students	teaching styles

DETAILED CHAPTER OUTLINE

I. Educational Goals
   A. Education is widely perceived to be an important avenue for advancement in society, and we need to think about the educational goals that various cultures establish.
   B. Members of different cultural groups need to know about themselves and their society.
   C. Education frames our worldviews and our particular ways of knowing.
   D. Education is not driven simply by the desire to teach and learn about ourselves.
      1. In colonial contexts, the colonial power often imposed its own educational goals and systems upon the colonized. These goals differed from what the colonized might have valued.
      2. For example, students were expected to listen to Bach, Beethoven, and Debussy rather than their own culture's music; to read Chaucer, Shakespeare, and Milton instead of their native literature; and so on.
      3. The path to success involved embracing and understanding the colonizer's culture, history, literature, and society rather than the native one.
   E. The educational experience in the United States reflects the nation's colonial legacy.
      1. This is despite the popular claim that the United States is a multicultural society populated by immigrants from all over the world.

2. For example, there is a tendency to value European writers, artists, and histories more than Asian writers, artists, and histories.

3. The reverberations of U.S. colonial history persist in the educational goals today, to the benefit of some and the detriment of others.

II. Studying Abroad

A. The traditional U.S. classroom setting is not the only educational context; many people become "international students" by studying in another country.

B. Many universities offer study-abroad programs to give their students international experiences.

C. International students engage directly in issues relevant to intercultural communication because the cultural norms in different educational settings vary widely.

D. Historical forces and the educational systems play an important role in international students' experiences.

1. Many students from former European colonies study at institutions in the former colonizing nation.

2. Students may do this because the educational system is similarly structured to their own and they know the language of the colonizing nation. This allows the students to move easily between institutions in the two nations.

III. Culturally Specific Education

A. The historical rise and development of educational institutions geared to various cultural groups is also relevant to intercultural communication.

B. The Morrill Act of 1890 established what are today known as HBCUs, or historically black colleges and universities.

1. Debates over the purpose of these educational institutions reflect the cultural attitudes inherent in education.

a. Some critics charged that these educational institutions focused on creating subservient Black workers in a White-dominated society, rather than being routes for empowering African Americans.

b. Black colleges received unequal funding from state or federal sources, and this inequality only served to perpetuate the historical inequality between Whites and Blacks.

C. Educational institutions were also established for White women and for Native Americans.

1. These colleges (HBCUs, womens' and Native American) were established for different reasons, but in each case education was intimately related to a specific culture and served different purposes for different students.

2. A person's cultural identity is reflected in his or her educational choices and experiences.

D. Not all of these colleges and universities have retained their original missions, yet many continue to draw the students for whom they were originally established.

1. The educational experiences of minority and majority students in these institutions are not the same as those of students who attend institutions initially established for White males.

2. Students' experiences at these different kinds of institutions reflect different histories, student composition, and social contexts.

E. Indian schools are an example of educational institutions that no longer exist but whose reverberations are still felt.

1. Indian schools were established to assimilate Native American children to White society by educating them off reservations in boarding schools.

2. Because these schools were intended to acculturate and assimilate Native Americans into the dominant White society, the education they received after being separated from their families and communities impacted their language usage, religious beliefs, attitudes toward education, and feelings of self-esteem.

3. The effects of education reverberate across generations, because lost languages, customs, traditions, and religions are difficult if not impossible for subsequent generations to recover.

F. Education is very influential in maintaining various cultural communities.

IV. Intercultural Communication in Educational Settings: Education is deeply embedded in culture, and expectations for the educational process are a part of culture.

A. Roles for Teachers and Students

1. Roles are very much a part of the cultural influences on education.

2. The classroom becomes a site for negotiation of cultural differences.

a. Teachers may be accustomed to students speaking up in class, while students may be accustomed to remaining silent.

b. The teacher may learn to lecture more rather than forcing class discussions, and the students may begin to speak up more in class.

3. Cultural differences between students and teachers can create confusion in the classroom when the expectations for student and teacher roles differ.

4. When students study in other cultural contexts, they may experience culture clashes based on several things:

a. Learning styles, which are the different ways that students learn in different cultures

b. Teaching styles, which are the styles that instructors use to teach

5. We are often unaware of our cultural assumptions about education until we are confronted with different ways of learning.

B. Grading and Power

1. The classroom is embedded with cultural expectations about power relations in the communication between instructors and students. The power difference may be greater or lesser in various cultures.

2. Intercultural conflicts may reflect differences in power relations. For example, a U.S. American exchange student may think it is appropriate to question a grade, but the host country teacher may find such questions disrespectful.

3. Culture plays an important role in the educational process, as the relationship between instructor and student is not uniform around the world.

4. Notions of "fair" and "unfair," such as expectations about grading systems, are culturally embedded.

V. Communication, Education, and Cultural Identity

A. There are debates over cultural identity, education, and the role of communication in reinforcing or challenging identities.

1. For example, a teacher who passes judgment and ridicules a student based on a cultural belief challenges the student's cultural identity.

2. This example demonstrates the alienation that students from other cultures may experience in the classroom.

B. Education itself is an important context for socialization and empowerment.

1. Education professor Ann Locke Davidson believes that while "education improves individual chances for social mobility . . . it work[s] less well for impoverished African American and Latino school children."

2. While we like to think that education provides equal opportunities for all students, inequities in the paths that students follow reflect differing patterns of treatment.

3. Experiences based on inequality are powerful forces in shaping students' identities, and students are attuned to these forces.

4. Students develop their identities within the educational context, and since other students from the same cultural background share many of these experiences, they shape a shared cultural identity.

5. Teachers may not have received the kind of education necessary to incorporate materials into the curriculum that reflect the diversity of their students.

VI. Social Issues and Education
   A. There is no way to escape the history of education and the ways this history has created cultural expectations for the educational process.
   B. The authors of this textbook are not suggesting that people should find a way to escape education. However, certain social issues should be considered as they bear upon intercultural communication.
      1. The educational process reflects cultural power.
         a. This is revealed in the curriculum, the way people communicate in the classroom, and the relationships between students and instructors.
         b. Everyone's culture is not treated the same in the curriculum.
      2. The structure of educational institutions, not the people in them, plays a significant role in the way that power functions.
      3. The educational system empowers some over others because of the way the system is set up. For example, the required history and literature classes taught in some colleges is Eurocentric, focusing on European or Western canons and views of history.
         a. This Eurocentric approach reinforces a Western worldview that challenges some student identities more than others and can create barriers to intercultural communication.
         b. Afrocentric history, one response to this problem, focuses on the African rather than the European experience and exposes African American students to an entirely different view of the world and their place in it.
   C. We must be willing to point out cultural differences that are creating problems in the educational process in order to change it.
   D. We need to create an environment in which cultural differences are assumed to exist and are discussed. We need to move away from the assumption that culture is irrelevant since everyone shares the same culture.

DISCUSSION QUESTIONS

1. What kinds of knowledge does a person from your culture need to succeed?

2. In high school, whose history did you study? Latinos'? African Americans'? European Americans'?

3. Why do students choose to study in another country?

4. Why did you choose this school and not another? On what criteria did you base your choice?

5. What might be some of the advantages and disadvantages to attending a college or university that is geared toward a particular cultural group?

6. How does education influence the maintenance of various cultural communities?

7. What are the expected roles for teachers and students in your school?

8. How can cultural differences and expectations based on student and teacher roles create confusion?

9. What are the expectations in your culture regarding speaking up in class, questioning your grade, or receiving a high grade?

10. Do you agree with education professors who believe that education does not provide equal opportunities for all students? Why or why not?

11. What are some of the intercultural communication issues that should be considered in education? Why?

12. How can we develop "dialogues of respect"?

13. Can you think of any cultural differences that are creating problems at your school? What could be done about them?

CLASSROOM EXERCISES AND CHAPTER ACTIVITIES

1. *International Student Exploration Exercise:* The purpose of this small-group exercise is for students to consider the challenges and benefits of studying in another country. Assign students to small groups and ask them to decide on a place they would all like to study in some day. Then have them create a list of challenges and benefits to studying in that country, and explain why they chose that particular country. After about 20 minutes, bring the class together and have each group share one item on its list. Depending on the time, continue to have students share their items. The items will be surprisingly similar regardless of where the students chose to study, and you may want to point this out to the students.

2. *International Student Exploration Assignment:* After students have completed the previous exercise, have them, individually or in small groups, pick a country they would like to study in. Students should research their chosen location and write a three-page paper focusing on the challenges and benefits raised in the previous exercise and any others they deem important. They can gather useful information about their destination from tourist bureaus, travel books, books that focus on specific cultures, and international student exchange programs. They might even interview someone who is an international exchange student and, if possible, someone from the country they have chosen for this assignment. If class size and time allow, have students present what they learned to the rest of the class.

3. *College Catalogue Comparison Assignment:* Ask students to go to their college or university library or Web site and look at a recent catalogue of course offerings, particularly those in the history and literature departments. Have students read the course descriptions for one of these discipline areas. Next, have them look at one of the college catalogues for a historically Black, women's, or Native American college or university on the Internet and read course descriptions for classes offered in the same department (history or literature). Ask students to compare the courses offered by the two schools. Then have them write a two- to three-page paper answering the following questions:

   a. Are the course offerings the same, or are they different? How do they differ?

   b. Are courses offered that specifically focus on African American or women's issues? (This will depend on which type of institution they choose.)

   c. Which curriculum or set of classes would best reflect your cultural identity and experiences? Why?

   d. What do the course offerings from each college/university say about the educational goals of each?

4. *College Catalogue Comparison Exercise Variation I:* Instead of having students research college catalogues, break the class into small groups and give each group two lists of course offerings from two different colleges or universities. One list may be from their

own institution, and the other from an HBCU, women's, or Native American institution (many of these college/university course offerings can be found on the Internet). Instead of having students write a paper, provide them with the suggested list of questions and have them answer the questions in small groups. Be sure one of the group members in each group records their answers. After 20 minutes or so, bring the class together and have groups share their findings. This could lead into a discussion focusing on culturally specific education and its relevance to intercultural communication.

SUGGESTED VIDEOS

1. *Unequal Education: Failing Our Children.* Distributed by Insight Media, New York, 1992. This student-produced documentary reveals the unequal educational opportunities in the New York City public schools. Focusing on a school in a middle-class neighborhood and a school in a working-class neighborhood, it contrasts the quality of the staff and the resources available to students. The video includes interviews with teachers, principals, and parents. (21 minutes)

2. *The Intercultural Classroom and Creating Community: A Different Place.* Produced by Jaime Wurzel; distributed by Intercultural Press, Yarmouth, ME, 1993. This two-part video depicts a classroom of international and U.S. students interacting with one another and their professor. In this dramatization, each of the participants enacts his or her cultural assumptions of appropriate classroom behavior. In the film, as in reality, these seldom-expressed conceptions of communication and learning lead to unresolved conflicts, mutual reinforcement of negative stereotypes, and negative educational experiences.

CHAPTER 13

Intercultural Communication and Health Care

LEARNING OBJECTIVES

After studying the material in this chapter, students should be able to:

Discuss the importance of intercultural communication in health care.

Understand some of the intercultural barriers to receiving health care faced by some people due to their cultural differences.

Describe why some groups do not trust the health care system in the United States.

Explain the power imbalances that exist in health communication.

Identify some of the intercultural ethics and health issues in the United States.

KEY TERMS

AIDS	euthanasia	prejudicial ideologies
alternative medicine	health care professionals	strict paternalism
benevolent deception	HIV	Tuskegee Syphilis Project
contractual honesty	medical jargon	unmitigated honesty
ethics committees	medical terminology	

DETAILED CHAPTER OUTLINE

I. The Importance of Communication in Health Care
   A. As the U.S. population ages and new medical technologies are developed, the significance of health care increases.
   B. U.S. Americans are beginning to seek out health care from a variety of sources, from traditional Western practitioners to more "exotic" Eastern and folk practices.
   C. Both patients and health care professionals (physicians, nurses, physical and occupational therapists, medical technicians) come from a variety of cultural backgrounds.
   D. Intercultural misunderstandings in health care communication arise daily.
   E. As the U.S. population becomes increasingly diverse, complexities arise in communicating about health issues.
      a. Health care professionals are communicating with people from differing cultural backgrounds, and vice versa.
      b. In some cultures, there may be stigmas associated with communicating about health issues, and subjects such as mental illness, AIDS, sexually transmitted diseases, impotence, and abortion may be avoided.
   F. Health care professionals and patients may not realize the importance of communication.
      a. Western physicians tend to rely heavily on physical symptoms to evaluate illness, rather than communicating with patients about what they are experiencing.

127

        b. Patients come to health care professionals to seek treatment and ask questions, but even native English speakers complain about the use of medical jargon by physicians.

        c. Health care professionals need to be especially careful using medical terminology with patients who are communicating in a second language.

        d. When cultural misunderstandings arise, inadequate treatment can result.

        e. Health care providers and patients operate out of an ethnocentric framework without realizing it, and assumptions about health care often have cultural roots.

    G. Treating patients is not always a matter of communication between physician and patient.

        a. In individualistic Western cultures, one-on-one communication generally works well, but other cultures may focus more on the family's role in health care.

        b. Most health care communication research has been limited to the physician–patient relationship, ignoring the importance of the professional–family interaction

        c. Health care professionals must be sensitive to cultural differences and must adapt their communication accordingly.

II. Intercultural Barriers to Effective Health Care

    A. Historical Treatments of Cultural Groups

        1. Widespread ideologies about different cultures have fostered differential treatment for some groups, especially racial and ethnic minorities, by medical professionals.

        2. Alleged racial differences historically have been used to justify a number of deplorable social practices, from slavery, to colonization, to immigration restrictions.

        3. Based on differential treatment, some cultural groups are justifiably suspicious of contemporary health care. The infamous Tuskegee Syphilis Project is one example.

           a. The Tuskegee Syphilis Project was conducted by the U.S. Public Health Service on unsuspecting African Americans in Tuskegee, Alabama, over a 40-year period.

           b. In this study, Black patients who had syphilis were given placebos (sugar pills) instead of medical treatment. They were not told they were part of a study that was establishing an experimental control group.

           c. This project and others have fueled suspicions about the medical community from many marginalized communities.

        4. The rise of AIDS (acquired immune deficiency syndrome) and HIV (human immunodeficiency virus) in the late 20th century provoked new fears among gays and minorities that the medical community would again provide differential treatment.

           a. Due to a history of homophobia, the gay community had a separate health care system in place that quickly responded to the AIDS epidemic, thereby saving many lives.

           b. The federal government's slow response to the AIDS epidemic has been widely discussed and critiqued.

           c. The HIV/AIDS epidemic highlighted the traditional lack of trust between the health care system and minority communities.

    B. Prejudicial Ideologies

        1. Prejudicial ideologies (sets of ideas based on stereotypes) affect both health care professionals and patients, and can present significant barriers to intercultural communication.

        2. Prejudicial remarks and attitudes may influence the quality of health care that patients receive.

        3. Health care professionals are hardly immune to prejudice, as nursing and medical school attendance do not purge people of homophobia, racism, sexism, or other kinds of prejudice.

4. Patients, too, often enter the health care system with prejudicial attitudes toward health care providers.
5. People may prefer to obtain medical information from their own communities out of mistrust for the medical professionals. Sometimes these communities provide significant alternative health care; other times they provide misinformation.
6. Due to mistrust, people also sometimes turn to alternative medicine (health care provided outside the traditional Western medical system).
   a. For some, this means returning to their traditional cultural medicinal practices, such as herbal remedies.
   b. For others, it means seeking out medicinal practices that are part of cultural traditions other than their own or new treatments altogether, such as acupuncture.

III. Power in Communication About Health Care
   A. Imbalances of Power in Health Communication
      1. Communication between physician and patient is often marked by an imbalance in power with regard to medical knowledge and access to treatment.
      2. These power imbalances are built into the health care structure in the United States, but physician–patient communication also reflects these power differences.
         a. For example, it is common for physicians to introduce themselves as "Doctor So-and-So" and to refer to patients by their first names.
         b. A physician may be irritated if a patient challenges this power imbalance by introducing him- or herself by title and calling the physician by his or her first name.
      3. There is potential confusion for patients when they meet physicians. The title of "doctor" does not indicate the role the person plays in providing health care.
      4. Patients may encounter many health care workers in a single day, exacerbating cultural differences in communication.
      5. The process of negotiating cultural differences may be especially difficult for the patient due to the brevity of each communication interaction.
   B. Health Care as a Business
      1. The health care industry in the United States is a huge business.
      2. This has implications for patients and has been the subject of heated public debates over the allocation of health care resources.
      3. One controversial issue is HMOs' rationing of health care resources; obtaining such resources often is not easy or automatic.
      4. The private health care system in the United States can be confusing for patients from countries in which health care is provided by the government and for some U.S. Americans as well.
      5. Because there is a power imbalance, patients need to recognize that HMOs are businesses, and it may not be enough simply to ask for many medical services, particularly for higher priced treatments.
   C. Intercultural Ethics and Health Issues
      1. With regard to communication ethics in health care, physicians can give information about the patient's health within four general frameworks.
         a. Strict paternalism reflects a physician's decision to provide misinformation to the patient when he or she believes it is in the best interests of the patient.
         b. Benevolent deception occurs when the physician chooses to communicate only part of a patient's diagnosis.
         c. Contractual honesty refers to the practice of telling the patient only what he or she wants to hear or to know.
         d. Unmitigated honesty refers to when a physician chooses to communicate the entire diagnosis to a patient.

2. The fear of malpractice suits guides many decisions related to ethics.
3. Some health care organizations use ethics committees staffed by health care professionals, religious leaders, and social workers to help make decisions about ethics.
4. Knowing the appropriate way to communicate with families and patients in the intercultural context can be complex.
   a. In some cultures, the family is involved in the health care and medical treatment of its members.
   b. In other cultures, medical information is confidential and is given only to the patient.
   c. Some patients may not want their families involved in their care if they have a miscarriage, are suffering from colon-rectal cancer, or are depressed.
5. Many medical procedures are very controversial, even among members of the same culture.
   a. For example, different religious groups, health care agencies, and citizens' groups have alternately supported and condemned Jack Kevorkian for assisting terminally ill individuals in committing suicide (euthanasia).
   b. Key issues in euthanasia include the amount of control a patient should have, the amount of power a physician should have if his or her ethical framework differs from the patient's, and the amount of power the state should have in making laws preventing or permitting euthanasia.

DISCUSSION QUESTIONS

1. Why are more and more people in the United States seeking out alternative forms of health care such as acupuncture?
2. What might be an example of how intercultural communication misunderstandings can arise between patients, their families, and health care professionals?
3. What medical jargon have you encountered in your interactions with health care professionals? Did it have an impact on your communication interaction?
4. In your opinion, why was the Tuskegee Syphilis Project allowed to continue for 40 years?
5. How do families differ with regard to health care expectations?
6. How might prejudicial ideologies (on the part of the health care professional and the patient) present barriers to intercultural communication?
7. Why do you think most insurance companies refuse to pay for alternative treatments such as acupuncture or chiropractic care?
8. What are some examples of power imbalances in the health care interaction?
9. If you were suffering from a disease, which ethical framework—strict paternalism, benevolent deception, contractual honesty, or unmitigated honesty—would you want your health care professional to use when communicating with you and your family? Why?
10. What are some of the key issues in the ethical debate regarding euthanasia?

CLASSROOM EXERCISES AND CHAPTER ACTIVITIES

1. *Communication About Health Care Interview Assignment:* This assignment focuses on exploring the intercultural communication challenges faced by health care professionals. Instruct students to interview a health care professional about his or her experiences with cultural differences in communication. Advise them to follow the suggestions and guidelines below and to answer the following questions in writing a two- to three-page paper.

   a. Whom did you interview, and what is her or his job as a health care professional?

   b. What cultural/ethnic group members does she or he interact with on the job?

   c. What challenges has he or she encountered in the communication process?

   d. How did he or she deal with these challenges?

   e. What advice does she or he offer to persons wishing to become health care professionals in the future regarding communicating interculturally with patients?

   f. What does the future hold for health care professionals with regard to the changing patient demographics?

   The following suggestions may help students set up and conduct their interview.

   Preparing for the Interview

   a. Plan the interview several weeks before the due date.

   b. Decide whom you want to interview.

   c. Call or contact the person to set a date for the interview. When you contact the person, be sure to explain the purpose of the interview. Ask if he or she is willing to help. If so, set the date, time, and place for the interview. Give the person an idea of how much time it will take, and ask if it's okay to take notes or tape-record the interview.

   d. Prepare your questions so that you are comfortable with their wording and are sure that they are clear and easy to understand. Short questions work better than detailed questions.

   e. Prepare any note-taking equipment. (Remember to take extra batteries for a tape recorder if you are using one and the interviewee agrees to be tape-recorded.)

   During the Interview

   a. Be professional. Dress comfortably but nicely to show respect for the interviewee. Ask ethical and thoughtful questions that demonstrate your respect for him or her.

   b. Before you begin the interview, establish rapport with your interviewee by spending a few minutes sharing information about yourself, the class, or other issues that will break the ice and create a convivial atmosphere.

   c. Start the interview by explaining its purpose and verifying that the person is comfortable with the method you have chosen for recording the information you elicit.

   d. As you ask the questions you have prepared, be sure to listen carefully to the answers and to ask follow-up questions if the interviewee does not provide the information you are seeking or gets off track. Be flexible in asking the questions, but try to keep the interviewee from going off on a tangent.

   e. Stick to the agreed-upon time limit to show respect for the interviewee's schedule.

   f. When the interview is finished, thank the interviewee for his or her time and help. It is also appropriate to send a thank-you note.

2. *Intercultural Communication Training Program for Health Care Providers Assignment:* This group project is designed to help students explore how health care providers can improve their intercultural communication skills. Students will prepare a short, mock training program for health care professionals on "What Health Care Professionals Need to Know About Serving a Diverse Patient Population." Assign students to groups of five or so members, depending on the size of the class, and tell them they will be expected to present a 7- to 10-minute program to the entire class. Students should start by discussing with their group members their own and others' experiences with health care professionals, and then decide on at least three suggestions for improving intercultural communication between patients and professionals. Next, the students should take their suggestions and determine the manner in which they want to communicate this information to the class. Students should pretend that the class is filled with doctors, nurses, or other health care providers who are there to learn more about intercultural communication and ways to serve a diverse patient population. Encourage students to have fun and be creative with this assignment, and to use all the resources available, such as video equipment, Power Point, Web site development, and role-plays. Students will probably need about 2 weeks to prepare their presentation, and depending on class size and length of class period, one to two class periods for presentations.

3. *Popular Culture Assignment:* This assignment is designed to utilize popular medical TV programs to highlight intercultural communication conflicts between health care professionals and patients. Instruct students to watch one of the popular medical TV programs such as *ER* or *Chicago Hope* and to pay attention to conflicts that result from poor communication between a health care professional and the patient (or the patient's family). Students should write a two- to three-page paper in which they do the following:

   a. Give the name of the show they watched.

   b. Describe an incident of a communication clash based on poor communication between a health care professional and a patient or his or her family. They should be sure to provide details such as who was involved in the clash, what happened, and what the outcome was.

   c. Discuss the basis for the clash—was it due to religious differences? Cultural differences? Gender differences? Ethnic differences?

   d. Provide suggestions for dealing with the clash. Could it have been avoided? How? What should the characters do to improve the situation?

SUGGESTED VIDEOS

1. *Tuskegee.* Distributed by Films for the Humanities, Princeton, NJ, 1998. Between the years of 1932 and 1971, the U.S. government used approximately 600 blacks from Macon County, Alabama, as human guinea pigs for syphilis research under the guise of treatment for "bad blood." Many participants were deliberately left untreated and died, even after a cure had been discovered. In 1997, President Clinton personally apologized to those who survived one of the 20th century's most barbaric medical experiments. This program, hosted by CBS News correspondent Richard Schlesinger, includes an interview with one of the last surviving participants, Herman Shaw; explains the role of Nurse Rivers; and presents the medical establishment's justification for disguising racism as legitimate medical research.

2. *America in Black and White: Health Care, the Great Divide.* Produced by *Nightline* and anchored by Ted Koppel, February 24, 1999. This segment of *Nightline* focuses on studies (particularly a new study in the *New England Journal of Medicine*) that show Blacks are suffering from medical problems at far higher rates than Whites. (60 minutes)

3. *Can You Hear Me?* Distributed by CCHCP (Cross Cultural Health Care Program), Seattle. This set of five culture-specific videos (*Understanding Arab Communities, Understanding East African Communities, Understanding Latino Communities, Understanding Russian Communities,* and *Understanding Somali Communities*) documents community forums and panel discussions with members of various communities. Topics discussed include immigration history, culture and religion, and cultural beliefs about medicine. (Times range from 34 to 95 minutes)

Part Three
Test Bank

CHAPTER 1

Studying Intercultural Communication

MULTIPLE-CHOICE QUESTIONS

1. The _____ imperative for studying intercultural communication refers to the need to understand differences in a diverse work environment, identify new business markets, and develop new products for differing cultural contexts.
   *a. economic
   b. technological
   c. peace
   d. demographic

2. The need to market products effectively in different countries illustrates the _____ imperative for studying intercultural communication.
   *a. economic
   b. technological
   c. peace
   d. demographic

3. The possibility of communicating with people from different cultures via e-mail, fax, and the Internet illustrates the _____ imperative for studying intercultural communication.
   a. economic
   *b. technological
   c. peace
   d. self-awareness

4. Juan, an engineer in a multinational corporation, e-mails coworkers from India and Taiwan on a weekly basis. Juan's communication illustrates the _____ imperative for studying intercultural communication.
   a. economic
   *b. technological
   c. peace
   d. demographic

5. Changes in the composition of the U.S. population illustrate the _____ imperative for studying intercultural communication.
   a. economic
   b. technological
   c. peace
   *d. demographic

6. John and Nancy were raised in Illinois and speak only English. Many of their neighbors, however, have immigrated from other countries and speak English as a second language. John and Nancy's desire to have a positive relationship with their diverse neighbors illustrates the _____ imperative for studying intercultural communication.
   a. economic
   b. technological
   c. peace
   *d. demographic

7. Violence, conflict, and tension between differing cultural groups in constant contact illustrates the _____ imperative for studying intercultural communication
   a. economic
   b. self-awareness
   *c. peace
   d. demographic

8. Ethnic conflict in Bosnia and the Soviet Union, as well as ethnic tensions in other multicultural nations, illustrates the _____ imperative for studying intercultural communication.
   a. economic
   b. ethical
   *c. peace
   d. demographic

9. Increased understanding of oneself as a cultural being illustrates the _____ imperative for studying intercultural communication.
   *a. self-awareness
   b. demographic
   c. ethical
   d. technological

10. Maria had never really thought much about her Italian heritage until she became friends with Aylin, a U.S. American of Middle Eastern descent. Through conversation and visits with Aylin's family, Maria gradually began to realize how many of her own behaviors were culturally determined. Maria's experience illustrates the _____ imperative.
    a. economic
    b. ethical
    *c. self-awareness
    d. demographic

11. People who believe that cultural differences are only superficial and that there are certain rules that apply across cultures are operating from a _____ position of ethics.
    a. political
    b. relativist
    c. judicial
    *d. universalist

12. People who believe that behavior can only be judged within the context in which it occurs are operating from a _____ position of ethics.
    *a. relativist
    b. cultural
    c. universalist
    d. demographic

13. Rebecca is appalled to learn that, in some countries, girls regularly marry before the age of 15. She believes that all females should be adults before they marry regardless of their culture because of issues of education, prenatal health, and economic rights. Rebecca has assumed the _____ position of ethics.
    a. relativist
    b. westernized
    *c. universalist
    d. politicized

14. Toni tells her Chinese friend Guiwen that he should not be angry about what he perceives as the superficial friendliness of many U.S. Americans without first understanding the cultural context of the behavior. Toni has taken a/an _____ position of ethics.
    a. explanatory
    b. universalist
    *c. relativist
    d. nonjudgmental

15. The process by which we "look in the mirror" to see ourselves as cultural beings is known as _____ .
    *a. self-reflexivity
    b. self-awareness
    c. journaling
    d. heterogeneity

16. The term _____ refers to the result of increased contact (through the Internet, media reports, and travel) among people around the world.
    *a. global village
    b. heterogeneity
    c. self reflexivity
    d. assimilation

17. The term _____ refers to the ability of southern and eastern European immigrants to "blend" into the general U.S. population.
    a. global village
    b. heterogeneity
    c. self-reflexivity
    *d. assimilatable

18. Principles of conduct that help govern the behavior of individuals and groups are known as _____ .
    a. morals
    *b. ethics
    c. values
    d. beliefs

19. _____ are the result of the tendency for members of particular ethnicities to settle in the same area (such as Latinos in Inglewood and East Los Angeles).
    a. Class structures
    b. Ethnic tensions
    c. Global villages
    *d. Enclaves

20. Economic disparity among ethnic groups in the United States can only be understood by looking at _____ .
    a. enclaves
    *b. class structure
    c. assimilatable groups
    d. economic mobility

21. The expansion of businesses into markets around the world is known as _____.
    a. immigration
    b. mobility
    c. heterogeneity
    *d. globalization

22. The anti-immigrant nativistic movements _____ .
    a. targeted immigrants of southern European descent only
    b. were not supported by the U.S. government
    *c. propagated violence against newer immigrants to the United States
    d. were a form of economic protection for enclave communities

23. The changes in the patterns of immigration during the last 40 years illustrate the fact that the population of the United States is becoming much more _____ .
    *a. heterogeneous
    b. classist
    c. nativist
    d. ethical

24. Martin and Nakayama describe the study of intercultural communication in order to proselytize others without their consent as a/an _____ issue about the application of intercultural knowledge.
    *a. ethical
    b. interpersonal
    c. religious
    d. demographic

25. Token stories of success and upward mobility (illustrated by Roseanne or the *Nanny* sitcom) reinforce _____ and perpetuate the myth of upward mobility.
    a. heterogeneity
    *b. class structure
    c. economic diversity
    d. assimilation

TRUE/FALSE QUESTIONS

26. Many U.S. companies provide little or no training before sending their workers overseas.   (T)

27. Anti-immigrant, nativist sentiment was well supported at the government level during the late 1800s.   (T)

28. The Chinese Exclusion Act officially prohibited Chinese from immigrating to the United States.   (T)

29. *Maquiladoras* are an example of how multinational corporations can benefit from lower labor costs while adhering to U.S. environmental policies.   (T)

30. Until the 1960s, most immigrants to the United States came from Europe.   (T)

31. "The Bistro" offered by America Online is one way in which the frequency of communication is increasing among peoples of the world   (T)

32. The majority of immigrants to the United States now come from Latin America or Asia.   (T)

33. Generally, all immigrants can assimilate in the American "melting pot."   (F)

34. The universalist position holds that cultural behavior can only be judged from the context in which it occurs.   (F)

35. In the next 20 years, the ethnic diversity of the U.S. population will be distributed more evenly across the nation.   (F)

ESSAY QUESTIONS

36. In what ways might economic conditions affect attitudes toward foreign workers and immigration policies?

37. How might the study of intercultural communication be helpful in understanding ethical issues involved in intercultural interaction?

38. Identify and discuss three ways in which we might become ethical students of culture.

39. Identify and discuss four of the six imperatives for studying intercultural communication.

40. Compare and contrast the universalist and relativist positions with regard to ethical intercultural interaction.

CHAPTER 2

Intercultural Communication: Building Blocks and Barriers

MULTIPLE-CHOICE QUESTIONS

1. The learned patterns of perception, values, and behaviors shared by a group of people are known as _____ .
   a. stereotyping
   b. perception
   *c. culture
   d. heterogeneity

2. The ways in which a culture judges good or bad, or right or wrong are often determined by _____ .
   a. stereotypes
   *b. values
   c. perceptions
   d. beliefs

3. The ways of looking at the world shared by people in a particular culture are known as _____ .
   a. stereotypes
   b. values
   *c. perceptions
   d. beliefs

4. White Americans think that there is greater equality between the races than do African Americans. This difference between cultural groups illustrates which of the following?
   *a. Culture is shared
   b. Culture is expressed as behavior
   c. Culture is dynamic
   d. Culture involves power

5. The idea that not all members of a particular group will behave or think in the same way illustrates that _____ .
   a. culture is shared
   b. culture is expressed as behavior
   *c. culture is heterogeneous
   d. culture involves power

6. Many Native American students are soft-spoken and hesitate to participate in classroom discussions. Amy, however, is a Native American who actively participates in class and often asks questions of her instructors. Amy illustrates that culture is _____ .
   a. shared
   b. expressed as behavior
   c. dynamic
   *d. heterogeneous

7. What is the symbolic process by which meaning is shared and negotiated?
   a. culture
   b. power
   *c. communication
   d. language

8. The fact that Berta uses her lips instead of her finger to point at an object across the room illustrates that communication is _____ .
   a. dynamic
   b. unintentional
   c. receiver oriented
   *d. symbolic

9. An "easy" class or quiz can mean different things to different people. This illustrates that communication _____ .
   *a. involves sharing and negotiating meaning
   b. is unintentional
   c. is receiver-oriented
   d. is symbolic

10. The fact that we are constantly sending and receiving messages that may change "in midstream" illustrates that communication _____ .
   a. involves sharing and negotiating meaning
   b. is unintentional
   *c. is dynamic
   d. is symbolic

11. Jeff accidentally insulted the parents of his roommate Mohammed by putting his feet up on the desk when they were visiting their dorm room. Jeff's behavior illustrates that communication is _____ .
   a. dynamic
   *b. unintentional
   c. receiver-oriented
   d. symbolic

12. Daniel offended a classmate by trying to help her with her books. She told him that he was sexist and that he should quit patronizing her. In trying to be helpful, Daniel has illustrated that communication _____ .
   a. involves sharing and negotiating meaning
   b. is unintentional
   *c. is receiver oriented
   d. is dynamic

13. Societies that are more likely to punish criminals than rehabilitate them probably see human nature as _____ .
   a. changeable
   b. basically good
   c. a combination of good and evil
   *d. essentially evil

14. Which relationship between humans and nature is illustrated by societies that place less emphasis on birth control, and tend not to interfere with rivers by building dams?
   *a. domination of nature over humans
   b. humans living in harmony with nature
   c. domination of humans over nature
   d. low access to technology

15. Kyle doesn't understand why people in some countries don't make greater use of agricultural technology and why, if they have large populations, more people don't practice birth control. Kyle probably lives in a society with a _____ orientation.
   a. domination of nature over humans
   b. humans living in harmony with nature
   *c. domination of humans over nature
   d. technological

16. Many Guatemalans place great emphasis on extended families and are more likely to consult with family members when making important decisions. This culture probably has a/an _____ relationship between humans.
   a. individualistic
   b. collectivist
   c. feminine
   d. masculine

17. A culture that values people being productive and keeping busy tends to have a _____ orientation to human activity.
   *a. doing
   b. puritanical
   c. growing
   d. being

18. Carmen would rather spend time interacting and relaxing with friends than working. In fact, she recently turned down a promotion because it would have meant she would see her family and friends less. Carmen probably grew up in a culture with a _____ value orientation toward human activity.
   a. doing
   b. puritanical
   c. growing
   *d. being

19. Shauna, age 27, has started to put money into an IRA. She doesn't plan to use this money until she retires. Shauna probably grew up in a culture with a _____ orientation toward time.
    *a. future
    b. past
    c. feminist
    d. financial

20. The extent to which less powerful members of a society expect and accept power is known as _____ , a cultural value that may distinguish cultures.
    a. masculinity–femininity
    b. uncertainty avoidance
    *c. power distance
    d. long-term orientation to life

21. Many people in Central America have a preference for gender-specific roles (for example, men should be primary breadwinners and women are responsible for the family). They probably have a/an _____ value orientation
    a. power distance
    b. uncertainty avoidance
    *c. masculine
    d. feminine

22. The degree to which people feel threatened by ambiguous situations and try to ensure certainty by establishing more structure is referred to as a/an _____ value orientation.
    a. power distance
    *b. uncertainty avoidance
    c. masculine
    d. feminine

23. Cultures whose members participate in religions like Hinduism and Buddhism, which emphasize virtue, tenacity, and perseverance, have a _____ orientation toward life.
    *a. long-term
    b. short-term
    c. feminine
    d. masculine

24. Jeremy is always polite and courteous to his instructors at school but tends to be a bit rowdy with his friends at parties. The differences in Jeremy's communication illustrate the importance of _____ .
    a. power distance
    *b. context
    c. ritual
    d. ethnocentrism

25. The belief that one's own cultural group is superior to all other cultural groups is known as _____ .
    a. prejudice
    b. stereotyping
    c. discrimination
    *d. ethnocentrism

26. Widely held beliefs or generalizations about a group of people are known as _____ .
    a. prejudice
    *b. stereotypes
    c. discrimination
    d. ethnocentrism

27. James believes that gay people are abnormal and overly concerned with sex, so he has never developed any friendships with people he knew were gay. James's attitude toward gays illustrates _____ , a barrier to intercultural communication.
    *a. prejudice
    b. stereotypes
    c. discrimination
    d. tokenism

28. People who go out of their way to engage in unimportant but positive intergroup behaviors in order to convince themselves and others that they are not prejudiced illustrate _____ , a subtle form of prejudice.
    a. stereotyping
    *b. tokenism
    c. arm's length prejudice
    d. ethnocentrism

TRUE/FALSE QUESTIONS

29. People in collectivist societies value more direct communication and active conflict resolution styles in order to maintain the group.   (F)

30. Groups with the most power determine the communication system of an entire society.   (T)

31. People of different age, gender, physical ability, or sexual orientation have relatively equal access to power in the United States.   (F)

32. People tend to communicate the same way regardless of the setting they are in or the person they are speaking to.   (F)

33. We learn to be cultural members slowly and subconsciously.   (T)

34. People who value quality of life, service to others, and support for the unfortunate tend to have a masculine value orientation.   (F)

35. A culture whose members believe that less hierarchy is better and that power should be used only for legitimate purposes tends to have a high power distance orientation.   (F)

36. Great Britain, Hong Kong and the United States have a low level of uncertainty avoidance.   (F)

37. Forces that attempt to change or retain existing social structures contribute to the political context.   (T)

38. Stereotypes are a normal product of our everyday thought processes.   (T)

ESSAY QUESTIONS

39. Identify, discuss, and provide examples of the three possible relationships between humans and nature according to Kluckhohn and Strodtbeck.

40. Compare and contrast the individualistic and the collectivist orientations toward relationships between humans.

41. Identify and discuss two ways in which communication reinforces culture.

42. Discuss the role of power in the intercultural communication process.

43. Identify and discuss four potential barriers to intercultural communication.

CHAPTER 3

History and Intercultural Communication

MULTIPLE-CHOICE QUESTIONS

1. Books that focus on political events in the past, such as Hitler's rise to power, are part of _____ histories.
   *a. political
   b. religious
   c. social
   d. family

2. Books that focus on the transmission and development of ideas or ways of thinking are called _____ histories.
   a. political
   *b. intellectual
   c. social
   d. family

3. As a part of her introduction to education class, Catherine finds that she is required to read about the development of the English educational system from medieval times. Catherine is reading a/an _____ history.
   a. personal
   b. social
   *c. intellectual
   d. institutional

4. Writers who attempt to understand everyday life experiences of groups in the past are documenting a/an _____ history.
   a. national
   b. institutional
   *c. social
   d. family

5. A book about the lives of women pioneers in the old West is an example of _____ history.
   a. national
   *b. gendered
   c. political
   d. social

6. Histories that are often not written down but passed orally from one generation to another are known as _____ histories.
   *a. family
   b. national
   c. political
   d. social

7. Jeff has a sword used by his great-great-uncle Frederick in the Civil War. When his father gave him the sword, he also told him the story of how Frederick died in the arms of his sweetheart, who tracked him down in a makeshift Army hospital. The history represented by Jeff's sword is known as a _____ history.
   a. national
   b. religious
   c. social
   *d. family

8. The history of Muslim immigrants to the United States and their settlement in the Midwest constitutes a _____ history.
   a. national
   *b. religious
   c. social
   d. family

9. Charlene's family did not immigrate to the United States until the late 1800s. Still, Charlene is very familiar with the story of Abraham Lincoln's boyhood. Charlene has learned _____ history.
   *a. national
   b. cultural group
   c. social
   d. family

10. The role of African slaves in the establishment of the 13 colonies constitutes a _____ history.
   a. national
   b. religious
   c. social
   *d. cultural group

11. Histories not typically included in national history but that explain current demographic and sometimes economic conditions of particular groups are known as _____ histories.
   a. personal
   *b. cultural group
   c. social
   d. sexual orientation

12. The unified story of humankind, which long dominated how people thought of the past, present, and future, is known as _____ .
   *a. the grand narrative
   b. Homo narrans
   c. religious history
   d. oral history

13. A book about the daily lives of Native Americans before European settlement is a form of _____ history.
   a. national
   b. gendered
   c. political
   *d. social

14. Stories concerning persecution of gays and lesbians during World War II are part of
_____ histories.
   a. national
   b. racial and ethnic
   c. social
  *d. sexual orientation

15. The attempt to document and understand the Japanese internment camps established in
the United States during World War II constitutes a form of _____ history.
   a. political
  *b. racial and ethnic
   c. intellectual
   d. sexual orientation

16. A massive exodus caused by war, famine, slavery, or persecution that results in the
dispersal of a unified group is known as a/an _____ .
  *a. diaspora
   b. colonization
   c. international exodus
   d. migration

17. A book that details the role of Chinese immigrants in the building of the railroad across the
United States in the 1800s is a form of _____ history.
   a. political
  *b. racial and ethnic
   c. social
   d. colonial

18. A book detailing the migration and resettlement of the Irish all over the world as a result
of the potato famine in the late 1800s is a form of _____ history.
   a. political
  *b. diasporic
   c. intellectual
   d. colonial

19. A history concerning the motivation and effects of White settlement in southern Africa is a
form of _____ history.
   a. political
   b. diasporic
   c. intellectual
  *d. colonial

20. A book that details the impact of Spanish settlement on Central and South America
constitutes a form of _____ history.
   a. political
  *b. colonial
   c. intellectual
   d. diasporic

21. Differences between Mexican Americans and Cuban Americans are influenced by their
    _____ histories.
    a. political
    b. diasporic
    *c. socioeconomic
    d. colonial

22. Jerrod's forebears migrated to Utah with Brigham Young. He is proud that his family
    helped to settle what is now Salt Lake City. The stories passed down to Jerrod by his father
    and grandfather constitute a _____ history.
    a. diasporic
    b. religious
    c. social
    *d. family

23. Accounts of past events that are not included in national or mainstream histories are
    known as _____ histories.
    *a. hidden
    b. religious
    c. social
    d. family

24. An explanation of why Spanish is spoken in most of the Western Hemisphere would
    constitute a _____ history.
    *a. colonial
    b. religious
    c. social
    d. family

25. An explanation of the role of poverty in the migration of people from Central America to
    the United States is a form of _____ history.
    a. colonial
    b. national
    c. social
    *d. socioeconomic

TRUE/FALSE QUESTIONS

26. Typically, we learn social histories in school.   (F)

27. Generally, a grand narrative includes stories of different ethnic groups, as well as the
    intellectual and social histories of a nation.   (F)

28. It is fairly easy to write about women's history so long as one has access to public
    documents and public records.   (F)

29. We are free to choose the languages we speak.   (F)

30. Most historical events are documented.   (F)

31. Diasporic migrations often cause people to cling more strongly to their group's identity.   (T)

32. Many Japanese are proud of the success of Japanese Canadians, Japanese Americans, and Japanese Peruvians.   (F)

33. Socioeconomic class distinctions are often overlooked in understanding the migration and acculturation of groups around the world.   (T)

34. History is constructed through narrative.   (T)

35. A book about the decision to drop the atomic bomb on Hiroshima is a form of social history.   (F)

ESSAY QUESTIONS

36. Why would it be important to examine the role of history in intercultural communication?

37. How might hidden histories affect intercultural interactions?

38. Compare and contrast family histories with national histories.

39. Why would U.S. Americans want to escape or ignore history?

40. Compare and contrast the effects of diasporic and colonial histories.

CHAPTER 4

Identity and Intercultural Communication

MULTIPLE-CHOICE QUESTIONS

1. Women who join social groups exclusive to women are highlighting their _____ identity.
   *a. gender
   b. age
   c. ethnic
   d. religious

2. In the United States, a 40-year-old man who lives with his parents and spends most of his time playing video games and chasing women is generally not seen as enacting his _____ identity.
   a. gender
   *b. age
   c. ethnic
   d. religious

3. Typically, _____ identity includes knowledge of a group's traditions, customs, values, and a feeling of belonging to that group.
   a. gender
   b. age
   *c. ethnic
   d. religious

4. Individuals who see themselves as connected to an origin outside the United States are often called _____ .
   a. global nomads
   b. assimilated Americans
   *c. hyphenated Americans
   d. minorities

5. Our _____ identity is determined by characteristics such as our height, weight, sex, and age.
   *a. physical ability
   b. age
   c. class
   d. gender

6. People who wear a crucifix around their neck are probably communicating their _____ identity.
   a. ethnic
   b. national
   *c. religious
   d. class

7. "Trailer park trash" or "White trash" are terms used to mark _____ differences in U.S. society.
   a. ethnic
   b. racial
   c. religious
   *d. class

8. Anu was born in the United States. Her parents were born in India. When Anu interacts with the children of other Indian immigrants, she is most likely enacting her _____ identity.
   *a. ethnic
   b. national
   c. religious
   d. class

9. Belle is from South Carolina. She is proud that she speaks with an accent and has no real desire to visit or live in the West. Belle affirms her _____ identity.
   a. ethnic
   b. national
   *c. regional
   d. class

10. The stage of minority identity development characterized by the lack of exploration of ethnicity is known as _____ .
    a. conformity
    b. resistance and separatism
    *c. unexamined identity
    d. integration

11. Manuel accepts the values and attitudes of the majority culture. Although he is Mexican American, he is often embarrassed by other members of his group. He has a strong desire to assimilate into the mainstream. Manuel is probably in the _____ stage of minority identity development.
    a. unexamined identity
    b. resistance and separatism
    *c. conformity
    d. integration

12. Simone, an African American, is not interested in or concerned with ethnicity. "Why would I need to learn about black history?" she asks. "I'm just into my own thing." Simone is probably in the _____ stage of minority identity development.
    *a. unexamined identity
    b. resistance and separatism
    c. conformity
    d. integration

13. In the _____ stage of minority identity development, individuals internalize the values and norms of the dominant group, and may have negative attitudes toward themselves or their group in general.
    a. unexamined identity
    b. resistance and separatism
    *c. conformity
    d. integration

14. In the _____ stage of minority identity development, individuals may reject the values and norms associated with the dominant group while embracing all the attitudes and values attributed to their own group.
    a. unexamined identity
    *b. resistance and separatism
    c. conformity
    d. integration

15. Bertina, a Native American, believes that Navajo customs and traditions provide the most effective responses to everyday issues. She rejects westernized medicine when she is sick and refuses to be cared for by anyone but a traditional healer. Bertina is probably in the _____ stage of minority identity development.
    a. conformity
    b. unexamined identity
    c. integration
    *d. resistance and separatism

16. A person with a strong sense of his or her own group identity and an appreciation of other cultural groups is probably in the _____ stage of minority identity development.
    a. unexamined identity
    b. resistance and separatism
    c. conformity
    *d. integration

17. Vivian, an African American, is proud to be Black. She admires, however, many Latin Americans' emphasis on family and applauds the successes of many Asian Americans. Vivian is probably in the _____ stage of minority identity development.
    *a. integration
    b. conformity
    c. resistance and separatism
    d. unexamined identity

18. A person who is aware of some physical and cultural differences but does not fear other racial or ethnic groups or feel a sense of superiority is probably in the _____ stage of majority identity development.
    a. resistance
    b. acceptance
    c. redefinition and reintegration
    *d. unexamined identity

19. A person who doesn't question the basic racial inequities in society and who may even believe that minority groups need help to assimilate is probably in the _____ stage of majority identity development.
    a. resistance
    *b. acceptance
    c. redefinition and reintegration
    d. unexamined identity

20. Ted, a White U.S. American, doesn't think of himself as being White. He knows that minority groups are economically disadvantaged and supports educational efforts to expose minorities to European music, art, and literature. Ted is probably in the _____ stage of majority identity development.
    a. resistance
    b. unexamined identity
    c. redefinition and reintegration
    *d. acceptance

21. When a person moves from blaming minority members for their conditions to blaming the social system as a source of racial or ethnic problems, he or she is probably in the_____ stage of majority identity development.
    a. acceptance
    b. unexamined identity
    c. redefinition and reintegration
    *d. resistance

22. Diana is comfortable being White although she can appreciate other groups. She recognizes that prejudice and racism are factors in our society but also realizes that blame, guilt, or denial doesn't really help eliminate racism. Diana is probably in the _____ stage of majority identity development.
    a. resistance
    b. acceptance
    *c. redefinition and reintegration
    d. unexamined identity

23. The relatively short-term feeling of disorientation or discomfort due to the unfamiliarity of surroundings or lack of familiar cues in an environment is known as _____ .
    a. adaptation
    *b. culture shock
    c. encapsulation
    d. identity formation

24. Duncan has a White father and a Korean mother. He feels torn between two different cultures. He has difficulty making decisions, is troubled by ambiguity, and feels pressure from both groups. Duncan is a/an _____ multicultural person.
    a. assimilated
    *b. encapsulated
    c. nomadic
    d. constructive

25. _____ multicultural people see themselves as choice makers. They seem to thrive on living in the margins of two cultures.
    a. Assimilated
    b. Encapsulated
    c. Nomadic
    *d. Constructive

TRUE/FALSE QUESTIONS

26. Gender is the same as biological sex.   (F)

27. Communication across age groups is not really intercultural communication.   (F)

28. Old age is revered in the United States, as well as many other societies.   (F)

29. The racial classification of a person is largely determined by biology.   (F)

30. A person in the redefinition and reintegration stage of majority identity development may minimize his or her communication with Whites and seek out interactions with people of color.   (F)

31. Culture shock occurs only to migrants who involuntarily cross cultural boundaries.   (F)

32. A multicultural person with a secure sense of self and exposure to more than one culture's norms and values is in the self-acceptance and assertion stage of multicultural identity development.   (T)

33. Individualism is a core symbol of Mexican American identity.   (F)

34. People with disabilities do not usually go through discernible stages of identity development because they are also members of larger cultural groups.   (F)

35. White people have an advantage of race privilege.   (T)

ESSAY QUESTIONS

36. What is the relationship between communication and identity?

37. How are racial categories constructed?

38. Identify and discuss three common characteristics shared by White people in the United States.

39. Why do U.S. Americans resist discussing class distinctions? What are the ramifications of lack of recognition of class?

40. What communication strategies are used to place someone in the class hierarchy in the United States?

CHAPTER 5

Verbal Issues in Intercultural Communication

MULTIPLE-CHOICE QUESTIONS

1. The study of the sound system of language, including how words are pronounced, is known as _____ .
   *a. phonology
   b. semantics
   c. pragmatics
   d. syntactics

2. The study of meaning, or how words communicate the meaning we intend to get across in our communication, is known as _____ .
   a. phonology
   *b. semantics
   c. syntactics
   d. pragmatics

3. The study of the structure of language, or how words are combined into meaningful sentences (for example, the cat white or the white cat), is known as _____ .
   *a. syntactics
   b. semantics
   c. pragmatics
   d. phonology

4. The study of how language is actually used in particular contexts is known as _____ .
   a. phonology
   b. semantics
   *c. pragmatics
   d. syntactics

5. Jamie is explaining the living conditions of undocumented immigrants. Her presentation illustrates which function of language?
   a. communicating feeling
   b. participating in rituals
   c. controlling others' behavior
   *d. giving information

6. Communication that is indirect because most of the meaning is internalized in the person is known as _____ communication.
   a. indirect
   b. low-context
   *c. high-context
   d. elaborate

7. When the bulk of a message is in the spoken words, the speaker is probably using the
    _____ communication style.
    a. indirect
    *b. low-context
    c. high-context
    d. affective

8. "In jokes" and meaningful glances used to communicate in long-term relationships are
    examples of _____ communication.
    a. indirect
    b. low-context
    *c. high-context
    d. affective

9. The _____ communication style emphasizes verbal messages that reveal a speaker's
    true intentions, needs, wants, or desires.
    *a. direct
    b. personal
    c. indirect
    d. contextual

10. Denise wants a new coat. Instead of asking her mother directly (which would be improper
    in her family) she openly admires the coats of others. Denise is using a/an _____ style
    of communication.
    a. direct
    b. personal
    *c. indirect
    d. instrumental

11. Many Arabic speakers use rich, expressive language in everyday talk. They are probably
    using a/an _____ style of communication.
    *a. elaborate
    b. succinct
    c. indirect
    d. exact

12. The _____ style of communication emphasizes cooperation and sincerity as a basis for
    human interaction.
    a. elaborate
    b. succinct
    c. indirect
    *d. exact

13. Languages such as Japanese that emphasize prescribed roles, status, and formality lend
    themselves well to the _____ style of communication.
    a. personal
    *b. contextual
    c. instrumental
    d. affective

14. Howard speaks several languages but tends to use English the most because it emphasizes personhood, informality, and symmetrical power relationships. Howard probably prefers the _____ style of communication.
    *a. personal
    b. contextual
    c. instrumental
    d. elaborate

15. Ramona is trying to convince her brother to let her use his car by telling him why she needs it and emphasizing the fact that she will "owe" him one. Ramona is using a/an _____ style of communication
    a. personal
    b. elaborate
    c. instrumental
    *d. affective

16. Changing our communication style to be more effective communicators in another culture is known as _____ .
    a. language acquisition
    b. translation
    *c. code switching
    d. semantics

17. Darrel is gay, but few of his coworkers are aware of this. At work, he uses communication strategies that revolve around trying to fit in and be accepted by a dominant group. Thus, he talks about his nephews when his colleagues talk about their kids, and he laughs at some jokes he doesn't really feel are funny. Darrel is using _____ communication in order to assimilate.
    a. assertive
    b. aggressive
    *c. nonassertive
    d. elaborate

18. Eduardo, a student who uses a wheelchair, goes to great lengths to prove that he is like the other students. He separates himself as much as possible from other people with disabilities, and he engages in self-ridicule to show that he is humble. Eduardo is using _____ communication in order to assimilate.
    a. assertive
    *b. aggressive
    c. nonassertive
    d. instrumental

19. Kelsey, who is Jewish, tries to blend with the dominant group at work as much as possible. When they offer her a slice of sausage pizza, she gently declines, pointing out that her religion tells her that she should not eat the meat of cloven-hoofed animals. Kelsey is probably using a/an _____ accommodation strategy.
    a. assertive
    b. aggressive
    *c. nonassertive
    d. indirect

20. Leona, an African American, hears one of her White friends use a phrase that has traditionally been used to disparage Blacks. She tactfully educates her friend about the history and meaning of the phrase because, while she doesn't wish to be offended, she also knows he meant no harm. Leona is probably using a/an _____ accommodation strategy.
    *a. assertive
    b. aggressive
    c. nonassertive
    d. indirect

21. Sankaran immigrated to the United States from India as a child. Although he speaks fluent English, he prefers to live, work, and socialize with people who look like himself. Sankaran has chosen to use a/an _____ separation strategy.
    a. assertive
    b. aggressive
    c. instrumental
    *d. nonassertive

22. _____ separation strategies, such as attacking and sabotaging others, are used by those for whom cocultural segregation has a high priority.
    a. Elaborate
    *b. Aggressive
    c. Assertive
    d. Nonassertive

23. People who speak more than two languages are considered _____ .
    a. bilingual
    *b. multilingual
    c. multicultural
    d. translators

24. The process of verbally expressing what is said or written in another language is known as _____ .
    a. translation
    *b. interpretation
    c. equivalency
    d. discourse

25. Cliff is in the process of producing an English target text that refers to an article written in Portuguese (source text). Cliff is engaged in _____ .
    *a. translation
    b. discourse
    c. equivalency
    d. interpretation

TRUE/FALSE QUESTIONS

26. The use of honorifics in English is limited to formal situations.   (F)

27. Groups of equal power within society's social structure are known as cocultural groups.   (F)

28. The exact style of communication values understatement, simple assertions, and silence.   (F)

29. The direct style of communication is often used when individuals wish to preserve the harmony of a relationship.   (F)

30. Groups with the most power in a society use a communication style that supports their perception of the world.   (T)

31. Nonassertive separation strategies are used by those who assume that segregation is a part of everyday life in the United States.   (T)

32. Labels are not really that important in establishing relationships.   (F)

33. Most bilingual people speak both languages at the same level of fluency.   (F)

34. Learning the language of a group you dislike is easier than learning the language of a more favored group.   (F)

35. A law stating that English is the only language to be used in educational settings would be a language policy.   (T)

ESSAY QUESTIONS

36. Explain the Sapir-Whorf hypothesis.

37. Under what circumstances might silence be a primary mode of communication in the United States?

38. Why are differences in social position central to understanding communication?

39. Discuss the power effects of labels.

40. Identify and discuss the issues of equivalency and accuracy in interpretation and translation.

CHAPTER 6

Nonverbal Issues in Intercultural Communication

MULTIPLE-CHOICE QUESTIONS

1. Stanley shakes his head no and ducks his eyes but doesn't say anything when his instructor asks him to turn in his essay. Stanley has used nonverbal behavior to _____ verbal behavior.
   a. contradict
   *b. substitute for
   c. complement
   d. reinforce

2. Lilly smiles, makes direct eye contact, and touches her partner Dolores frequently. Lilly's nonverbal behavior is communicating _____ .
   *a. relationship messages
   b. status
   c. power
   d. deception

3. People in _____ cultures stand closer together while talking, have more direct eye contact, and speak in louder voices than many people in the United States.
   *a. contact
   b. east Asian
   c. noncontact
   d. northern European

4. Sufen, an immigrant from Taiwan, feels uncomfortable whenever her boss, an Italian American, talks to her. She feels that her boss stands too close and talks too loud for the space they are in. Sufen's feelings are probably a result of _____ cultural differences
   a. collectivist vs. individualistic
   b. monochronic vs. polychronic
   *c. contact vs. noncontact
   d. verbal vs. nonverbal

5. The "bubble" around us that marks the territory between ourselves and others is known as _____ .
   a. an emblem
   b. an adaptor
   *c. personal space
   d. a regulator

6. Which of the following is not true about the eye contact of most U.S. Americans?
   a. They look away from their listeners most of the time.
   b. They look directly at their listeners to signal a conversation turn.
   c. They look at their listeners every 10 to 15 seconds.
   *d. They tend to avert their eyes during conversation.

7. Gestures that have a specific verbal translation (for example, nodding one's head to indicate agreement) are known as _____ .
   *a. emblems
    b. adaptors
    c. regulators
    d. illustrators

8. Hamid holds his hands together to give his friend Ben an idea of how much food was served at the international student dinner yesterday evening. As he speaks, Hamid is using _____ .
    a. emblems
    b. adaptors
    c. regulators
   *d. illustrators

9. Kerry starts to gather her books, pens, and papers together before the instructor has finished speaking. She looks at her watch in an obvious way when the instructor is looking in her direction. Kerry is using _____ to communicate.
    a. emblems
    b. adaptors
   *c. regulators
    d. illustrators

10. Gestures that are related to managing our emotions are known as _____ .
    a. illustrators
   *b. adaptors
    c. regulators
    d. emblems

11. People with a _____ concept of time tend to regard time as a commodity.
    a. polychronic
    b. regional
    c. capitalist
   *d. monochronic

12. Casey is obsessed with punctuality. He gets up at 7:30 every morning, goes to basketball practice at exactly 8:20, takes a 1-hour lunch, and comes to class at exactly 12:00 every Tuesday. He knows that being late to class can be interpreted negatively. Casey is probably from a _____ culture.
    a. polychronic
    b. regional
    c. capitalist
   *d. monochronic

13. People with a _____ orientation toward time tend to view time more holistically and will often interrupt a task to talk to a friend, which means that many times things are not finished "on time."
   *a. polychronic
    b. monochronic
    c. capitalist
    d. regional

14. Which of the following is NOT typically communicated by nonverbal behaviors?
    a. status
    b. relational messages
    c. deception
    *d. content information

15. _____ is the particular way in which communication constructs meanings of various places.
    a. Prejudice
    *b. Cultural space
    c. Popular culture
    d. Home

16. A form of cultural space that communicates social class is _____ .
    *a. home
    b. neighborhood
    c. region
    d. city

17. A person from Montreal who identifies more strongly with the province of Quebec than with her country, Canada, demonstrates _____ , a form of cultural space.
    a. home
    b. neighborhood
    c. nationalism
    *d. regionalism

18. _____ is a way of changing cultural space that is fleeting, temporary, and usually desirable.
    a. Migration
    *b. Traveling
    c. Reading
    d. Regionalizing

19. According to Basso, for the Western Apaches, which of the following is a context in which silence is likely to be used?
    a. showing enthusiasm and excitement
    b. making tribal decisions
    *c. courtship
    d. performing tribal duties

20. Which of the following is true about cultural spaces?
    a. The influence they have on our identities is static.
    b. Generally, cultural spaces are designated by physical markers.
    c. Cultural spaces can be accepted or rejected; they are never forced on us.
    *d. We negotiate relationships to the cultural meanings attached to particular spaces we inhabit.

21. When people are loyal to a particular demographic area that holds significant cultural meaning, they are _____ .
    a. building postmodern cultural spaces
    *b. expressing regionalism
    c. utilizing a cultural space
    d. creating personal space

22. Jonah tells Katrina he is glad to see her but doesn't smile or look at her frequently and seems preoccupied. Jonah has used nonverbal behavior to _____ verbal behavior.
    *a. contradict
    b. substitute for
    c. complement
    d. reinforce

23. Nodding our head while saying yes illustrates that nonverbal communication can _____ verbal communication.
    a. contradict
    b. substitute for
    c. complement
    *d. reinforce

24. Which of the following is NOT true about nonverbal behavior?
    a. It can communicate status and power.
    b. It must be interpreted using the context in which it occurs.
    *c. It is possible to gauge meaning from a specific nonverbal behavior.
    d. It communicates deception.

25. Which of the following is NOT true about eye contact?
    *a. Native Americans use a lot of eye contact in place of verbal communication.
    b. It shortens the distance between two people.
    c. It can be used to regulate interpersonal distance.
    d. It communicates meanings about respect and status, and often regulates turn taking.

TRUE/FALSE QUESTIONS

26. Women are more likely than men to carry their books close to their body and take up less space when sitting.   (T)

27. Direct eye contact can create distance between people because it makes them feel uncomfortable.   (F)

28. When misunderstandings arise, we are more likely to look at the nonverbal communication.   (F)

29. Silence is generally not appropriate in social situations in which relationships are ambiguous because U.S. Americans tend to reduce uncertainty through communication.   (T)

30. Prejudice is often based on aspects of nonverbal communication.   (T)

31. In hate crimes, the victim's appearance is more significant than her or his specific cultural heritage.   (T)

32. Polychronic cultures value being punctual, completing tasks, and keeping to schedules.   (F)

33. Among the Japanese, silence communicates awkwardness and may cause people to feel uncomfortable.   (F)

34. The contexts that form our identity are a form of nonverbal communication.   (T)

35. Once determined, cultural spaces are relatively unchanging.   (F)

ESSAY QUESTIONS

36. Compare and contrast contact cultures with noncontact cultures. What are the intercultural implications of these differences?

37. Compare and contrast monochronic and polychronic time orientations. What are the intercultural implications of these differences?

38. Identify and discuss Basso's five contexts in which silence is appropriate.

39. Discuss the role of neighborhood as a cultural space in U.S. cities.

40. Identify and discuss the ways through which cultural space can be changed.

CHAPTER 7

Popular Culture and Intercultural Communication

MULTIPLE-CHOICE QUESTIONS

1. Which of the following is true about people's responses to popular culture?
   a. In general, people cannot resist popular culture.
   b. The study of popular culture is considered by most people to be worthy of serious attention.
   *c. People are often unaware of the complex nature of popular culture.
   d. The United States imports much of its popular culture from other countries.

2. Those systems or artifacts that most people know about and share are known as _____ .
   *a. popular culture
   b. media cultural texts
   c. high culture
   d. low culture

3. What initially motivated the exportation of U.S. popular culture?
   a. the desire to share new information and technological advances
   b. requests from countries that did not have high-quality entertainment
   c. a need to help people from other cultures understand the benefits of democracy
   *d. the decision to use it to advertise U.S. products

4. In the study of White and Black job applicants, how did interviewers who were influenced by negative stereotypes of Blacks differ in their behavior?
   a. They spent more time interviewing some applicants.
   b. They showed more immediacy behaviors.
   *c. Their speech deteriorated.
   d. They were more outgoing.

5. To what does cultural imperialism refer?
   a. the idea that many White people have superiority over people of color
   b. the technological advancement of the United States in media forms
   c. the resistance of people in the United States to popular culture forms from other countries
   *d. the dominance of U.S. popular cultural forms throughout the world

6. _____ produces products of popular culture (for example, movies, cartoons, Pokémon) as commodities that can be economically profitable.
   a. Cultural imperialism
   *b. The culture industry
   c. High culture
   d. A cultural forum

7. Intercultural communication scholars are interested in popular culture because _____ .
   a. it gives us true representations of other people
   *b. most people rely on popular culture for information about others
   c. people all over the world assign the same meanings to popular culture texts
   d. there is little cultural variation in the way people negotiate their relationships to popular culture

8. Details concerning the age, sex, and income of a magazine's readership are known as a/an _____ .
   a. cultural identity
   b. abstract demographic
   c. form of media imperialism
   *d. reader profile

9. Which statement is NOT true about popular culture and information about cultures?
   *a. People tend to think popular culture presents true information about their own culture.
   b. People use popular culture texts to learn about other cultures.
   c. People tend to think popular culture presents true information about other cultures.
   d. People use popular culture texts to negotiate their relationships with cultural identities.

10. According to the study on how interviewers respond to Black and White job applicants, Black job applicants _____ .
    a. were less qualified than White applicants
    b. did not have interviewing skills
    c. were less immediate than White applicants
    *d. were reacting to the interviewers

11. Which statement is true about popular culture and stereotypes?
    a. Sometimes we unconsciously accept stereotypes presented in the media.
    *b. Popular culture reinforces existing stereotypes.
    c. We resist stereotypes projected by popular culture.
    d. Popular culture is the main reason stereotypes persist.

12. Female African American characters who appear as "scenery" in the background of television shows serve to perpetuate _____ .
    a. cultural imperialism
    b. media imperialism
    c. social roles
    *d. stereotypes

13. Which of the following is true about how people resist cultural texts?
    a. A person's preference for popular culture is based more on media sensitivity than on cultural values.
    *b. Refusal to participate in popular culture is one form of resistance.
    c. Motivation to participate in popular culture is unrelated to a person's social role.
    d. Resistance may be motivated by displeasure over media representations of certain social issues.

14. Which of the following is true about the Navajo G.I. Joe doll?
    a. It is a form of cultural imperialism.
    b. It serves as a cultural text.
    *c. It is a way in which the history of an underrepresented group is made available to the public.
    d. It reaffirms stereotypes.

15. Manusov and Hegda found that having some cultural information and positive expectations _____ .
    a. motivates migrants to be overconfident about their knowledge of a culture
    b. leads to more rigid stereotyping than having no information
    c. leads to greater levels of disappointment and frustration for migrants
    *d. may lead to more in-depth conversations than having no information

16. The popularity of _____ suggests that not all popular culture comes from the United States.
    a. Mickey Mouse and Donald Duck
    b. Disneyland and Disney World
    *c. Pokémon and Hello Kitty
    d. Batman and Robin

17. Who tends to be most influenced by popular culture portrayals of another cultural group?
    a. people who have been very exposed to the other group
    b. people who have a tendency toward ethnocentric attitudes
    c. people who have experience with the culture of the other group
    *d. people who have limited experience with the other group

18. The impact that U.S. and Western media have had on the rest of the world is known as _____ .
    a. electronic colonialism
    b. media imperialism
    *c. cultural imperialism
    d. consumerism

19. _____ has been reconceptualized as popular culture.
    *a. Low culture
    b. High culture
    c. Cultural identity
    d. Colonialism

20. Electronic colonialism is _____ .
    a. domination by one country through political, economic, and cultural exploitation
    b. domination through the spread of cultural products
    *c. domination or exploitation using technological forms
    d. domination or control through media

21. Popular Mexican American music in Los Angeles illustrates _____ .
    a. the ways in which folk culture becomes popular culture
    b. the subtleties of cultural imperialism
    c. the ways in which culture industries manipulate various media
    *d. the ways in which marginalized cultural groups are able to express themselves in innovative, alternative ways

22. The fact that we are bombarded with popular culture every day and everywhere illustrates that it is _____ , a characteristic of popular culture.
     a. folk culture
     b. stereotypical
     c. ambiguous
    *d. ubiquitous

23. Which of the following is NOT true about the consumption of popular culture?
     a. Public texts do not have to win over the majority of people in order to be popular.
    *b. Unpredictability in advertising has been removed through consumer profiling.
     c. We participate in those texts that address issues relevant to our cultural groups.
     d. We actively seek out and choose texts that serve our needs.

24. Which of the following is true about resisting popular culture?
     a. The majority of people refuse to engage in particular forms of popular culture.
    *b. Some acts of resistance may be related to social roles.
     c. It is easy to resist exposure to popular media.
     d. Cultural politics are rarely a factor in choosing to resist a form of popular culture.

25. The practice of marketing U.S. goods through movies on foreign screens is referred to as _____ .
    *a. cultural imperialism
     b. high culture
     c. cultural identity
     d. colonialism

TRUE/FALSE QUESTIONS

26. U.S. television programs that cross cultural and linguistic frontiers are successful because they appeal to basic human values.   (F)

27. Television is more a reflection of reality than a forum for discussing and working out ideas on a variety of topics.   (F)

28. There is a great deal of research on why U.S. television programs are so successful in other cultures.   (F)

29. People resist the use of popular culture as a forum for dealing with social issues.   (F)

30. Cultural groups are generally depicted accurately in popular culture.   (F)

31. The U.S. film industry makes more money on their films outside the United States than they do inside.   (T)

32. Generally, a large number of people have to be interested in something for it to be considered popular culture.   (F)

33. White Americans are so often portrayed in popular culture that it is difficult to stereotype them.   (T)

34. When non-Americans watch U.S. television shows for entertainment (such as *Dallas* or *Beverly Hills 90210*), they don't consider the story a reflection of reality in the United States.   (F)

35. Most language teachers discourage the use of popular culture to improve language skills because it teaches slang and inappropriate speech varieties.   (F)

ESSAY QUESTIONS

36. Identify and discuss four characteristics of popular culture.

37. Identify and discuss the manner in which popular culture serves cultural functions connected to cultural identities.

38. Identify and provide examples of the ways in which someone might resist popular culture.

39. Identify and discuss at least four ways of thinking about cultural imperialism. What are the ramifications for intercultural communication from each of these perspectives?

40. What are the intercultural effects of underrepresentation of various groups in popular culture?

CHAPTER 8

Culture, Communication, and Conflict

MULTIPLE-CHOICE QUESTIONS

1. A perceived or real incompatibility of goals, values, expectations, or processes among two or more independent parties is known as _____ .
   a. avoidance
   b. compromise
   *c. conflict
   d. interaction

2. Irwin is unsure of how to handle a conflict with his girlfriend, Wenshu. She wants to spend their vacation with family while he would like to take a trip to a place they've never been before. They haven't argued, but Irwin is confused about how to resolve their different desires. Irwin is discovering that there is a great deal of _____ in intercultural conflicts.
   a. confrontation
   *b. ambiguity
   c. mediation
   d. pacifism

3. When individuals become aware that their feelings and emotions are incompatible, they are most likely experiencing _____ conflict.
   *a. affective
   b. value
   c. cognitive
   d. goal

4. Philip has decided to move in with his girlfriend. His parents are highly critical of his decision because they feel that living together before marriage is morally unacceptable. Philip and his parents are experiencing _____ conflict.
   a. affective
   *b. value
   c. cognitive
   d. goal

5. A situation in which people have incompatible preferences for a course of action is a/an _____ .
   a. affective conflict
   b. value conflict
   c. cognitive conflict
   *d. conflict of interest

6. Ben and his wife, Jenny, disagree over what kinds of investments they should make for long-term financial security. Ben wants to invest more heavily in risky ventures while Jenny prefers more secure options such as CDs or savings bonds. Ben and Jenny have a/an _____ .
   a. affective conflict
   *b. conflict of interest
   c. cognitive conflict
   d. goal conflict

7. When people disagree about a preferred outcome or end state, they are involved in _____ conflict.
   a. affective
   b. value
   c. cognitive
   *d. goal

8. Lisa and her roommate, Kristen, argue over how often they should clean their apartment. Kristen doesn't mind things being out of place or an occasional sweater on the couch. Lisa, however, prefers a more orderly environment in which everything has a place and is in it. Lisa and Kristen are experiencing _____ .
   a. affective conflict
   b. value conflict
   *c. cognitive conflict
   d. conflict of interest

9. A person with a high concern for self and a low concern for others is likely to use a/an _____ style of managing conflict.
   a. integrating
   b. obliging
   c. avoiding
   *d. dominating

10. Juanita and Jorge generally try to be open and direct in conflict situations because they have a high concern for both self and the other. Juanita and Jorge tend to use a/an _____ style of resolution.
   *a. integrating
   b. obliging
   c. avoiding
   d. compromising

11. Marita tends to play down the differences and incompatibilities between herself and her boss. She frequently tries to satisfy what she thinks are her expectations before her boss has even expressed them. Marita is using a/an _____ style of resolution.
   a. integrating
   *b. obliging
   c. avoiding
   d. compromising

12. People who value _____ believe that the best response is to recognize conflict and work through it in an open, productive way so that opportunities are redistributed, tensions released, and relationships renewed.
    a. pacifism
    *b. confrontation
    c. avoidance
    d. compromise

13. Jeong Hwa asked her friend Su Lee to talk to her roommate about playing her music too loud late at night. Jeong Hwa has used a/an _____ to resolve her conflict.
    a. individualistic approach
    b. pacifist approach
    c. collaborative approach
    *d. intermediary

14. In _____ conflict, individuals carefully narrow the conflict to try to understand what the specific problem is.
    a. destructive
    *b. productive
    c. value
    d. cognitive

15. Abdul's most recent argument with his friend Don escalated from where to have dinner to a critique of Don's inability to make decisions. Abdul and Don have engaged in _____ conflict.
    *a. destructive
    b. productive
    c. value
    d. cognitive

16. A _____ atmosphere in a relationship will promote coercion, suspicion, rigidity, and poor communication.
    a. productive
    b. cooperative
    *c. competitive
    d. destructive

17. _____ conflict arises from unequal or unjust social relationships between groups.
    a. Economic
    *b. Social
    c. International
    d. Interpersonal

18. In _____, individuals work together to bring about social change, such as when consumers boycotted grapes during the 1990s as a protest against treatment of migrant workers.
    a. international conflicts
    b. social conflicts
    *c. social movements
    d. environmental conflicts

19. The use of traditional stereotypes in either/or thinking often results in _____ .
    a. avoidance
    *b. polarization
    c. dominance
    d. dialogue

20. When people differ in ideologies on specific issues, such as spousal roles, they are most likely engaged in _____ conflict.
    *a. value
    b. cognitive
    c. affective
    d. goal

21. The person who uses the _____ style of conflict resolution usually has a moderate degree of concern for self and others.
    a. dominating
    *b. compromising
    c. integrating
    d. obliging

22. In dominant U.S. cultural contexts, the person who uses a/an _____ style of conflict resolution supposedly has a low concern for self and others.
    a. dominating
    b. compromising
    *c. avoiding
    d. obliging

23. Which of the following is not true of the conflict styles of people from individualistic societies?
    a. They tend to be more direct in their communication.
    b. They tend to be more concerned with saving their own self-esteem.
    *c. They tend to emphasize extended families and loyalty to groups.
    d. They tend to use more controlling confrontational and solution-oriented conflict styles.

24. Which of the following is true of conflict in general?
    a. Conflict is found primarily in individualistic cultures.
    b. Conflict is always viewed as destructive to relationships.
    *c. Men and women deal with conflict differently.
    d. There are few cultural differences in how people from other cultures approach conflict.

25. The key to creating a cooperative atmosphere is to _____ .
    a. encourage people to think of innovative and creative solutions
    b. step back and explore other options or delegate the problem to a third party
    *c. create an atmosphere based on exploration, not argumentation
    d. identify one's own preferred conflict style

TRUE/FALSE QUESTIONS

26. Mexican managers tend to be more indirect and polite than U.S. managers in expressing their disagreements.   (T)

27. Conflict strategies usually relate to how people manage their self-image in relationships.   (T)

28. Although people with a dominating style may be loud and forcefully expressive, they are generally effective in resolving conflict.   (F)

29. The compromising style of conflict resolution is seen as most effective in most conflicts because it attempts to be fair and equitable.   (F)

30. People tend to use a particular conflict style in their interactions regardless of the particular context or situation.   (F)

31. In both Amish and Japanese cultures, people tend to see conflict as good and are concerned with individuals preserving their own dignity.   (F)

32. When it comes to conflicts of value and opinion, Japanese use the avoiding style more with acquaintances than with best friends.   (T)

33. A cooperative atmosphere relies on effective argumentation.   (F)

34. In the Buddhist, Taoist, and Confucian traditions, people tend to avoid direct expression of feelings, confrontation, and verbal aggression.   (T)

35. White males and females tend to focus on the importance of taking responsibility for their behavior.   (T)

ESSAY QUESTIONS

36. Identify and discuss the different levels at which conflict occurs throughout the world.

37. What makes intercultural conflict different from other kinds of conflict?

38. Identify and discuss the basic principles of the "peacemaking" approach.

39. Identify and discuss the manner in which men's and women's communication styles may lead to conflict.

40. Compare and contrast productive versus destructive conflict management styles.

41. In what ways might an economic argument against immigration hide a racist argument?

42. Identify and discuss four of the seven suggestions for dealing with conflict.

CHAPTER 9

Intercultural Relationships in Everyday Life

MULTIPLE-CHOICE QUESTIONS

1. Which of the following is NOT a benefit of intercultural relationships?
   a. They can help to break stereotypes.
   b. They may teach us something about history.
   *c. They are easier to maintain than same-culture relationships.
   d. They may help us acquire new skills.

2. Talal, a Middle Eastern student, finds himself attracted to Guo Hongwu, a Chinese student in his economics class. After several conversations, he has found that, despite their different cultural backgrounds, they have many of the same opinions about and experiences in the United States. Talal and Hongwu's relationship illustrates the _____ rationale for relationship formation.
   a. heterosexual
   *b. similarity
   c. difference
   d. physical attraction

3. When we seek out people who have different personality traits, we are looking for a/an _____ relationship.
   *a. complementary
   b. intercultural
   c. compromising
   d. conflictual

4. Which of the following is NOT true about U.S. romantic relationships?
   a. Honesty and individuality are more important than harmony and collectivism.
   b. Understanding, respect, and sincerity are more important than togetherness, trust, and warmth.
   *c. Physical attraction and passion are not as important as similar backgrounds and compatibility.
   d. In intimate relationships, it is important to be open and to talk things out.

5. Which of the following is NOT true about gay relationships?
   a. Men in gay relationships tend to seek emotional support from same-sex friendships.
   b. Close friendships may be more important to a gay person than to a straight person due to discrimination and hostility.
   c. Although their friendships start with sexual attraction and involvement, they often last after the sexual involvement is terminated.
   *d. They are formed primarily for physical intimacy.

6. The "be yourself" approach to intercultural communication in which the person is not conscious of differences and does not need to act in any particular way is known as _____ .
   a. conscious incompetence
   *b. unconscious incompetence
   c. unconscious competence
   d. conscious competence

7. When communication goes smoothly but we're not sure why, we are probably communicating with _____ .
   a. conscious incompetence
   *b. unconscious competence
   c. unconscious incompetence
   d. conscious competence

8. Which of the following is NOT true about the similarity principle in relationship formation?
   a. We are attracted to people who hold beliefs similar to ours.
   b. It doesn't matter if people are truly similar as long as we think they are.
   *c. There must be a certain degree of physical similarity for a relationship to last.
   d. When people think they are similar, they have higher expectations for future interactions.

9. Matt just finished his first conversation with an international student from Rwanda. He found that things went smoothly without his having to think about what he was saying even though he was a bit nervous about the interaction before it happened. Matt's experience illustrates _____ .
   a. conscious incompetence
   *b. unconscious competence
   c. unconscious incompetence
   d. conscious competence

10. Suzette is methodical and analytical when preparing for meetings with the Chinese managers of her company. She pays careful attention to seating and protocol, and tries to learn as much as she can before, during, and after each interaction. Suzette probably communicates with _____ .
    a. conscious incompetence
    b. unconscious competence
    c. unconscious incompetence
    *d. conscious competence

11. Elizabeth, a U.S. American student, and Ahmad, an international student from Turkey, find that although they are of different faiths, their attitudes about the role of religion in everyday life are very much alike. This realization illustrates _____ , a theme in intercultural relationships
    a. competence
    *b. similarity
    c. involvement
    d. a turning point

12. Experiences or conversations that move a relationship either forward or backward are known as _____, a theme in intercultural relationships.
    a. competence
    b. similarity
    c. involvement
    *d. turning points

13. Tamaya and Monique make certain they take time to talk to each other every day and plan weekly activities together. They share many of the same friends, and in their conversations, they often share their feelings concerning personal issue. Tamaya and Monique's friendship illustrates _____, a theme in intercultural relationships.
    *a. involvement
    b. similarity
    c. competence
    d. a turning point

14. The most desirable style of interaction in intercultural marriage, _____, is based on agreement and negotiation.
    a. compromise
    b. obliteration
    *c. consensus
    d. submission

15. Roger and Adair are in an intercultural marriage. They have both agreed to give up certain aspects of their culture, but now Adair is starting to resent giving up some of the things she grew up with. Roger and Adair have probably used the _____ style of interaction in intercultural marriage.
    a. obliteration
    *b. compromise
    c. consensus
    d. submission

16. Keiko, who grew up in Japan, and Wahid, who grew up in Egypt, met and married in the United States. They have decided to stay in the United States and "become American" rather than negotiate the differences between their two cultures. What style of interaction have they adopted?
    *a. obliteration
    b. compromise
    c. submission
    d. consensus

17. The _____ style of interaction in intercultural marriage occurs when each person gives up some of his or her culturally bound beliefs in order to accommodate the other.
    a. obliteration
    *b. compromise
    c. submission
    d. consensus

18. Which of the following does NOT characterize an intercultural alliance?
    a. identification of power and unearned privilege
    b. orientations of affirmation
    *c. the use of compromise and submission in making decisions
    d. acknowledgment of the impact of history

19. The most common style of interaction in intercultural marriage, _____, occurs when one partner abandons his or her own culture in favor of the partner's culture.
    a. compromise
    b. obliteration
    c. consensus
    *d. submission

20. Which of the following is a characteristic of people interested in forming coalitions?
    a. emotional independence
    *b. commitment to personal involvement
    c. lack of knowledge of ethnic history
    d. an ability to speak to groups of people concerning intercultural issues

21. Darrell, the father of five children who has been married for 16 years, is friends with Joe, a gay man who has been in a relationship with the same man for 8 years. Darrell says that before he met Joe he thought that all gays were simply interested in sex but that his friendship and conversations with Joe have taught him otherwise. Joe and Darrell's friendship is an example of how intercultural friendships can _____ .
    *a. help to break stereotypes
    b. teach us something about history
    c. teach us more general information
    d. help us acquire new skills

22. In what ways are intercultural relationships similar to intracultural relationships?
    a. There is a similar amount of anxiety during the early stages of the relationship.
    b. They take the same amount of work and effort.
    *c. They pass through the same developmental stages.
    d. They are based on the same notions of attraction.

23. Which of the following is a greater concern among people in intercultural marriages than those in intracultural marriages?
    *a. defining gender roles and raising children
    b. achieving relational satisfaction and sexual intimacy
    c. finding comfortable living arrangements
    d. coping with illness

TRUE/FALSE QUESTIONS

24. There is often more anxiety in the early stages of intercultural relationships than in intracultural relationships.   (T)

25. Generally, relationships across age groups, levels of physical ability, class, or race have the same amount of anxiety in the initial stages.   (F)

26. A lack of previous contact with members of a particular cultural group may lead to more anxiety than a few negative experiences. (F)

27. Actual similarity is a greater factor than perceived similarity in relationship formation. (F)

28. The term "friend" has more or less the same meaning for all cultural groups. (F)

29. Even though they are shorter lived, gay relationships tend to be happier and more mutually productive than many opposite-sex relationships. (T)

30. People in intercultural marriages are more likely to disagree about how to raise their children than people in intracultural marriages. (T)

31. Asian American men and African American women are more likely than Asian American women and African American men to marry outside their cultural group. (F)

32. Once a person has developed one intercultural relationship, it's generally easier to develop other intercultural relationships. (T)

33. The people in the majority have the most to gain from cross-cultural relationships. (F)

ESSAY QUESTIONS

34. Identify and discuss the challenges in intercultural relationships.

35. Identify and discuss the benefits of intercultural relationships.

36. What challenges face people in intercultural friendships?

37. How are gay relationships different from "straight" relationships?

38. Identify and discuss the four levels of intercultural communication competence.

CHAPTER 10

Intercultural Communication and Tourism

MULTIPLE-CHOICE QUESTIONS

1. Tomás, a rural Guatemalan, is tired of seeing missionaries visit his village for three-day revivals. When a group of eco-tourists stops by his store, he very aggressively questions them and their motives for being there and chooses not to tell them of a more accessible road to their destination. Tomás's attitude toward the eco-tourists demonstrates _____, an attitude of residents toward tourism.
   *a. resistance
   b. retreatism
   c. boundary maintenance
   d. revitalization

2. John doesn't like the fact that his hometown is invaded every summer by strangers. He knows that the town's economy is dependent on tourism, but he keeps his distance by avoiding contact with tourists. John's attitude toward tourists demonstrates _____, an attitude of residents toward tourism.
   a. resistance
   b. revitalization and adoption
   c. boundary maintenance
   *d. retreatism

3. The Amish, Hutterites, and Mennonites do not really desire a lot of interaction with tourists. They may interact with tourists on a limited level, but by and large they have learned to ignore or endure them as they go about their daily lives. These groups have taken a _____ response to tourism.
   a. resistance
   b. revitalization
   *c. boundary maintenance
   d. retreatism

4. Costa Ricans have embraced tourism—particularly eco-tourism—as a means of stabilizing their economy. The benefits have been so substantial that many residents of communities near tourist attractions have accepted tourism as part of their social and cultural fabric. The Costa Ricans have taken a _____ attitude toward tourism
   *a. revitalization
   b. retreatism
   c. boundary maintenance
   d. resistance

5. When community members avoid contact with tourists on a social level but accept it on an economic level, they probably have a _____ attitude toward tourism.
   a. revitalization and adoption
   *b. retreatism
   c. boundary maintenance
   d. resistance

6. _____ is illustrated when community members resent or have an aggressive or antagonistic attitude toward tourism.
    a. Resistance
    b. Revitalization and adoption
    c. Boundary maintenance
    *d. Retreatism

7. When community members choose to regulate the interaction between themselves and tourists, they demonstrate the _____ response to tourism.
    *a. boundary maintenance
    b. revitalization
    c. resistance
    d. retreatism

8. Communities that accept tourism as part of their social and cultural fabric and actively invest money to draw tourists probably have a _____ response to tourism.
    a. boundary maintenance
    *b. revitalization and adoption
    c. resistance
    d. retreatism

9. Which of the following is NOT true of tourist–host encounters?
    a. Most encounters are short-term and transitory.
    *b. Most encounters occur between people of similar socioeconomic levels.
    c. Most encounters are limited by time and space.
    d. Most encounters are business exchanges that lack novelty or spontaneity.

10. When talking about his last tour of Turkey as part of a tour group, Clyde complained, "Sure, I saw some interesting things, but I didn't really get to know anyone. Most of my conversations were pretty simple. The most I talked to anyone was when I was trying to buy a carpet." Clyde's comments most clearly illustrate which of the following characteristics of tourist–host encounters?
    a. Most encounters are short-term and transitory.
    b. Most encounters occur between people of different socioeconomic levels.
    c. Most encounters are limited by time and space.
    *d. Most encounters are business exchanges that lack spontaneity or depth.

11. Heba, an Egyptian woman visiting the United States, is surprised to find that she does not overhear many conversations as she walks along city streets. Heba's surprise is the result of a difference in the norm for _____ .
    a. dress
    b. shopping
    *c. comportment on the street
    d. religious expression

12. Which of the following is NOT a communication challenge in a tourist context?
    a. expectations for appearance in public
    *b. expectations for private interactions
    c. expectations for linguistic ability
    d. expectations for the negotiability of price when shopping

13. Which of the following is NOT a cultural variable involved in shopping?
    a. whether one should touch the merchandise
    b. differences in resources between tourist and host
    c. whether one should bargain for merchandise
    *d. the gender roles of salespeople

14. Christina returned to the United States from a trip to China earlier than anticipated. She is rather negative about her trip and doubts she'll return. Which of the following is probably NOT a factor in her experience?
    a. physiological aspects of traveling
    b. the difference between her own culture and that of her Chinese hosts
    *c. the availability of books concerning communication with the Chinese
    d. her language ability

15. Which of the following is a symptom of culture shock?
    a. desire for intercultural interaction
    *b. anger or frustration with service people
    c. struggles to learn the local language
    d. interest in learning more about the local culture

16. Lack of spontaneity in tourist–host encounters is explained by all of the following EXCEPT _____ .
    a. differing social backgrounds between hosts, tourists, and service providers
    b. time limitations
    c. inadequate linguistic abilities
    *d. space limitations

17. Which of the following is NOT a nonverbal communication challenge in tourism contexts?
    a. expectations for appearance in public
    *b. expectations for linguistic ability
    c. expectations for smiling at strangers
    d. expectations for the touchability of merchandise when shopping

18. Which of the following is true of bargaining in many cultures?
    a. Socioeconomic class issues don't matter.
    b. It's relatively easy to decide what price is a fair price.
    *c. It is part of a larger relational emphasis, a way that people are connected.
    d. Only tourists are really expected to bargain.

19. Which of the following would NOT be useful in building the intercultural skills of tourists?
    a. learning a few words of the local language
    b. gathering knowledge about the culture before visiting
    c. learning about local customs that may affect communication during the visit
    *d. practicing speaking up when they don't understand something

20. Tony has planned his trip to Europe using guide books and other people's experiences. His schedule includes as many places as he can manage based on the available train schedules. He is so motivated to have a good trip that he has even learned a few phrases in French and German. What is one other suggestion for building intercultural skills that might benefit Tony?
    a. Practice explaining American customs.
    b. Practice bargaining in shops.
    *c. Practice staying flexible and tolerating ambiguity.
    d. Practice speaking up when he doesn't understand something.

TRUE/FALSE QUESTIONS

21. There are often power differentials involved in tourist encounters.   (T)

22. With the spread of U.S. goods, shopping norms are more or less the same all over the world.   (F)

23. Culture shock tends to occur independently of the differences between the host culture and the visitor's home culture.   (F)

24. Language is not often a problem for tourists because English is spoken in most parts of the world.   (F)

25. A person with a resistance response to tourism may be overtly hostile or aggressive.   (T)

26. In the United States, expectations for appearance in public are very informal.   (T)

27. Most people will embrace tourism because of its economic benefits.   (F)

28. It's virtually impossible to learn anything about a culture in a short period of time.   (F)

29. Most tourists can engage in social interaction and have meaningful conversations with local people.   (F)

30. Tourist encounters are spontaneous because the people interacting are from different cultures.   (F)

ESSAY QUESTIONS

31. Identify and discuss the different groups that come into contact in tourism contexts.

32. Identify and discuss the characteristics of tourist–host encounters.

33. Identify and discuss the suggestions for improving tourists' intercultural communication skills.

34. What issues might be involved in culture shock for a tourist?

35. Compare and contrast resistance and revitalization as responses to tourism. What impact would each of these have on the intercultural encounter?

CHAPTER 11

Intercultural Communication and Business

MULTIPLE-CHOICE QUESTIONS

1. Which of the following is NOT a factor in the increasing diversity of the U.S. workforce?
   a. The market is more diverse.
   *b. Multinational companies have greater access to the U.S. population.
   c. The population of people of color is growing faster than that of the majority group.
   d. The number of people with disabilities wanting to work has increased.

2. Which of the following is NOT a factor in the global business context?
   a. The Internet has affected the costs of conducting business.
   *b. Popular culture is increasingly marketable.
   c. Societies around the world are becoming increasingly interconnected.
   d. Latin American and Asian economies present business opportunities.

3. Omar is confused by his new boss, Ted, who doesn't seem to act like a boss. "He's always asking for suggestions, and he told us to call him by his first name," he told a colleague. "Do you think he really knows what he is doing?" Omar probably comes from a culture that values _____ .
   a. low power distance
   b. a collectivist orientation
   *c. high power distance
   d. an individualistic orientation

4. Jessica really likes working for her boss, Juanita. "She acts very informally and lets me call her by her first name," she told her mother. "In fact, the first day I met Juanita, I didn't even know she was the manager because she dresses just like the rest of us!" Jessica and her boss both probably come from cultural groups that value _____ .
   *a. low power distance
   b. a collectivist orientation
   c. high power distance
   d. an individualistic orientation

5. People from cultures that value _____ tend to feel that an organization functions best when the differences in power are clearly marked.
   a. a collectivist orientation
   b. low power distance
   *c. high power distance
   d. an individualistic orientation

6. People from cultures that value _____ tend to feel that power distances should be minimized and that an egalitarian view is best.
   *a. low power distance
   b. high power distance
   c. a collectivist orientation
   d. an individualistic orientation

7. Ke Guiwen is visiting the United States from China. As he visits several companies and talks to both workers and managers, he is surprised to realize that, although U.S. workers seem to have more autonomy than the employees in his company, they also tend not to work together to complete tasks. Ke Guiwen's reaction is probably due to a/an _____ orientation in his culture.
   *a. collectivist
    b. communist
    c. high power distance
    d. individualistic

8. In countries with _____ views, workers are expected to perform certain jobs with clearly defined responsibilities.
    a. collectivist
    b. low power distance
    c. high power distance
   *d. individualistic

9. A boss who tries to preserve harmony on his work team and who encourages his subordinates to fill in for one another when they can probably has a/an _____ orientation toward work.
    a. low power distance
   *b. collectivist
    c. high power distance
    d. individualistic

10. Which of the following is a characteristic of cultural groups that value high power distance?
    a. Bosses and workers should intermingle.
    b. Interaction is less formal than in groups that value low power distance.
   *c. Status is readily identifiable.
    d. Everyone is on a first-name basis.

11. A person who values working hard over socializing with friends and family is most likely _____ .
    a. Australian
    b. Italian
   *c. German
    d. Mexican

12. In cultures in which relationships are of a higher priority than task accomplishment, _____ .
    a. tasks rarely get done
    b. business meetings tend to be quick and to the point
   *c. people spend a greater amount of time getting to know one another than working.
    d. interactions are formal

13. Which of the following is NOT a suggestion for dealing with increasing linguistic diversity?
    a. Don't assume that someone speaking a language other than English is talking about you.
    b. Avoid using jargon when speaking to speakers of English as a second language.
    c. Use a simple but not simple-minded vocabulary.
   *d. Don't worry about learning another language because most people in the business world will know some English.

14. Erica is helping Taeko, an international student from Japan, fill out an application. "Look," she says in a loud voice, "this is very easy. All you have to do is write in the little boxes." Which suggestion for dealing with linguistic diversity has Erica violated?
    a. Don't assume that someone speaking a language other than English is talking about you.
    b. Avoid using jargon when speaking to speakers of English as a second language.
    *c. Remember not to be condescending and not to raise your voice.
    d. Use shorter words when possible.

15. A person with a/an _____ style of communication would probably not feel comfortable giving straightforward information in a problem situation.
    a. direct
    *b. indirect
    c. formal
    d. informal

16. John explains a mishap in the factory to his supervisor, Shi Xian. John tells him exactly where the miscommunication occurred and who was at fault. Now, John is trying to understand why his boss seems more cold and distant and why he is getting less desirable assignments. John may be learning _____ .
    a. to use a less indirect style of communication
    *b. that social harmony is sometimes valued more than honesty
    c. that reporting bad news will damage his career prospects
    d. to be more formal in his interactions

17. A person whose culture supports delaying or "adjusting" bad news to avoid upsetting the recipient of the information has probably learned _____ .
    a. to lie
    *b. that social harmony is a high priority
    c. to be more formal in his or her communication
    d. that honesty is the best policy

18. Which of the following is NOT a suggestion for effective communication in a culture that values harmony over honesty.
    a. Ask questions in such a way that other people can't figure out what you really want to hear.
    b. Engage other people in conversations in such a way that the information you need will just "fall out."
    c. Ask more than one person for directions.
    *d. Relax when someone tells you not to worry.

19. Which of the following is NOT true of people in a culture that values formality?
    a. They attach great importance to courtesy.
    b. High-level officials should be treated with solemnity and respect.
    *c. It is not necessary to dress formally so long as you act formally.
    d. Avoid excessive familiarity, especially in initial meetings.

20. The most important reason companies are likely to address diversity issues is _____ .
    a. a moral obligation to redress a history of sexism, racism, and intergroup tensions
    *b. legal and social pressure
    c. it's time to level the playing field between the races
    d. having a diverse workplace keeps employees happy

21. The Americans with Disabilities Act _____ .
   *a. requires employers to make "reasonable" accommodations for employees with disabilities
   b. is a means of dealing with reverse discrimination
   c. requires employers to have people with disabilities make up a certain percentage of their workforce
   d. gives people with disabilities preferential treatment

22. Which of the following is NOT a suggestion for building intercultural skills in the workplace?
   a. Identify the ways in which your workplace is diverse.
   b. Be flexible, and try to see the other person's point of view.
   *c. Remember not to be condescending and not to raise your voice.
   d. Establish a standard of communication that everyone must learn.

TRUE/FALSE QUESTIONS

23. In the United States, the population of people of color is growing faster than that of the majority group population.   (T)

24. Members of a cultural group that values low power distance are more likely to want bosses to act like bosses and workers to act like workers so that there is no confusion about the chain of command.   (F)

25. In Japan, a specific job is assigned to each individual so that all can contribute equally to the final product.   (F)

26. Individualism in the Greek workplace may be even more developed than in the U.S. workplace.   (T)

27. People in Mexico tend to value time with friends and family more than work.   (T)

28. In the United States, the highest priority is on smooth relationships and the process of task accomplishment rather than completion of the task itself.   (F)

29. It's important to say things the way you usually would to speakers of English as a second language so that they can learn the different pronunciations.   (F)

30. Most cultural groups tend to be more formal in business contexts than U.S. Americans.   (T)

31. In Mexico, it's okay to call your teacher by his or her first name.   (F)

32. In the United States, it doesn't really matter which values you hold or which communication style you use so long as you can get the job done.   (F)

ESSAY QUESTIONS

33. Identify and discuss the intercultural communication issues relevant to domestic growth.

34. Compare and contrast the "live to work" and "work to live" attitudes toward work and material gain. What impact might these attitudes have on intercultural communication?

35. How might the use of a direct style of communication in a workplace in which indirect communication is the preferred style affect the quality and effectiveness of interactions?

36. Discuss the role of power in relation to the language and communication style in the workplace.

37. Identify and discuss the reasons companies address affirmative action and diversity issues.

CHAPTER 12

Intercultural Communication and Education

MULTIPLE-CHOICE QUESTIONS

1. Which of the following is NOT true of education in U.S. society?
   a. If you cannot read or write, it is difficult to succeed.
   *b. The educational experiences of college students are more or less the same across colleges.
   c. Educational institutions have the potential to reproduce social inequality.
   d. It contains the remnants of a colonial educational system.

2. Which of the following is true about the colonial educational system?
   *a. It is often imposed upon the colonized at the expense of their own culture.
   b. A person acquiring an education in such a system has less power than one who is taught in a system embracing the native culture.
   c. The educational curricula tend to reflect the society in which the system is established.
   d. The system no longer exists.

3. _____ give college students international experience.
   a. Colonial educational systems
   *b. Study abroad programs
   c. Intercultural communication courses
   d. Language courses

4. The Morril Act of 1890 _____ .
   *a. established what are today known as historically Black colleges and universities
   b. mandated separate but equal college education for all races
   c. has little lingering effect on today's educational institutions
   d. provided for the participation and eventual success of Blacks through the colonial educational system

5. Native American children were taken from their families and sent to _____ in an attempt to assimilate them.
   *a. boarding schools
   b. colonial schools
   c. other countries
   d. colleges and universities

6. The different ways in which students acquire knowledge in different cultures are known as _____ .
   a. teaching styles
   b. education systems
   *c. learning styles
   d. books

7. Cheree, a professor of communication, prefers to engage her students in discussion rather than lecture for the full class period. She believes that students learn more when they are actively engaged. Cheree's _____ is common in the United States.
   *a. teaching style
   b. grading system
   c. learning style
   d. passive strategy

8. Which of the following is NOT true about grading and power across cultures?
   a. The power difference between instructor and student varies from culture to culture.
   b. In the United States, relationships between student and instructor are less formal than in other cultures.
   *c. Instructors in different cultures evaluate students' work similarly.
   d. Intercultural conflict can result from differing grading expectations.

9. Which of the following is true about the relationship between education and cultural identity?
   a. The experience of students of color is consistently integrated into the curriculum.
   *b. Schools work less well for impoverished students of color.
   c. Students are not aware of the effects of educational experiences in shaping their identities.
   d. All teachers who do not see the need to incorporate materials that reflect the experiences of people of color in their classrooms are racist.

10. Colleges that require courses focusing on Western views of history and literature tend to be _____ .
   *a. Eurocentric
   b. classical studies
   c. inclusive
   d. Afrocentric

11. Which of the following is true about Afrocentric history?
   a. It is empowering for European American students.
   *b. It highlights the role of Africans in significant historical accomplishments.
   c. It is part of the standard curriculum in most schools.
   d. It is equally inclusive and fair to all groups.

12. Which of the following is NOT a suggestion for improving the educational process in the United States?
   a. We need to be willing to point out the cultural differences that are creating problems.
   b. We have to assume that cultural differences are present.
   *c. We need to stop talking and start changing the system.
   d. We need to discuss cultural differences.

13. Which of the following is true of culturally specific education in the United States?
   a. Institutions such as Alabama State University received the same funding as their White counterparts.
   b. Historically Black colleges and universities established by the Morrill Act empowered African Americans.
   *c. The quality of education available in these institutions is as valuable as the education provided in more mainstream colleges.
   d. The educational experiences in these institutions are identical to those in institutions established for White males.

14. Which of the following aspects of the educational system is not a potential source of intercultural conflict?
     a. teaching and learning styles
     b. admission standards
     c. the curriculum
     *d. the value placed on education

TRUE/FALSE QUESTIONS

15. According to *Workforce 2000,* racial differences in college are decreasing as a result of the elimination of legal barriers based upon race.   (F)

16. An education is not as important as intelligence and a little luck in getting ahead in society.   (F)

17. Educational goals for different groups are largely driven by members' need to know about themselves and the society in which they live.   (T)

18. Educational choices are made independently of culture.   (F)

19. There is no real power difference between instructors and students.   (F)

20. The majority of today's curricula are sensitive to the multiple economic, social, and cultural variable in students' lives.   (F)

21. Everyone's culture is treated more or less the same in a standardized curriculum.   (F)

22. Afrocentric history gives students a different perspective on history.   (T)

23. An educational system is used to socialize and enculturate members of a society.   (T)

24. Black colleges were originally little more than vocational schools.   (T)

ESSAY QUESTIONS

25. In what ways does the educational system in the United States reflect a colonial history?

26. Compare and contrast the roles for teachers and students in the United States. How might these vary across cultures?

27. Why would it be necessary to study the educational process in an intercultural communication course?

28. In what ways might an educational curriculum affect the self-esteem and cultural identity of a student?

29. In what ways might culturally specific educational systems perpetuate the inequality of a society?

CHAPTER 13

Intercultural Communication and Health Care

MULTIPLE-CHOICE QUESTIONS

1. Which of the following is NOT a reason intercultural communication skills are important in the health communication context?
   a. The population is increasingly diverse.
   b. Assumptions made about health care are often cultural.
   *c. Members of particular cultures are more likely to seek traditional, culture-specific cures.
   d. Certain health issues have different kinds of stigmata across cultures.

2. For a patient communicating in a second language _____ .
   a. having a doctor who speaks loudly will help comprehension
   *b. medical terminology can be confusing
   c. it is best to bring in a translator
   d. the medical vocabulary is likely to be familiar from language classes

3. The case of Setsuko, the Japanese woman who became depressed but did not ask directly for treatment, illustrates that _____ .
   *a. assumptions about health care are often cultural
   b. medical terminology can be confusing to speakers of English as a second language
   c. a cultural bias exists in the role of the family in health care
   d. people are treated differently based on their culture

4. Which of the following is true about the history of medical treatment of minority cultural groups?
   *a. Medical studies were used to justify social policies.
   b. Members of minority groups have long been able to find members of their culture among service providers.
   c. Medical studies were used to loosen immigration restrictions.
   d. Gay people with AIDS and HIV rejected minority status to receive treatment within the framework of mainstream health care.

5. According to Larry Gross, AIDS taught us that _____ .
   a. homophobia increased with the AIDS epidemic
   b. all people with AIDS receive inadequate attention
   *c. people will begin to pay attention when famous and important people are involved
   d. the U.S. health care system is quick to respond to a crisis

6. Which of the following was NOT an effect of the Tuskegee Syphilis Project?
   a. reinforced suspicion about the medical community from marginalized communities
   b. advanced cases of syphilis
   c. community-based AIDS treatment centers
   *d. acquisition of medical data establishing White superiority

7. Health care provided outside of the traditional Western medical system is called _____ .
    a. stigmatized care
    *b. alternative medicine
    c. managed care
    d. witchcraft

8. The fact that many White southerners believe Prozac is addictive illustrates _____ .
    a. that white southerners aren't very well educated
    *b. that people who mistrust medical professionals will often turn to their own communities for information
    c. that regional identities play only a small role in the health care setting
    d. a self-fulfilling prophecy

9. Which of the following is NOT true about the communication between a physician and a patient?
    a. It is marked by an imbalance in medical knowledge.
    b. It is marked by an imbalance in access to treatment.
    *c. It is easier when the patient meets a wide variety of health care professionals.
    d. The communication patterns reflect power differences.

10. Which of the following is true about health care in the United States?
    a. It is available to all people.
    *b. The health care industry is a huge business.
    c. Patients needing expensive treatments need only request them from their doctors.
    d. It is modeled after the French health care system.

11. A physician's decision to provide misinformation to a patient when the physician believes this is in the patient's best interests is known as _____ .
    *a. strict paternalism
    b. contractual honesty
    c. benevolent deception
    d. unmitigated honesty

12. Dr. Garcia decides not to tell a patient she has terminal cancer because he feels that that knowledge would cause her condition to deteriorate more rapidly. Instead, he tells her she is suffering from weak kidneys and low blood sugar. Dr. Garcia has used the _____ framework for providing patients with information.
    a. unmitigated honesty
    b. contractual honesty
    *c. strict paternalism
    d. benevolent deception

13. _____ occurs when a physician chooses to communicate only a part of a patient's diagnosis.
    a. unmitigated honesty
    b. contractual honesty
    c. strict paternalism
    *d. benevolent deception

14. Dr. Lee tells Jim he has prostate cancer but does not tell him he has an advanced case. Dr. Lee has used the _____ framework for providing patients with information.
    a. unmitigated honesty
    b. contractual honesty
    c. strict paternalism
    *d. benevolent deception

15. The communication practice of only telling the patient what he or she wants to hear is known as _____ .
    a. unmitigated honesty
    *b. contractual honesty
    c. strict paternalism
    d. benevolent deception

16. Sarah tells her doctor, "I only want to hear about successful operations of this type. Do not tell me about what might go wrong." If the physician complies with Sarah's wishes, he or she is operating from the _____ framework for providing patients with information.
    a. unmitigated honesty
    *b. contractual honesty
    c. strict paternalism
    d. benevolent deception

17. _____ happens when a physician chooses to communicate the entire diagnosis to a patient.
    *a. unmitigated honesty
    b. contractual honesty
    c. strict paternalism
    d. benevolent deception

18. Lynn asks her doctor to tell her everything he knows about her condition. She thinks not knowing the truth will be more painful than having all the facts. Lynn is asking her doctor to use the _____ framework for providing patients with information.
    *a. unmitigated honesty
    b. contractual honesty
    c. strict paternalism
    d. benevolent deception

TRUE/FALSE QUESTIONS

19. AIDS is easily discussed around the world because it is so widespread.   (F)

20. Westernized medicine has a cultural bias.   (T)

21. The Western model of communication in health care settings has traditionally included the family.   (F)

22. In the past, medical studies about racial differences were used to justify immigration restrictions, slavery, and other social inequalities.   (T)

23. The Tuskegee Syphilis Project was terminated when a health care worker leaked information to a newspaper.   (F)

24. Health care professionals can generally keep their prejudices out of their professional life.   (F)

25. In order to get services, generally, all you have to do is ask your HMO.   (F)

26. Some health care professionals prefer to engage in strict paternalism as a protection against lawsuits.   (F)

27. Fear of malpractice suits guides many ethical decisions.   (T)

28. Health care professionals are usually members of the dominant culture.   (F)

ESSAY QUESTIONS

29. Why would it be important to look at intercultural communication in the health care context?

30. How has the historical treatment of cultural groups affected current members' willingness to seek treatment for medical conditions?

31. What is the role of prejudicial ideologies in the health care setting?

32. Compare and contrast benevolent deception with unmitigated honesty in the health care setting.

33. How might culture affect the arguments for and against euthanasia?